THEATRE:
the AGE *of* *Garrick*

Published in conjunction
with an exhibition at the
COURTAULD
INSTITUTE
GALLERIES

24 March to 30 May 1994

*English mezzotints from the collection of
the Hon. Christopher Lennox-Boyd*

Christopher Lennox-Boyd

Guy Shaw

Sarah Halliwell

Supported by Glaxo Holdings plc

LONDON
CHRISTOPHER LENNOX-BOYD
1994

Published by Christopher Lennox-Boyd

ISBN 0 9523264 0 X

Designed and printed by Expression Printers Ltd, N5 1JT
Typeset in Adobe Caslon

Acknowledgements

First and foremost we should like to thank Dennis Farr and John Murdoch, the past and present directors of the Courtauld Institute Galleries for inviting us to hold the exhibition here in the Courtauld Institute. Among the many people at Somerset House who have made this exhibition possible we must single out Dr Colum Hourihane and Barbara Hilton-Smith, who initiated the exhibition, Susan Blake, Jane Benson, June Hoare, William Bradford and Philippa Alden.

Next our thanks must go to our sponsors. Glaxo Holdings plc has with great generosity funded the production of the catalogue, the mounting of the show and publicity; Elizabeth Browne has been of great help, not least for her continuing enthusiasm for the project. The D'Oyly Carte Charitable Trust's generous donation helped to provide the additional illustrations to the catalogue.

We owe a debt for assistance with research, advice or photography to numerous individuals and institutions:

Tim Clayton and Richard Sharp, who are working on a book covering all prints of the theatre in this period, have put a great deal of their research at our disposal for which we are most grateful. We are particularly grateful for the kindness and patience of the staff of the Print Room at the British Museum, Dr Jim Fowler and his colleagues at the Theatre Museum and Dr Jeanne T. Newlin and her colleagues at the Harvard Theatre Collection. We should also like to thank the staff at the Bodleian Library, the British Library and the London Library.

We have been very fortunate to have been able to draw upon the valuable assistance of Adam Chadwick at the closing stages of the project and we should also like to thank Emma Bird and Vicky Bruce, who restored many of the prints; their skill and advice has made an important contribution to the success of the exhibition. We should also like to thank Louisa Metcalfe-Gibson, Henrietta Makinson, Kim Britten, Colette Harris and Virginia Hill for their support and enthusiasm at the beginning of the work.

Michael Dudley and his hard working staff at the Ashmolean Museum photographed the prints and extra illustrations were kindly provided by Louise Rhodes at the British Museum, Naresh Kaul at the British Library, Isabel Sinden at the Victoria & Albert Museum, Michael Dumas at the Harvard Theatre Collection, Westminster Libraries and Archives, Norwich Central Library, and York Central Library.

Finally, we cannot thank Tina Schwarz and her colleagues at Expression Printers Ltd enough for their magnificent skill and patience in producing this catalogue.

Acknowledgements for additional illustrations

By permission of The British Library: 12, 21, 28 , 40, 48 , 52, 56, 108, 111, 118, 120.
Courtesy of The Trustees of The British Museum: 59, 78, 82, 127, 136.
Courtesy of The Board of Trustees of The Victoria & Albert Museum: 9, 50, 53.
Courtesy of The Harvard Theatre Collection: 48, 54, 56, 76, 80, 103, 139.
Courtesy of The Print Room, Museum Street, London: 68.
Courtesy of Westminster City Archives: 88, 141.
Courtesy of Norfolk County Council Library and Information Services: 45.
Courtesy of York Central Library, North Yorkshire County Council Libraries: 4.

Introduction

The Age of Garrick (1745–80) was a time of great transformation both on the English stage and in English art. While Garrick was captivating theatre audiences with his new naturalistic style of acting, English painting was progressing from being dull and second-rate to equalling the best in Europe. At the same time David Garrick revitalised the English stage, transforming all aspects of the theatre, from acting to management. Art and the stage are by no means separate: both deal with illusion and both create a visual experience in an attempt to convince. We are fortunate that there were painters in England who were capable of recording, with such imagination and accuracy, how Garrick and his contemporaries looked and played.

The aim of this exhibition is to display theatrical prints and present some of the interesting aspects of mezzotint production and of print publishing. Mezzotint is a method of engraving that, although developed in the Low Countries, is universally associated with England. It became popular for the English to collect 'heads' – portraits of the famous and notorious – since they were barred by faith from owning religious images. A school of engravers led by John Smith (c. 1662–1742) produced hundreds of portrait mezzotints, which inevitably included actors and actresses. Most of the great mezzotint engravers worked in London and were English or Irish; they produced works that rank among the greatest reproductive prints – prints that translate an image in one medium, usually coloured, into another, often on a different scale. Mezzotint is a superb way of transferring facial expression from an oil painting or pastel and for this reason it is a superb medium for theatrical prints. Mezzotint is a method of creating graduated tones not by building up shadows, as in line engraving, but by working down the highlights. This is achieved by engraving the copper plate with a rocker so that it prints black overall, burnishing it where it needs to be lighter.

We are able to follow the production and marketing of a mezzotint from the examples displayed. First, the engraver made a reduced copy of the chosen picture to ascertain the correct proportions (p. 67) and then he began engraving. Progress was hard to monitor on the copper and so 'working proofs' were taken off at different stages, some of which survive (p. 142). Most of these show the print finished in parts, but with some highlights still needing work; faces are usually dusky and dress plainer than in the finished print (p. 84). The last proofs, almost completed, might well have been sent to the painter or the publisher for their comments. The engraver or painter could have 'touched' the proof, drawing in suggested changes either in outline or emphasis (p. 22). Many of these 'touched proofs' survive, providing a fascinating insight into engravers' methods. When the engraving was completed, the 'inscription space' at the bottom of the print still printed grey and needed to be cleaned; at this point, most engravers roughly scratched their name, and that of the painter, in this space (p. 109). Throughout the eighteenth century there was a vogue for collecting prints in these early states; to most collectors a 'scratched letter proof' bore a guarantee that it was a fine early impression. In proof state the print was considered ready to be shown at one of the societies that organised exhibitions; the Society of Artists annual exhibition was usually chosen (p. 58). Here it was seen by connoisseurs, painters and, more importantly, by publishers: many mezzotints were the private speculations of the engravers, sometimes in partnership with the painter. If an engraver managed sell the plate (p. 89) to a publisher, he could then recoup his investment and know that his work would be efficiently marketed. The final tasks would be to send the plate to a specialist 'writing engraver' and then to a printer (p. 58).

There was a sophisticated system of distribution: in some cases 'flyers' were sent out like modern brochures; prints were advertised in newspapers, where provincial agents were sometimes listed, and in Dublin and Edinburgh, printsellers advertised London stock. Chapmen travelled to country fairs with the cheaper prints and a large number of retail print shops existed in London. Their names are often recorded but facts about them are sparse, as is the case with the majority of eighteenth century tradesmen. The Copyright Act of 1734 gave protection for twenty eight years to the 'designer' of the print if he added 'Published according to Act of Parliament'. This Act was soon amended, requiring the date of publication to be added as well; when this protection was extended to others, like engravers or printsellers, they were required to provide names and addresses. When a print was successful and a large number of impressions were printed, it would wear down quickly and so would be sent to an engraver for repair and re-working. The engraver would supervise or perform this if he still had some control, but when the plate belonged to a commercial publisher, any re-working would be done by an apprentice or a journeyman engraver.

Engraved copper-plates were items of considerable value, forming the capital of the publisher; a good engraver could be paid £150 for a 16 x 20 inch plate. They were sold on in the event of death, bankruptcy of financial embarrassment and it is possible to follow their progress from one business to another (p. 8 and p. 70). When the plates changed hands they often received the new publishers' names. Alongside the production of fine engravings, there was a market for cheap copies of famous prints, a market dominated by publishing houses of Sayer and of Bowles. Most of these inferior copies pirated fashionable portraits, but a number of theatrical scenes were plagiarised.

At least three London printsellers issued catalogues of their stock of older prints: Walter Shropshire, John Thane and the proprietor(s) of the Magazin des Estampes. Where appropriate we have noticed the difference in price between their fine proofs and impressions on offer by publishers. The three dealers dealt with serious print collectors like Joseph Gulston, one of whose prints is exhibited (p. 18). Another print shown may have been in an eighteenth century collection: James McArdell's *Romeo and Juliet* (p. 49) once belonged to the Print Room at Dresden and had presumably been acquired before 1790, when collecting English mezzotints was fashionable throughout Europe.

During Garrick's career the reputation of English engraving changed. In 1740 French prints were all the rage and collected avidly everywhere, but by 1780 their dominant role was taken over by English works. William Woollett was the first engraver whose work was collected abroad, but by the 1750s the mezzotints of James McArdell were sought after. Then came the great mezzotint engravers John Dixon, Valentine Green, John Raphael Smith and the Watsons, whose works are seen here. The export boom that followed was led by John Boydell, the self-publicist, a print-publisher who rose to be Lord Mayor of London. He was less involved with publishing theatrical prints than his rival Robert Sayer, but most of the engravers who scraped theatrical mezzotints worked for him at some time.

The theatre played a large role in eighteenth century life; even those who lived far from a theatre were bombarded with reviews and notices in newspapers, magazines and books. Throughout the period the stage was censored: the 'Licensing Act' of 1737 stipulated that all new plays and any alterations to existing plays had to be licensed by the Lord Chamberlain. In addition, performances were only permitted at two theatres when previously there had been five: these two survivors, the Theatres Royal in Covent Garden and on Drury Lane, had been granted Royal letters patent after the Restoration in 1660, and were usually referred to as the 'Patent Houses'. The Lord Chamberlain could also grant licences to other theatres, usually on stringent conditions; the Duke of York was able to obtain a limited licence for Samuel Foote to produce plays in a theatre in Haymarket. Fairs governed by Royal Charter, such as 'Bartholomew Fair' (p. 2) and 'May Fair' were allowed to provide booths where plays, usually of a low nature, could be performed; many players started their careers in this way. Music was not censored and this did much to encourage musical comedy. The act was intended to prevent seditious plays, by forbidding the imposition of any admission charge for drama. It was easy to circumvent: for example, Henry Giffard, an actor from Dublin, found an ingenious solution; he simply provided a paid concert with a play presented 'free' in the middle. He survived five years at his playhouse in Goodman's Fields, during which time he gave Garrick his debut, but the 'patentees' who managed the two licensed houses finally managed to suppress him. Foote succeeded with a similar ploy when he offered 'A cup of Tea – at theatre prices', charging for refreshment rather than drama (see p. 95).

There were permanent companies in other major cities like York, Bath, Norwich (p. 44) and Bristol. Travelling companies toured county towns such as Ipswich, where Garrick was first billed under the name of 'Lyddal'. There were flourishing theatres in Dublin, while in Scotland the theatre was technically illegal until 1767. The provincial, Irish and Scottish stages have left few visual relics. There were amateur theatricals, although they were less evident than they were to become in the 1780s, and prints recording these are extremely rare.

Although today we go to the theatre to see one play, be it *Medea* or *Five Guys called Moe*, the Georgian playgoer was presented with a group of performances, rather like an old-fashioned cinema programme with a 'B' movie and a cartoon. The visit started with a main-piece which might have a prologue and an epilogue; this could be interspersed with a number of interludes and the visit would end with a short three act after-piece. Plays changed daily because the number of playgoers was limited and the theatres vast, rather like present day opera and ballet, and there was nothing like the amount of contemporary drama that is offered today. The best of plays from the time of Shakespeare onwards were performed regularly, most of them ruthlessly adapted to contemporary taste, a fate suffered even by Shakespeare: the final scene of an already altered *Romeo and Juliet* had extra lines added and *King Lear*, amongst other alterations, had a happy ending. Garrick increased the number of Shakespearean plays and contemporary work that was presented, but Jonson, Mrs Centilivre, Congreve, Rowe and Vanburgh were all staples.

Theatrical mezzotints depict scenes from all types of plays and operas, new and old. After-pieces, light or satirical, provided opportunities for Shuter, Moody, Weston and Garrick himself to shine and for this reason there are numerous prints of them. Among the large plates showing actors on the stage are to be found plays both famous and forgotten. Plays by Shakespeare such as *The Merry Wives of Windsor* (p. 14), *Macbeth* (p. 81), *King Lear* (p. 27) and *King John* (p. 69) were illustrated together with now forgotten works like Garrick's *Lethe* (p. 22), Cumberland's *The West Indian* (p. 46) and Foote's *The Mayor of Garrat* (p. 33). In the comedies the scene portrayed is not always that in which leading players perform: when Major O'Flaherty attacks Varland in *The West Indian*, we are seeing two minor characters rather than the protagonists. This happens to be the most memorable scene; it would have been mere coincidence had it been the most important one too. This also applies when single figures are portrayed: search the synopses of *The Beaux Stratagem* (p. 84) or *The Wonder! a Woman Keeps a Secret* (p. 89) and you will not find the characters 'Foiguard' or 'Gibby', who mean nothing in the play. Another form of theatrical entertainment, the equivalent of the music-hall of the next century, was a rich source for prints; figures like Matthew Skeggs (p. 142) and the rope dancer Anthony Maddox (p. 141) became celebrated figures. Even prologues, epilogues (p. 92) and pantomimes (p. 74) were the subject of prints. Theatrical prints were important as souvenirs to those who had seen the plays and wished to have a record of memorable performances.

The theatrical wardrobe consisted of worn-out suits and dresses, although leading actresses like Mrs Abington received allowances for fine clothes and some of the men acquired cast-off finery. For a small part of the repertory specific dress was worn, for example, 'Gibby' (p. 89) was played in Scot's dress, while the Irishman in *The Register Office* (p. 63) wore a worn coat. Both *King John* and *Richard the Third* had required 'Elizabethan' dress even before Garrick devised costumes which were more in period: thus King John (p. 69) seems to have adopted Richard the Third's sur-coat (p. 67). Plays with oriental settings were performed in 'Turkish / Eastern' dress, even if set in China; 'Roman' dress was worn for classical and pseudo-classical scenes (p. 144); for Italian renaissance parts there was the curiously striped 'Iachimo' suit as worn by Turbutt as Sosia in *Amphitryon* (p. 1). However, most plays were acted in contemporary dress as worn by Macbeth and Lady Macbeth (p. 81).

Stage setting was an important adjunct to realistic acting: Garrick improved theatre lighting, introducing dimming and inset footlights that increased the distance visible on the darkened stage. For his pantomimes he let his stage designer de Loutherbourg's imagination and invention run free; the results must have been spectacular (p. 74). Unfortunately most of the effects were impossible to capture in prints and are consequently lost to us.

Although most leading players of Garrick's life-time are to be seen in this exhibition, there are a number of absentees: not every theatrical print after Zoffany has been exhibited since space did not permit this; the print of Spranger Barry in the part of Hamlet is lacking from this collection; Charles Macklin, Garrick's other great rival, was never engraved in mezzotint even as Shylock, his greatest role. Some of the greatest performances were reproduced in line engravings and etchings, but not in mezzotint, for example, Hogarth's engraving of *The Beggar's Opera* in 1728; this is also the case with his famous picture of Garrick as Richard the Third starting from his couch, which revolutionised the depiction of the actors in role. Frontispieces to editions of plays, both in series like 'Bell's British Theatre' and in separate editions, show actors and actresses in roles not seen in mezzotint.

Biography of David Garrick

David Garrick was born in Hereford in 1717, and brought up at Lichfield. At the age of twenty he came to London to become a wine merchant. Fascinated by the stage, he played in amateur theatricals, wrote epilogues and his first farce, *Lethe* (p. 22). In March 1741 Henry Giffard gave him a professional opening in a pantomime at his theatre in Goodman's Fields. Garrick replaced Richard Yates, who was ill, with sufficient success to be taken on when Goodman's troupe played at Ipswich and he subsequently attempted, unsuccessfully, to join one of the patent houses. In the following year Garrick played the part of Richard the third at Goodman's Fields, and for a season he filled the small theatre, to the loss of the larger theatres. His technique was naturalistic and revolutionary, and most people greeted his performances with enthusiasm: Pope, for example, wrote, 'that young man never had his equal', adding prophetically, 'and never will have a rival'. Garrick stayed at Goodman's Fields until it was forced to shut early in 1742, playing occasionally at Drury Lane. After an extremely successful summer season in Dublin, he became a member of the company at Drury Lane and in 1747 invested in a share of the theatre's patent. His company thrived and for over twenty years dominated the London stage. Garrick was as popular with the Pit and Galleries as with the Boxes, although this did not prevent trouble: the theatre was wrecked in 1755 when the audience opposed foreign dancers during the war with France. The theatre was badly damaged again in January 1763 when Garrick tried to dispense with the practice of half-price admission for late-comers. The labours of a manager, combined with disputes with his partner, John Lacy, wore Garrick down and later that year he took time away from the stage and travelled in Europe. Fearing that he would lose his place to rivals and protégés like William Powell (p. 98), Garrick returned to London in 1765, bringing with him new ideas for lighting. Unfortunately his health declined and he decided to reduce the amount of tragedy he played. By the 1770s many of the players with whom he had performed successfully had left the stage, and he himself was ageing. During the summer of 1776 Garrick acted many of his greatest parts for the last time, ending with Don Felix in *The Wonder* on 10 June. He spent his retirement visiting friends at their country seats. While spending Christmas with Lord Spencer he collapsed and was taken to London, where he died on 20 January 1779. He was buried in Westminster Abbey; his pall bearers included the Duke of Devonshire, four other peers and his patron Sir Watkin Wynne (p. 67).

James McArdell was one of the first wave of Irish mezzotint engravers to arrive in London in 1746. Born in Cow Lane in Dublin, now known by the more genteel name of Greek Street, in 1728 or 29, he was taught either by John Brooks or Andrew Miller (p. 1). After scraping his first three mezzotints, he travelled to London together with Richard Houston and Brooks. Almost immediately they prospered and were soon joined by Charles Spooner and Richard Purcell. Before long it was evident that McArdell was the most able engraver, a fact which was confirmed when in 1752, the Duke of Grafton permitted him to engrave van Dyck's portrait of the two sons of the Duke of Richmond. McArdell worked successfully both for the printsellers and later for himself. He made theatrical prints for most of his life, beginning with '*Benjamin Hallet*' (p. 140) in 1748. In 1754 he engraved '*Garrick as Hamlet*' (p. 52), his first plate after Benjamin Wilson, and in the same year produced his first plates after Sir Joshua Reynolds, two portraits of the Duke and Duchess of Leinster. In a short but highly productive career, McArdell engraved thirty eight prints after Reynolds, twenty one after Thomas Hudson and fourteen of theatrical sitters. Dying young and intestate in 1765, most of his plates were eventually acquired by Robert Sayer.

His style was precise and clear, and he varied it to suit the painter; a print after Wilson looked very different to one after Hudson. Reynolds thought highly of him, employing him to engrave '*Lady Charlotte Fitzwilliam*' the only print Reynolds ever published himself, claiming that 'by this man shall I be immortalised'.

Benjamin Wilson was an artist whose contribution to theatrical painting was to reproduce the darkness of the theatre in a realistic way. His paintings of Shakespearean scenes show all the shadows of a poorly lit stage. Born in Leeds, he was a great admirer of Rembrandt and produced the famous etching in Rembrandt's style that deceived Hudson and other connoisseurs. Most of his subject paintings are permeated with a Rembrandtesque gloom, which successfully concealed Wilson's poor, sometimes appalling (p. 50), draughtmanship. By the 1750s he was among the leading portrait painters, succeeding Hogarth as Serjeant-Painter to the King in 1764. He had a greater interest in the theatre than any other contemporary artist, managing the Duke of York's private theatre in James Street, Westminster. Throughout his life he maintained a great interest in chemistry and electricity and was elected F.R.S. in 1751. By about 1770 he had abandoned painting for scientific research and he died in 1788.

Johann Zoffany was born Johannes Josephus Zauffaly near Frankfurt in 1733. His continental training taught him composition which was important for a theatrical painter. He came to England in 1754 where he found no better employment than painting clock faces, although he eventually became a drapery painter in Benjamin Wilson's studio. Rescued by Garrick from this drudgery, he set up as a theatrical painter and produced a series of large pictures of groups of actors on the stage. Starting with Garrick and Cibber as Jaffeir and Belvidera (p. 55), these paintings proved eminently suitable for engraving as mezzotints. Throughout the 1760s he produced a regular flow of these paintings and other conversation pieces. When these went out of fashion he moved to India, returning in 1789, a wealthy man. He painted little on his return, but arranged that some of his paintings of India were engraved as mezzotints by Richard Earlom. He died in 1818.

Robert Sayer had the most extensive print publishing business in eighteenth century London, although his trade did not include as many prestigious prints as that of John Boydell. He published and re-published many prints after major paintings as well as a horde of lesser plates, copies and piracies. In this he had a rival in Carington Bowles, but Bowles produced far fewer fine plates. In addition Sayer produced numerous maps, pattern-books and general stationery.

Sayer was born in 1725 and acquired the business of Philip Overton in Fleet Street. Overton's business had principally been that of a wholesale stationer, but Sayer expanded his trade. Over the next decades he astutely purchased copper-plates, including a large share of those by James McArdell. On another occasion he seems to have acquired a one-third share of the Finlayson-Zoffany theatre plates. In 1766 he issued a general catalogue of his stock. As his trade grew he took a former apprentice, John Bennett, into partnership in 1774; in order to make reasonable terms Sayer had an inventory of his stock taken, and from this issued a catalogue in 1775. After Bennett's death Sayer continued to trade alone, before taking on his former apprentice, Robert Laurie (p. 77), and James Whittle, to run the business. He retired to Bath, where he died on 29 February 1794, leaving the business to be sold to Laurie & Whittle on special terms. The next year they issued their own catalogue and remained in partnership until Laurie's retirement in 1812 when R.H. Laurie joined as a junior partner, becoming sole proprietor in 1818. The business became more map-oriented and still survives as Imrays, publishers of charts and yachtsmen's guides.

Sayer seems to have been ruthless and none too honest; he was capable of falsifying proofs and altering plates if commerce warranted. Like the Bowles family, his descendants joined the ranks of the gentry.

Christopher Lennox-Boyd

Abbreviations

<table>
<tr><td>BL</td><td>British Library</td></tr>
<tr><td>BM</td><td>British Museum</td></tr>
<tr><td>C</td><td>Fitzwilliam Museum, Cambridge</td></tr>
<tr><td>CLB</td><td>Private collection of Christopher Lennox-Boyd</td></tr>
<tr><td>H</td><td>Harvard Theatre Collection</td></tr>
<tr><td>TM</td><td>Theatre Museum, London. The National Museum of the Performing Arts</td></tr>
<tr><td>NPG</td><td>National Portrait Gallery, London</td></tr>
<tr><td>PRO</td><td>Public Record Office, London</td></tr>
<tr><td>V&A</td><td>Victoria & Albert Museum, Department of Prints and Drawings</td></tr>
</table>

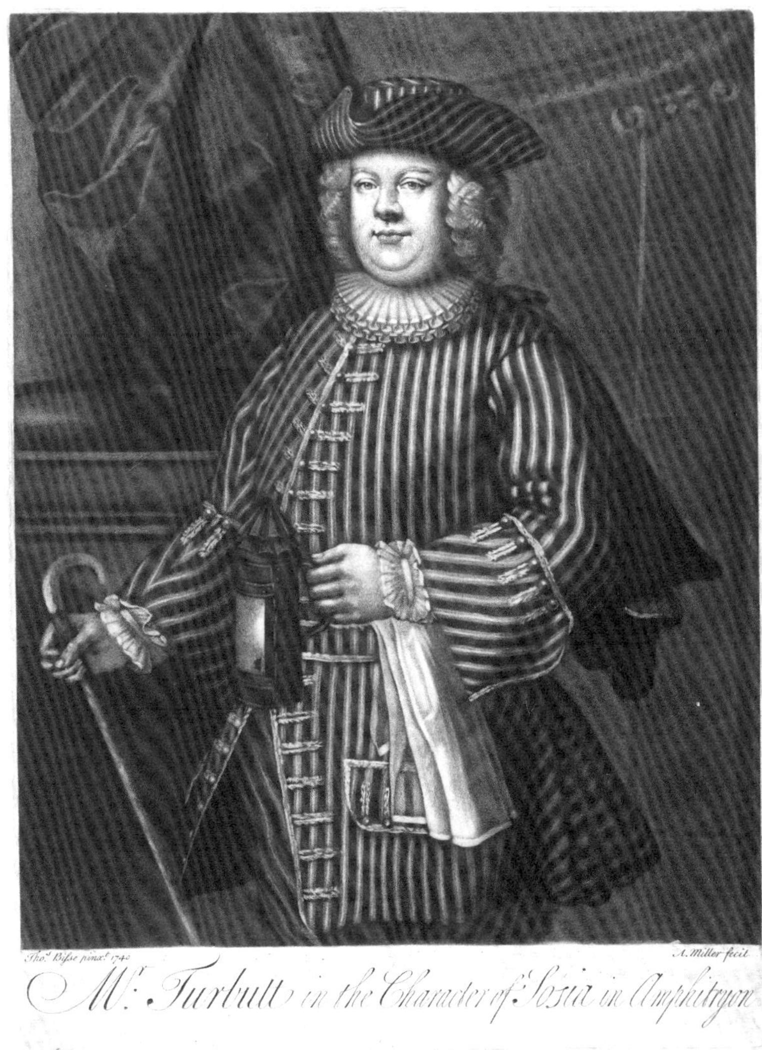

1 M.' Turbutt in the Character of Sosia in Amphitryon

Engraved by Andrew Miller after Thomas Bisse

318 x 250 I; 355 x 252 Pl.

References: CS 57; O'D 1; Hall 1

1. Finished proof with the engraved inscription: *"Tho.' Bisse pinx! 1740 *** A. Miller fecit. / M.' Turbutt in the Character of Sosia in Amphitryon".*
Impressions: CLB P8,492 (impression exhibited); BM; H.

2. Republished by Henry Overton[1]: *"Printed for and Sold by H. Overton at the White Horse without Newgate London".*
Impressions: BM.

This is the only recorded work after Thomas Bisse and no other details are known about this artist. The portrait of Robert Turbutt in the character of Sosia, painted in 1740, is characteristic of theatrical portraiture to this date. In the same way that a folio bible in the hand of a popular preacher indicates his calling, Miller paints Turbutt holding a lamp; his striped dress is as clear an indication of his vocation as are the lawn sleeves worn by a bishop.

Andrew Miller is said to have been trained by John Faber in London but their styles are quite different. He practised engraving in London for a few years, but shortly after he engraved this print he went to Dublin, where he stayed until his death in 1763. When in Ireland he advertised in the newspapers that Faber had been his master, but there is no evidence to support this claim. Miller engraved four portraits of actors; in London he engraved mezzotints of John Harper and of Joe Miller and later in Dublin he engraved two copies of Faber's prints of Margaret Woffington and David Garrick. John Brooks, probably the most important engraver in Ireland at the time and the man who had trained many of the great Irish mezzotint engravers, left Dublin for London in 1757. His departure allowed Miller to fill his place as the leading mezzotint engraver.

☞ Dryden's play, based on Plautus, takes its name from the central character Amphitryon who, expecting to arrive home the following day from a successful campaign, sends his slave Sosia in advance to inform his wife, Alcmena. Jupiter, in order to enjoy the favours of Alcmena, assumes the form of her husband and forestalls him by ordering Mercury to assume the form of Sosia, thus keeping out the true Sosia. The comedy derives from the complications arising from the successive arrival at Amphitryon's palace of two indistinguishable Amphitryons and two indistinguishable Sosias, and their final confrontation.

All plates by Miller, with the possible exception of his print of Joe Miller, are rare. The price asked for an impression of '*Turbutt in the Character of Sosia*' by Robert Grave[2] in 1809, £1 11s 6d, suggests that this print was considered rare even then, especially since he listed other theatrical prints of a similar size by Miller at 10s 6d.

Little is known about Turbutt who is first recorded in 1733. An entry in *The General Advertiser* of 27 February 1746 mentions that on the day before

> died, after a lingering illness, Mr Robert Turbutt, belonging to the Theatre Royal in Drury Lane, and Master of the Swan Tavern in Smithfield, a facetious and agreeable companion, greatly and justly esteem'd by all that knew him for his Sincerity where he proffess'd a friendship.

Sosia was the part he chose for his benefit on 12 May 1740. He was presumably the Turbutt who had a booth at Bartholomew Fair in 1741.

More is known about Turbutt's son, who was sentenced to hang for the theft of a silver pint mug. In his defence it was said that he had been under immense stress since his wife was in labour at the time. Garrick and the principal actors at Drury Lane petitioned the King on his behalf in early October 1765, and he was reprieved. When one of the cast – and the inference was that it was Weston – was asked what they thought of the matter, he replied that there was nothing unusual about it, since it was just another case of an actor having one more cup than he should.

[1] Henry Overton, printseller (fl. 1751–c. 1765).
[2] Robert Grave the younger (d. 1825), printseller in Tottenham Court Road.

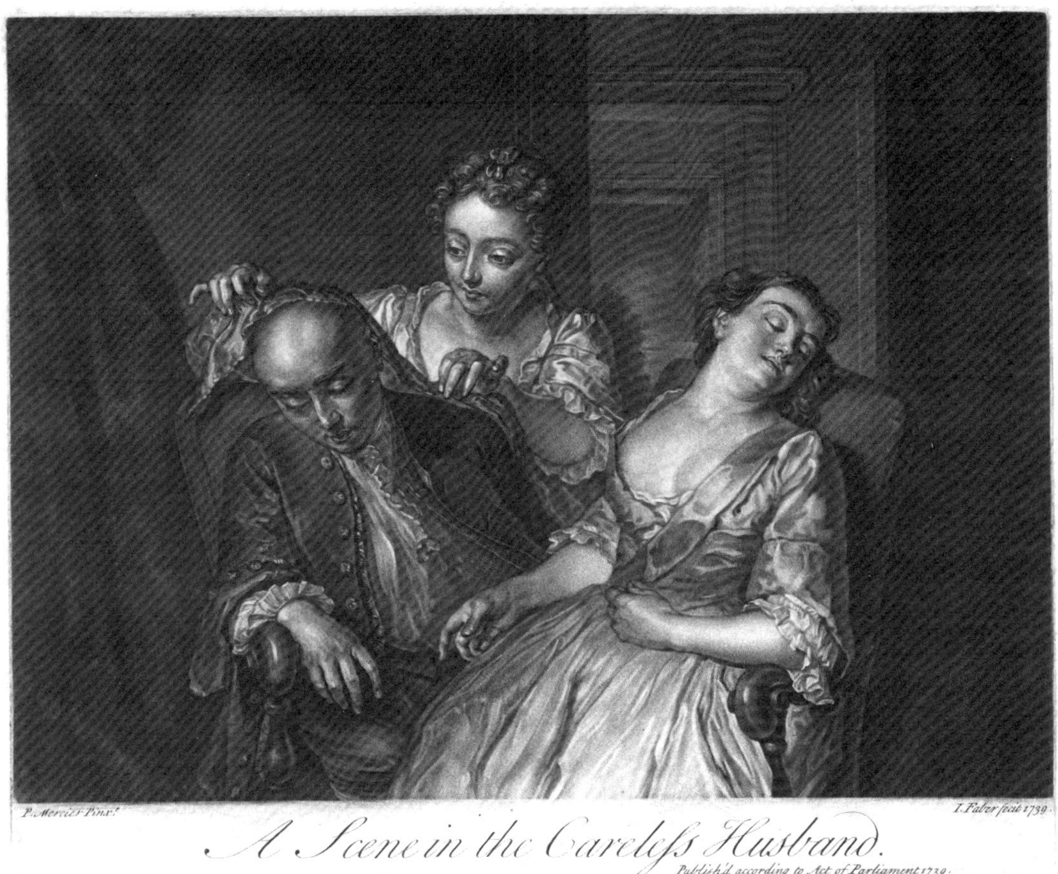

2 A Scene in the Careless Husband

Engraved by John Faber jun.
after Philip Mercier

Published by John Faber jun. 1739

249 x 326 I; 276 x 328 Pl.

References: CS 414

1. With the engraved inscription: *"P. Mercier Pinx! *** I. Faber fecit 1739. | A Scene in the Careless Husband. | *** Publish'd according to Act of Parliament 1739.".*
Impressions: CLB P5,932 (impression exhibited).

It is difficult to know whether the print illustrates a scene in a play or a book; it could even show actual players on the stage. Equally it could be mistaken for a simple domestic scene. A Scene in the Careless Husband and its pair A Scene from the Recruiting Officer are imaginative representations of scenes in plays. It is possible that the inspiration for these two pictures stemmed from Philip Mercier's theatrical interest, for in 1733 he became a shareholder in John Rich's[1] new theatre at Covent Garden. Mercier's picture does not represent theatrical portraiture, being closer to book illustration. By 1740 he had abandoned the competitive field of portrait painting for the riskier practice of fancy pictures. He had already worked with John Faber, who engraved a number of his portraits. In May 1739, subscriptions for the first eight mezzotints by Faber after Mercier's fancy paintings were being advertised in York, where he eventually set up his studio (see over). Over the next decade he published at least another sixteen prints.

John Faber junior (1684–1756) was the son of a mezzotint engraver. His output consisted overwhelmingly of portraits, or 'heads' which were skilfully and sensitively engraved, but somewhat homogenised by Faber's lack of imagination.

In *The Careless Husband* by Colley Cibber,[2] Sir Charles Easy, who neglects his wife and carries on intrigues with her maid and Lady Graveairs, is brought to contrition by discovering that his wife's kind and gentle treatment of him is due not to ignorance of his infidelities, but to her virtue and sense of duty. The coquette, Lady Modish, is encouraged to accept the suit of her honourable

3

lover, Lord Morelove, by a plot which excites her jealousy and persuades her that Morelove, weary of her contempt, is about to give her up.

Mercier's picture shows a moment in Act V, Scene IV with the characters Mrs Edging, Sir Charles Easy and Lady Easy; the last is supposed by some to be a portrait of Mrs Clive.

This Day are publish'd,
PROPOSALS *for Printing by* SUBSCRIPTION,
EIGHT Prints in Metzotinto, done by Faber, after Mr. Mercier's Paintings, reprefenting, 1. A School of Boys. 2. Another of Girls. 3. A Scene in the Recruiting Officer. 4. A Scene in the Carelefs Hufband. 5. A Lady at her Toilet. 6. A Venetian Courtezan. 7. Cupid in the Character of Bacchus. 8. Bacchus in the Character of Cupid.

Each Subfcriber to pay Half a Guinea at the time of fubfcribing, and Half a Guinea on delivery of the Prints. They fhall be printed on a fine French Royal and Imperial Paper. The original Paintings may be feen at Mr. Mercier's, in the Great Piazza in Covent-Garden, by whom Subfcriptions are taken in ; as alfo by Mr. Brindley, Bookfeller to his Royal Highnefs the Prince of Wales, in New Bond-Street ; Mr. Regnier, Printfeller, in Newport-ftreet, near Long-Acre ; Mr. Tiney Printfeller, in Fleet-ftreet ; and at Read's Lace-Chamber on Ludgate-Hill, London.

N. B. Five of the above Plates are already done, and Specimens may be feen of them at the above Places ; the other three are near finifh'd, and will be ready to deliver to the Subfcribers next Week.

Specimens are alfo to be feen, and Subfcriptions taken in, by WARD and CHANDLER, Bookfellers in *York*.

---

[1] John Rich (1687?–1761), impressario, manager of Covent Garden.

[2] Colley Cibber (1671–1757), actor, manager of Drury Lane and playwright, was the father-in-law of Susannah Cibber (see pages 11–13, '*Mrs Cibber in the Character of Cordelia*'.).

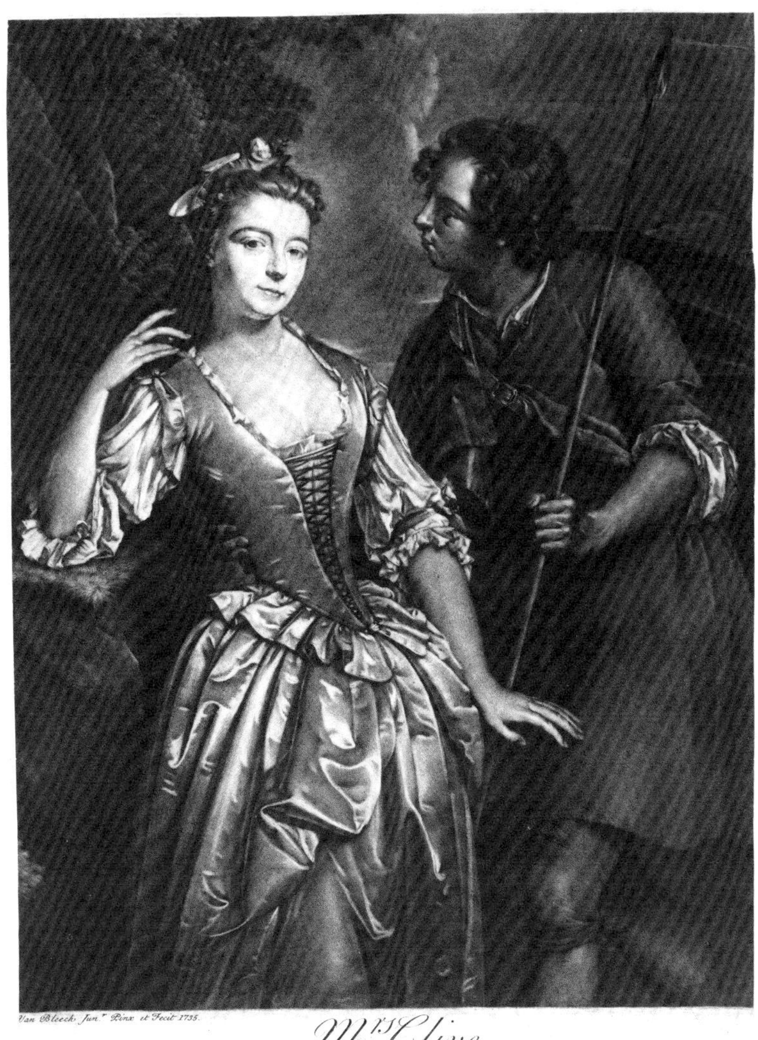

3 Mrs Clive in the Character of Philida

Painted and engraved by Peter van Bleeck jun.

[Published by Peter van Bleeck jun. c. 1735]

316 x 233 I; 344 x 234 Pl.

References: CS 2; O'D 1; Hall 9

1. With the engraved inscription: "*Van Bleeck Junr Pinx et Fecit 1735. | Mrs Clive | in the Character of Philida.*"
Impressions: P26,496 (impression exhibited); BM; H.

In 1735 George Vertue[1] recorded a dispute between Peter van Bleeck and John Faber, instigated by the former. Further details of this are provided by two undated newspaper cuttings in the theatre collection at Harvard:

> The Print of Mrs Clive, in the Character of PHILIDA[2] (lately published by Mr. Faber) failing in the likeness, obliged Mr. Van Bleeck, jun (the Painter) to have the same done over, by another Hand, and may now be had of Mr. Sympson,[3] at the Dove in Russel-Court, Drury Lane.

Faber replied:

> Mr. VAN BLEECK, Jun. Painter, having asserted, that I have in a Print of Mrs. Clive, in the Character of Phillida fail'd in the Likeness, and that he has been obliged to have the same done by another Hand, meaning his own; I submit it to all Judges, which of us has most fail'd; the Painter, in his Copy after nature, or I in imitation of his Picture; and at the same Time take leave to acquaint the Publick, that I always acknowledge my Print unlike Mrs Clive, it being impossible to take a likeness where none was found. The Publick may

soon be convinc'd of this, when they see a Print of Mrs Clive, which, I hear, will shortly be published from a painting by an eminent Hand; and this I think sufficiently proves that the first was never approv'd. In the mean Time I would desire the Curious to examine two Prints lately published of Oliver Cromwell, from an Original Painting of Sir Peter Lely, the one by Mr. VAN BLEECK, jun. and the other by JOHN FABER.

The print by 'an eminent hand' to which Faber was alluding was presumably the mezzotint by Alexander van Haecken of Mrs Clive which shows her seated, holding a music book on her knee.[4] This print was still being published by Bowles & Carver[5] at the end of the century, an indication of the plate's success. Despite Faber's description of van Haecken as 'eminent', it is interesting to note that Vertue records two portraits of Senesino and Farinelli, both engraved in 1735, as being van Haecken's first works in mezzotint.

Catherine, or Kitty, Clive was born in 1711, the daughter of William Raftor, an impecunious lawyer from Kilkenny who had settled in London. She had little education, but a forceful personality. She came to the attention of Colley Cibber, then manager of Drury Lane, who employed her there when she was seventeen years old.

She achieved great success in 1729 as Phillida in Cibber's *Love in a Riddle*; the piece had seemed doomed to failure until Clive entered and changed the mood of the audience. Although the piece was later withdrawn after all, she had made an enormous impact.

Even when her brief marriage to George Clive, a barrister, had ended, her character was 'then and to the last unblemished'.[6] Kitty Clive remained at Drury Lane until 1741, becoming increasingly popular. Like Mrs Cibber, she was a great favourite of Handel, and sang at the first production of his oratorio *Samson* in 1742. Her forte was 'well-marked characters of low or middle life, and impersonation'. Her attempts at more serious parts did not meet with critical approval; one critic complained that, 'the applause she received in Portia was disgraceful both to her and the audience'.[7] Similarly, Davies lamented: 'Of Mrs Clive's [O]Phelia I shall only say, that I regret that the first comic actress in the world should so far mistake her talents as to undertake it'.[8] This type of criticism unfortunately did not deter her from playing parts which did not suit her: 'Mrs Clive, particularly happy in low humour, with a most disagreeable face and person, was always the joy of her audience when she kept clear of anything serious and genteel'.[9]

She was an invaluable comic actress, being equally successful in roles, 'from the high bred Lady Fanciful to the vulgar Mrs Heidelberg; country girls, romps, hoydens and dowdies; superannuated beauties, viragos and humorists'.[10] She remained almost constantly with Garrick's company from the time of her engagement in 1746 until she retired in April 1769. Although Mrs Clive was not always easy to deal with, being jealous and capricious, she and Garrick respected one another's talent and even maintained a correspondence. She entertained a variety of distinguished visitors at her house at Strawberry Hill; Dr Johnson admired her greatly, considering her 'the best actress I ever saw', while Goldsmith claimed that, 'She has more true honour than any actor or actress

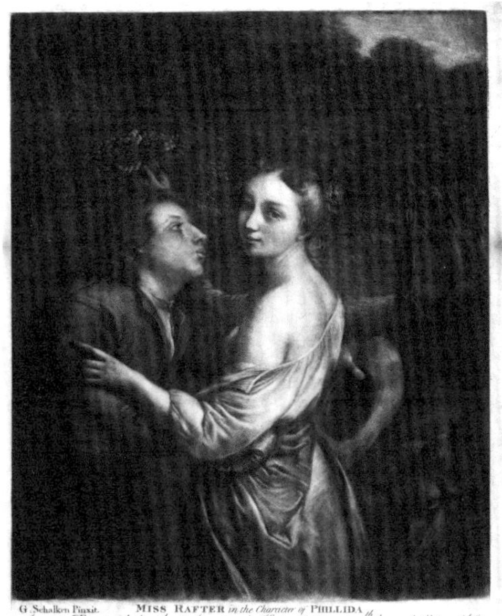

Miss Rafter in the Character of Phillida

280 x 226 I; 322 x 226 Pl.

References: CS ENA II, 19; O'D 5; Hall 12

1. With the engraved inscription: "MISS RAFTER in the Character of PHILLIDA / G. Schalken Pinxit. *** // [in two columns] See native Beauty clad without disguise, / No art, t'allure a paltry Lovers Eyes, / No stiff, sett Airs, which but betray the mind, / But unaffected Innocence, we find: Happy the Nymph w.th Charms by Nature blcft, / But happicr Swain, who of the Nymph pofest, / Can taste the Joys, which she alone can bring, / And live in Pleasures which alternate spring."
Impressions: CLB; BM; H.

1. *Walpole Society*, Vol. XXX (1948–50), Vertue VI, p. 192.
2. C S 85.
3. Joseph Sympson Sen., an eminent printseller.
4. C S 4.
5. Bowles & Carver printsellers at 69 St. Paul's Churchyard (1793–1832).
6. Theodore Martin in DNB.
7. Gentleman, I, p. 297.
8. *Dramatic Miscellanies*, III, p. 127.
9. Gentleman, II, p. 497.
10. Davies, II, p. 197.
11. After Colley Cibber's *Love in a Riddle* was howled off the stage in 1729, he used part of the plot to create his successful after-piece *Damon and Phillida*.
12. C S E.N.A. II, p. 1628, no. 19.
13. *ibid*.
14. Edward Evans (1789–1835), printseller.

on the English or any other stage that I have seen'. She died in December 1785.

In addition to those mentioned above, there are three further mezzotint plates of Mrs Clive in the character of Phillida from Colley Cibber's *Damon and Phillida*.[11] These were supposedly also engraved by John Faber and van Bleeck. What is more remarkable is the attribution of the original painting to Godfrey Schalken, who had died five years before Mrs Clive was born.

The first plate, in reverse to the painting, was only known to Chaloner Smith from a single impression which was probably cut;[12] he records it as measuring about 322 x 252 mm and states that 'the workmanship is admirable and in the style of Van Bleeck'. The second plate, in the same direction as the painting, is only known in a state with the engraver's name erased[13] (see left). Chaloner-Smith had seen copies of this plate, but only in a worn state. The third plate was published by the famous printseller Edward Evans[14]. In both the last two plates the composition closely resembles Schalken's picture, which was sold in the sale of Jacques de Roore at The Hague on 4 September 1747, but the face of the girl has been altered, perhaps in an attempt to achieve a better likeness of Mrs Clive. The larger plate could well have been engraved by Faber, although no impressions are known with the engraver's name and all impressions recorded are on late paper. Both plates are listed in Evans's catalogue for 1853.

In spite of her great success, Clive was rarely engraved in character. There is a large etching, published by Charles Mosley in 1751 after a drawing by Thomas Worlidge, in which she is seen as the Fine Lady in *Lethe*, and a small portrait of her as Mrs Heidelberg in *The Clandestine Marriage*.

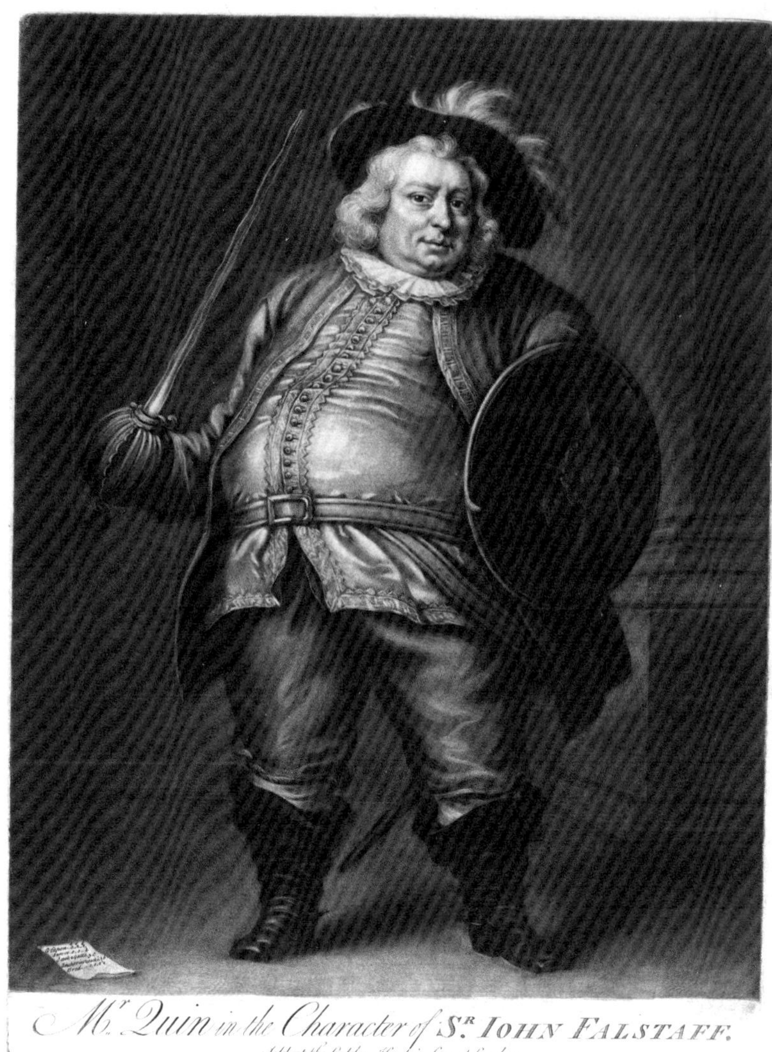

4 M.ʳ Quin in the Character of Sʳ John Falstaff

[Painted?] and engraved by James McArdell

Published by James McArdell
[distributed by 1751]

Re-published by Robert Sayer

330 x 251 I; 352 x 253 Pl.

References: CS 149; R 149; G 173; O'D 5;
Hall 11

1. With the engraved inscription: *"M.ʳ Quin in
the Character of S.ᴿ IOHN FALSTAFF. | Sold at
the Golden Head in Covent Garden.".*
Impressions: CLB P8,484 (impression exhibited).

**2. Extensively re-worked; boots, shield and
coat below shield now much darker.**
Impressions: CLB.

3. Re-published by Robert Sayer: *"*** J.,
M.ᶜArdell delin. et fecit. | M.ʳ Quin in the Character
of S.ᴿ JOHN FALSTAFF. | London, Printed for*

McArdell's mezzotint was available by at least September 1751 when a small group of his portraits was advertised in George Faulkner's Dublin Journal[1] by Thomas Silcock, at his shop in Nicholas Street, Dublin and a fellow Irishman, Paul Smith of Crane Lane (see over). No advertisements for this print have been found in the English newspapers. It seems that McArdell, who had arrived in London in the late 1740s, only began to advertise his own work from 1754. As well as Smith and Silcock, two mezzotint engravers, Andrew Miller and Michael Ford, marketed McArdell's prints in Dublin. Ford advertised that he annually travelled to England in order to purchase stock and pressed his clients to furnish him with their requests. For this purpose it seems that both Silcock and Ford raised 'subscriptions' which enabled them to apply to an engraver or printseller in England for a precise number of impressions.

The subject of this print is the same as that used for a painting which is now at the Folger Shakespeare Library. Some time after McArdell's death in 1765 the plate was acquired by Robert Sayer and was extensively re-worked.[2] Sayer added McArdell's name to the print and claimed that McArdell was not only the engraver but also the draughtsman; at the same time Sayer replaced McArdell's address with his own publication line. In the past the Folger paint-

Rob! Sayer, Map & Printseller, at N.° 53 in Fleet Street.".
Impressions: BM.

4. [Re-published by Laurie & Whittle].
Worn, with the addition of '53' in the bottom r. of the inscription space.
Impressions: CLB.

JUST imported, and are only to be fold by Paul Smith in Crane lane, and Thomas Silcock in Nicholas ftreet, the original Mezotinto Prints of his Royal Highnefs the Prince of Wales, the Duke of Dorfet, the Bifhop of Ely, Counfellor Erskine, Capt. Coram, and Mr. Quin in the Character of Falftaff, (all) done by the ingenuous Mr. James M'Ardill.
    N.B. The Print of the Duke of Dorfet is fold for 1s. 7d. Halfp.

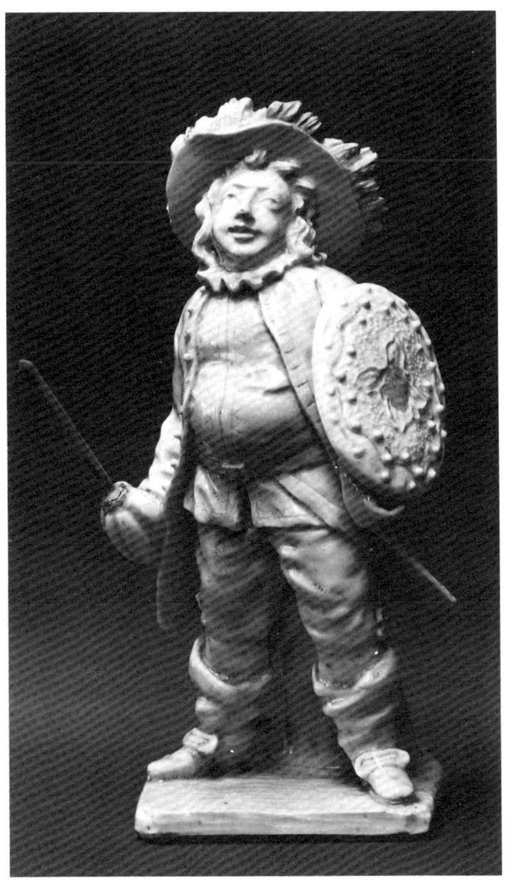

ing was attributed to McArdell on the strength of Sayer's claim, but the attribution must remain tentative, especially since no other painting by McArdell is known. The print and the painting differ and since no conclusive link can be made to McArdell it is possible that the painting is a fine oil copy either from a drawing or indeed from the mezzotint.

The plate was listed in Saver & Bennett's catalogue for 1775, priced at 2s. The number '53', added later to the then worn plate, corresponds to the catalogue entry in Laurie & Whittle's 1795 catalogue. In 1773 Walter Shropshire[3] listed a fine impression in his stock at 5s and the Magazin des Estampes listed one the following year at 3s 6d. Quin's reputation in this part and the absence of any alternative publication guaranteed sales of the print until the end of the century. The mezzotint may also have been used as a memorial print when Quin died. This reputation was also reflected in the manufacture of numerous Bow, Derby and Staffordshire porcelain figures;[4] these were so popular that the Derby factory manufactured six different sizes to cater for customers' varying tastes and purses – even Garrick owned one (see over).

Falstaff was regarded as one of Quin's finest roles, for it was suited to both his bulk and his character. Davies believed that Quin was only ever exceeded in the part by John Henderson, and that he had the perfect manner and build to play Falstaff, especially in the scene in which he had to lift the dead Hotspur[5], although this, he points out, could also cause certain problems:

> Quin had little or no difficulty in perching Garrick upon his shoulders, who looked like a dwarf on the back of a giant. But, oh! how he tugged and toiled to raise Barry from the ground! As they were rivals, and sometimes jarred, we may, without breach of charity, suppose, that Hotspur sometimes enjoyed the sweat of Falstaff.[6]

Born on 24 February 1693 in Covent Garden, James Quin was the grandson of Mark Quin, Lord Mayor of Dublin in 1667. He was taken there in 1700 or 1701, and attended Trinity College for a short time. It transpired that his parents' marriage had been invalid and he was unable to inherit their real property; he was thus forced to try his luck on the stage. He is billed at Covent Garden by February 1715 and played both there and at Drury Lane until September 1742, after which date he performed exclusively at Covent Garden. It is likely that his relationship with the manager there, John Rich, was particularly strong, for in 1721 Quin had saved his life during a stage brawl; Quin was involved in a number of similar incidents over the years, and in fact was twice charged with manslaughter.

Garrick and Quin were thrust together on the stage for the first time in 1746–7. Arthur Murphy asserts that during the entire season, although there may not have been a friendship, there was no outright dispute between the two men.[7] Davies explains that 'A Close intamacy [sic] between Garrick and Quin could not be expected during the time their rivalship lasted' as, 'Before Mr. Garrick snatched the laurel from the brow of Quin, he was accounted sole monarch of the stage, nor could he bear the dethronement very patiently'. Quin, the older man with greater experience who had ruled the stage for years, believed that Garrick was a new religion and that the audiences would in the end 'come back'; Garrick retorted, 'Pope Quin, who damns all churches but his own, Complains that heresy infects the town ... It is not heresy, but reformation'.[8]

Surprisingly, it does seem that Quin was able to sustain some of his position, adapting to the changes and possibly to a degree even joining Garrick's 'reformation'; this prompted one critical observer to look at Quin in a new light:

> ... I remember when ... some years ago, we were eternally repining at the wretched condition of the stage. Quin was at the head of the fraternity; but a very different man from what he is at present, and merely a bad copy of Booth; with all his mouthing and pageantry, but without his musical elocution, or his dignity. Whether Time or Emulation has had the greatest hand in Improving him, I know not; but certain it is, that he is improved, beyond what you will really imagine. He has got much more variety, and much more spirit ... '.[9]

Either Quin learned new tricks or Garrick realised that Quin could still enhance his company, for as late as 1750–1 he attempted to poach him from the rival company at Covent Garden. Although he was now under threat from the rise in popularity of Spranger Barry at Covent Garden, Quin was still in command. He used Garrick's application to his advantage, forcing Rich to increase his salary to the highest level of his entire career.

Quin played characters in both tragedy and comedy although it was felt that he was better at tragedy, when he was able to show sentiment and gravity of action rather than passion.[10] Cruelly, Gentleman felt that, as Othello, Quin had 'not a very probable external appearance to engage Desdemona ...'.[11] Despite the complaints that his performances were monotonous, he was able to enthral the audience with his powerful voice and a skilful use of tone and cadence, particularly when he delivered passages from Milton.

After Quin's last performance in 1751 he retired to Bath, although he returned to play Falstaff for Lacy Ryan's benefit the following year. After his retirement, he actually became a regular and welcome visitor to Garrick's house at Hampton.

He died in January 1766, at Bath.

[1] *The Dublin Journal*, 10–14 September 1751.
[2] It is likely that Sayer acquired this print after 1766 since McArdell's plates do not appear in Sayer's catalogue for that year.
[3] Walter Shropshire (d. 1785), book and print seller.
[4] Bradshaw *Derby*, pp. 314–6.
[5] *Henry IV part I*.
[6] *Dramatic Miscellanies*, I, p. 274.
[7] Murphy, I, p. 127.
[8] *ibid*.
[9] *The Museum, or Literary and Historical Register*, 28 Feb. 1747.
[10] Davies, II, p. 111.
[11] Gentleman, I, p. 151.

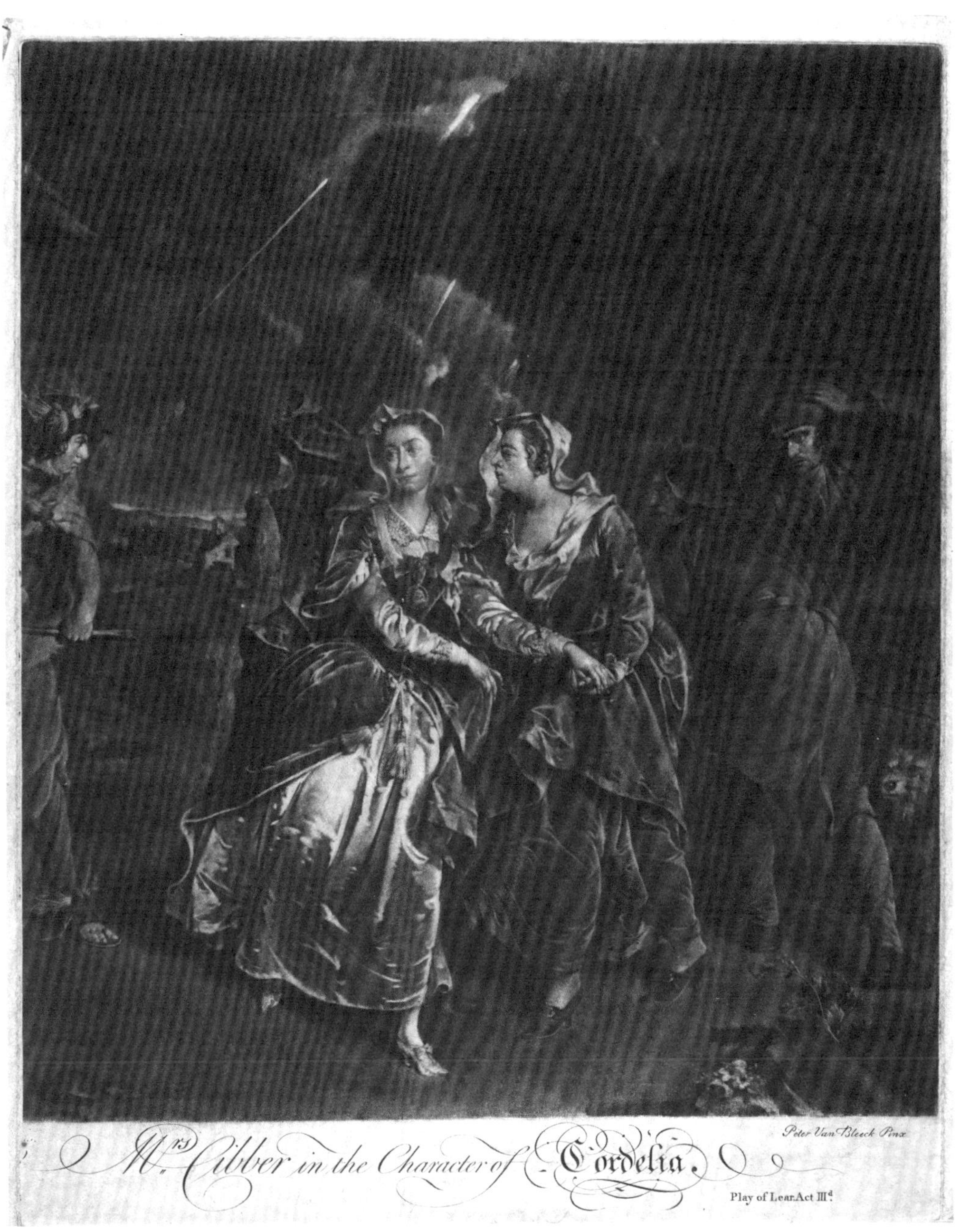

5 M.rs Cibber in the Character of Cordelia

Painted and engraved by Peter van Bleeck

Painted 1755

[Published by Peter van Bleeck]

405 x 404 I; 445 x 404 Pl.

References: CS 1; O'D 6; Hall 8

1. Before all letters.
Impressions: BM.

2. With the engraved inscription: *"Peter Van Bleeck Pinxt 1755. M.rs Cibber in the Character of Cordelia Play of Lear, Act III.d".*
Impressions: CLB P32,314 (impression exhibited); BM; TM; H.

The style of engraving in this print is atypical of van Bleeck, but Chaloner Smith and others accept the attribution. It seems to be his last print, done almost twenty years after the bulk of his work. The mezzotint is taken, in reverse, from a painting which is now at the Yale Center for British Art. A huge canvas over nine feet square, it illustrates a further advance in theatrical depiction; whereas Hogarth's Garrick as Richard III (1746) and Wilson's Garrick as Hamlet (1754) each depict a single instant, van Bleeck manages to record a succession of events and the movement of the players as they act their parts.

There is no clear evidence to suggest that this plate ever passed into the hands of a major printseller; nevertheless, all impressions in the third and fourth states were printed on wove paper. Wove paper was not commonly used for mezzotints in England until the early 1790s, which suggests that impressions were taken from the plate at a much later date; by this stage there is considerable wear

11

3. The plate reduced 59 mm on l., removing van Bleeck's name and half of the date. *Peter Van Bleeck Pinx* engraved top r. of the inscription space and the remainder of the inscription strengthened.
Impressions: TM; H.

4. With the remaining part of the date erased.
Impressions: CLB; BM.

to the plate. In the third state the plate has been cut down on the left side, removing the hovel and half of the figure. In addition the background between Edgar and Cordelia has been altered: the storm-blasted tree has been removed and replaced by a smaller one and a cottage and tower have been added in the distance. Had the background not been altered when the plate was cut down, the tree would have left an imbalance which would have directed the eye towards a detached fragment on the left hand side.

The painting, which is now in poor condition, seems at one stage to have been folded to show just the two central figures, but interestingly it has also been cut down on all sides. The background is the same as in the altered state of the mezzotint, which suggests that the picture may have been repainted, although this does not seem to be the case from a superficial inspection.

If, as suggested, the plate did fall into the hands of another printseller after van Bleeck's death in 1764, it could well have been cut down at this stage, possibly because it had been damaged. The alterations to the mezzotint were certainly made before 1799, since William Richardson[1] offered an impression of this print in his sale catalogue for that year, 'before the plate was reduced', which sold to [James?] Robson for 5s 6d.

In this scene from Act III, Cordelia has returned to England and wanders the heath in search of her father, accompanied by her maid Arante. She is about to be saved by Edgar, disguised as poor Tom, from two ruffians employed by Edmund.

The scene is taken from Nahum Tate's 1681 version, *King Lear and His Three Daughters*, which included a love affair between Cordelia and Edgar, the omission of the Fool and a happy ending. Francis Gentleman commented that these changes were acceptable as 'Shakespear's King Lear much wanted such assistance'.[2]

Susannah Maria Cibber was forty when van Bleeck painted her as Cordelia, a part she continued to play for some years. Even in her last season she was described as beautiful; it was said that, 'she preserved all the appearance of youth long after she had reached middle life'.[3] She was born in 1714, the sister of Dr Arne the composer. She first appeared on the stage in 1732–3 as a singer at the Haymarket Theatre and is recorded as receiving a benefit at Drury Lane the following season.[4]

Charles Burney thought her voice, 'a mere thread, and [her] knowledge of music inconsiderable', but he praised its expressiveness. She was a favourite of Handel and it was claimed that the beauty of her voice once provoked an enraptured Bishop to exclaim, 'Woman! thy sins be forgiven thee!'.[5] Her acting soon won sufficient acclaim for her to be ranked alongside Mrs Clive in tragic parts. Quin recognised her talents and declared: 'that woman has a heart, and can do anything where passion is required'.

In 1734 she unwisely married Theophilus, Colley Cibber's son. Aware that an acquaintance, William Sloper, had designs on his wife, Theophilus engineered an affair between the two, with the intention of suing for damages. Initially thwarted in his aim, Theophilus had to force Susannah to stay with Sloper at gun-point. At the trial, the minute and sordid details of the affair were made public. Theophilus claimed £5,000 in damages, but although he won the case his behaviour was found to be so despicable that he was awarded a mere £10. He tried again with more success at a later date, but Susannah remained with Sloper for the rest of her life. Theophilus's loss was compounded when, to spare her further embarrassment, the managers of both patent theatres made an agreement with her to exclude him from any engagements whilst she was in the company.

In 1746–7 she was at Covent Garden, where she acted with Garrick, Quin and Mrs Pritchard, which according to Horace Walpole was 'the best company that perhaps ever was together'.[6] Her performance as Juliet to Barry's Romeo during the remarkable twelve night battle with Garrick and George Anne Bellamy in 1750 (see p. 49), was greeted with delight. She returned to Drury Lane for the 1753–4 season and remained there until her retirement. Her health declined rapidly which often prevented her from appearing; the fact that she gave little or no notice at all infuriated the managers.

Although she and Garrick were essentially fond of each other, after her death he wrote that she had been:

> the greatest female plague belonging to my house. I could
> easily parry the artless thrusts and despise the coarse language
> of some of my other heroines; but whatever was Cibber's
> object, a new part or a new dress, she was always sure to carry
> her point by the acuteness of her invective and the steadiness
> of her perseverance.[7]

Her last full season was 1764–5. She died the following year and was buried in the cloisters of Westminster Abbey, in spite of being Roman Catholic. Davies believed that:

> … the harmony of her voice was as powerful as the animation
> of her look – in grief and tenderness, her eyes looked as if
> they swam in tears – in rage and despair they seemed to dart
> flashes of fire – [she] was the most pathetic of all actresses,
> and the only Cordelia of excellence.[8]

[1] William Richardson (fl. 1778–1808), print and book seller. Stock sold 23 April 1814.
[2] Gentleman, I, p. 352.
[3] Davies, II, p. 109.
[4] Genest, V, p. 100.
[5] *The Festival of Wit*, I, p. 5.
[6] DNB.
[7] *ibid*.
[8] *Dramatic Miscellanies*, II, p. 320.

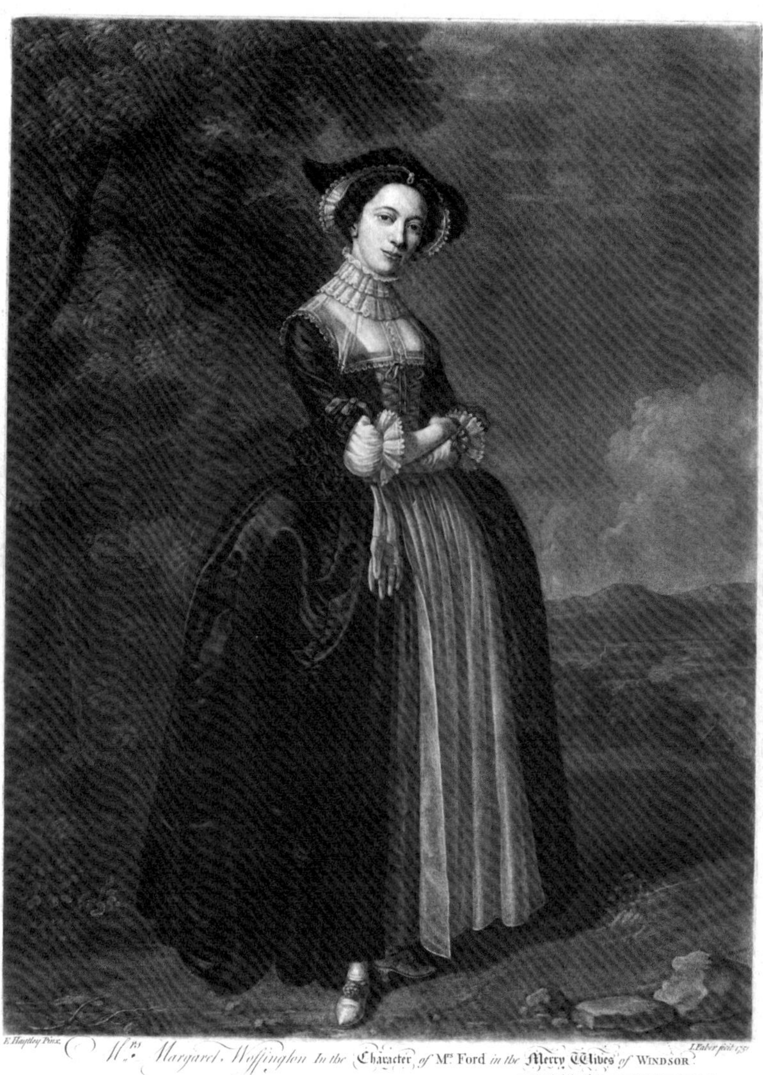

6 M.rs Margaret Woffington in the Character of M.rs Ford in the Merry Wives Of Windsor

Engraved by John Faber jun.
after Edward Haytley

[Published by] sold by John Faber jun.

484 x 351 I; 506 x 354 Pl.

References: CS 392; O'D 4; Hall 33

1. With the engraved inscription: "*E Haytley Pinx. *** I. Faber fecit 1751 / M.rs Margaret Woffington In the* Character of M.rs Ford *in the* Merry Wives of WINDSOR. / *** *** *Sold at the Golden Head near the Church Bloomsbury Square.*". Impressions: CLB P34,789 impression exhibited; BM; TM.

2. The plate cut down to 307 x 250 I; 350 x

Little is known of Edward Haytley's career but he was of sufficient eminence in 1746 to be invited to give two paintings to the Foundling Hospital. The size of this plate, 20 x 14 inches, is unusually large for a portrait of this period. Vertue[1] mentions that Faber had engraved larger plates (such as the portrait of Walpole of the same size) which were to cost 5s. The print was distributed by Faber until his death in 1756 when the plate was acquired by Ryall & Withy, together with several others. The copper-plate seems to have remained with Robert Withy after the dissolution of the partnership in 1758–9, although impressions were printed for John Ryall. In 1766 Withy retired from printselling to pursue a second career as a 'stockbroker'. Only the catalogue for the second part of the sale of his stock-in-trade has survived; the sale was held by Charles Paterson on 20 August 1766 and the following two days. It is plausible that lot 613, described simply as a copper-plate of 'Mrs Woffington', refers to this print since no other print of Mrs Woffington was published by Ryall & Withy. The plate appears to have been lost in a fire before 1806.[2] In his catalogues for 1769 and 1770 Shropshire listed a very scarce proof impression of this print priced at 12s, presumably the un-cut version.

250 Pl. The image reduced to an half length and the inscription re-engraved: "*I. Haytley Pinx! *** I. Faber fecit 1751. | M:s Margaret Woffington | In the* Character *of* M:s Ford *in the* Merry Wives of WINDSOR. | *** *** *Price 2. Shil. Sold at the Golden Head near the Church Bloomsbury Square.*".
Impressions: CLB; H.

3. Re-published by Ryall & Withy with the price erased: "London Printed for John Ryall & Rob: Withy, at Hogarth's Head, in Fleet Street.".
Impressions: NPG.

4. The publication line altered to: "London Printed for John Ryall at Hogarth's Head in Fleet Street.".
Impressions: BM.

☞ In Shakespeare's *The Merry Wives of Windsor*, Falstaff, who is 'out at heels', decides to court the wives of Ford and Page, two gentlemen living at Windsor, since they control their husbands' finances. Falstaff's discharged followers, Nym and Pistol, warn the two wives who, having received identical love-letters from Falstaff, decide to torment him. Firstly, they hide Falstaff from Ford in a basket, cover him with foul linen and have him thrown into a ditch. Next, they disguise him as the 'fat woman of Brentford', causing him to be soundly beaten by Ford. The husbands, having also been fooled twice, now learn of the plot and a final meeting in Windsor Forest is suggested to Falstaff. Accosted by mock fairies, he is finally seized and exposed by Ford and Page, but all ends happily, even for Falstaff.

The *Merry Wives of Windsor* was a popular play which provided Peg Woffington with one of her most successful roles, Mrs Ford. She played this part with increasing success throughout her career, later on in memorable partnership with Edward Shuter as Falstaff. She first played the part in 1748, the year in which this print was first published.

Margaret Woffington is said to have been born in Dublin in October 1718, the daughter of John Woffington, a journeyman bricklayer. As a child Peg was part of Madame Violante's[3] entertainments, which consisted largely of rope-dancing, after which she took up her mother's occupation of fruit selling. At the age of ten she was again hired by Mme Violante for a lilliputian company. She was noticed whilst playing Polly in *The Beggar's Opera*, and engaged at Aungier Street Theatre in Dublin, where she acted and danced between acts.

Woffington's first major part was Ophelia in February 1737 at the Smock Alley Theatre in Dublin. In May 1742 she played Cordelia to Garrick's Lear at Drury Lane, returning to Dublin with him the following month. She was often Garrick's leading lady at Drury Lane and they lived at 6 Bow Street, together with Charles Macklin, an arrangement which was short-lived. In the autumn of 1745 their affair was over, and from 1747 Garrick neither acted with her, nor engaged her at Drury Lane. Their relationship was the source of much gossip. Garrick wrote:

> Woffington, I am told, shews my letters about; pray have you heard any thing of that kind? What she does now, so little affects me, that, excepting shewing my letters of nonsense love to make me ridiculous, she can do nothing to give me a moment's uneasiness – the scene is changed – I'm altered quite.[4]

Mrs Clive and Mrs Pritchard proved to be Woffington's greatest rivals and she was forced to vie for parts and precedence which led to bitter feuds. In 1752–3 she returned to Dublin where she was an enormous success. Her last performance was in 1757 when she revealed her failing health to an astonished audience. She was too ill to play Gertrude to Barry's Hamlet in May, according to Tate Wilkinson, and she died the following year. She was buried in Teddington, where she had lived. She was vivacious and witty, renowned both for her beauty and for her numerous affairs.

L. P. Boitard engraved a watch-paper for Robert Sayer from this mezzotint. Watch-papers were small, measuring about 60 x 60 mm, with a circular image about 38 mm in diameter in the middle. These could be cut out and inserted in the back of a watch-case where they would keep out dust, allowing moisture to pass in or out freely. Sayer advertised them in his 1766 catalogue at 3d plain or 6d coloured; seven of his list of sixty-one titles were copied from theatrical portraits. Since they most often survive cut for use information about them is sparse, but we know that Sayer was not the only publisher to issue them.

---

[1] *Walpole Society*, Vol. XXX (1948–50), Vertue VI, p. 196.

[2] In *Robert Grave's Catalogue of Prints*, 1806, p. 51; it is described as 'the plate destroyed by fire'.

[3] Madame Violante (1682–1741), rope dancer, gymnast, actress and manageress visited Dublin in 1727.

[4] *Letters*, no. 37, 23 Oct. 1745.

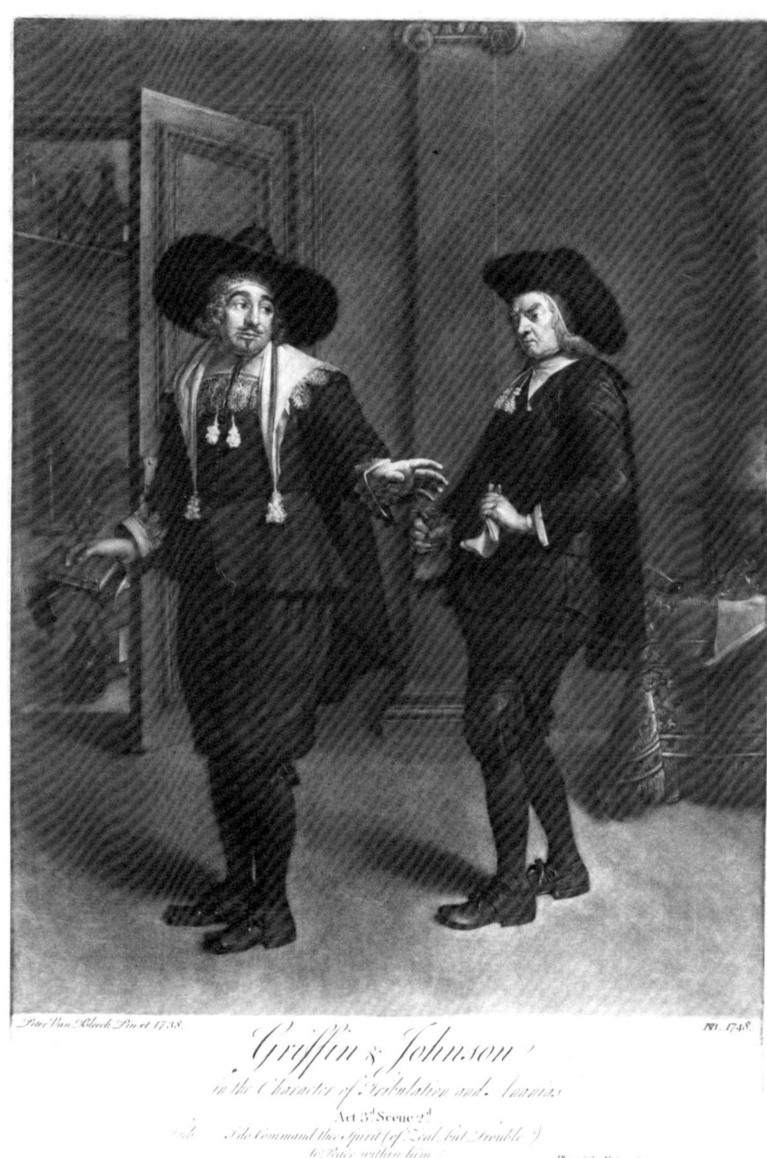

7 Griffin & Johnson in the Character of Tribulation and Ananias

Painted and engraved by Peter van Bleeck

[Published by Peter van Bleeck 1748]

411 x 306 I; 473 x 307 Pl.

References: CS 5; O'D 1; Hall 1

1. Finished proof before all letters.
Impressions: C .

2. With the engraved inscription: *"Peter Van Bleeck Pinxt. 1738. ✱✱✱ PVB. 1748. / Griffin & Johnson / in the Character of Tribulation and Ananias / Act 3ᵈ Scene 2ᵈ / Trib,, I do Comand thee Spirit (of Zeal, but Trouble) / to Peace within him. / ✱✱✱ Play of the Alchemift".*

This is the first mezzotint to show actors 'upon the boards'. The print of Garrick, Burton and Palmer in the same play (see page 60) published thirty-three years later shows little increase of sophistication in the depiction of the subject. By the time van Bleeck published this print, both actors had been dead for some years, and although he was careful to indicate on the print that the picture had been painted whilst the actors were still alive, it is not clear why the publication was delayed.

George Vertue considered that van Bleeck meant the print to 'show his skill in those two branches of Art – painting and scraping'.[1] Both Walter Shropshire and the Magazin des Estampes listed an impression of this print in their catalogues for 1774 at 10s 6d, one being described as 'very fine & rare', the other 'scarce'.

The play maintained a constant place in the repertory and performances were given most seasons, with five in 1747–8 and two in 1748–9. The two actors, Griffin and Johnson, complemented each other well and, as was often the case, the actors' success resulted in their being identified with the characters. Garrick's later interpre-

16

Impressions: CLB P9,396 (impression exhibited); BM; TM; H.

3. With the plate pitted, worn and clumsily re-worked; the inscription re-touched with the word *Character* altered to *Characters*.
Impressions: CLB; BL.

☜ In Ben Jonson's *The Alchemist*, Love-wit, during an epidemic of the plague, leaves his house in London in the charge of his servant, Face. The latter, with Subtle, the Alchemist, and Dol Common, his consort, use the house as a place for deluding and cheating gullible people, by holding out to them promise of the 'philosopher's stone'. Among their victims are: Sir Epicure Mammon, a greedy voluptuous knight; Tribulation Wholesome, and Ananias, puritans; Dapper and Drugger, a clerk and a tobacconist, and Kastril, the quarrelsome lad who wants a good match for his sister Dame Pliant. Surly, the gamester, who sees through the fraud, attempts to expose it by presenting himself disguised as a Spaniard, and the unexpected return of Love-wit puts Subtle and Dol to sudden flight. Face makes peace with his master by resourcefully marrying him to Dame Pliant.

The print was advertised in the *General Advertiser* on 3 December, 1748:

The Picture of the late Inimitable Griffin and Johnson, painted by Mr. Van Bleeck, of Covent Garden, in the Characters of Tribulation and Ananias, so much esteem'd for the Likeness of Features and Lively Representation of the Attitudes, in that celebrated Play of the Alchymist, has lately been taken off in Metzotinto; is now publish'd and may be had at his Lodgings.

tation of the part of Abel Drugger, a natural fool, is a fascinating contrast to Griffin and Johnson who,

> ... were much admired for their just representation of the canting puritanical preacher and his solemn deacon the botcher; there was an affected softness in the former which was finely contrasted in the fanatical fury of the other ... there should be seen a fine print of them in their characters, from a painting of Van Bleeck ... they are very striking resemblances of the comedians.[2]

Benjamin Griffin, here playing Tribulation, was born in 1680 in Yarmouth, the son of the rector of Buxton and Oxnead. He was originally apprenticed to a glazier in Norwich and left to join a company of strolling players in 1711–12, appearing at Lincoln's Inn Fields in 1715. He took the part of Polonius in September 1721 at Drury Lane, where he remained until his death in February 1740. He was most successful in playing characters of 'choleric and eccentric old men', and was 'a comedian excellent in some characters'.[3] His only other part of primary importance was the original Lovegold in the *Miser*.

Benjamin Johnson, who appeared as Ananias, was born about 1665. Originally a scene painter, he joined the Drury Lane company in 1695 but went to the Haymarket in 1706 where he proved to be particularly successful in plays by his namesake. He was admired for his ability to concentrate on his part whilst on the stage, a rare thing amongst actors in this period, who would converse with each other or even with members of the audience when they were not speaking their lines:

> His large speaking blue eyes he fixed steadily on the person to whom he spoke, and was never known to have wandered from the stage to any part of the theatre. Johnson was the Hemskirk or D. Teniers of the theatre; the honest Dutch painter, who contents himself with giving a portrait of mere nature.[4]

Johnson remained on the stage until he was seventy-seven, his last appearance being in May 1742. Some confusion exists over the date of Johnson's death which seems to have been in July 1742.

[1] *Walpole Society* XXII (1933–4), Vertue III, p. 141.
[2] *Dramatic Miscellanies*, II, pp. 108–9.
[3] DNB.
[4] *Dramatic Miscellanies*, III, p. 135.

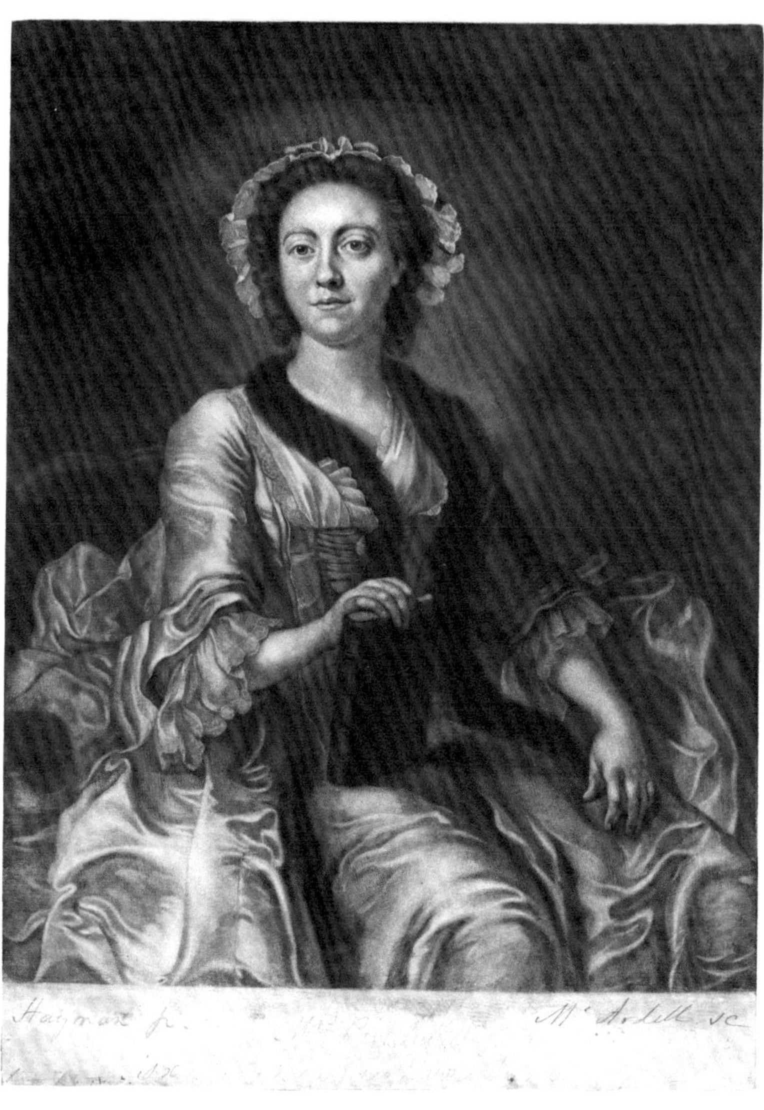

engraved inscription: "*F. Hayman Pinx.*,̣ *1750* *** *J.ˢ M.ᶜ Ardell fecit. | M.ʳˢ Pritchard. |* *** *Publish'd April 25 1762*".
Impressions: CLB P8,543 (impression exhibited); BM; H ; TM.

5. With the added scratched price '2s' to l.
Impressions: CLB.

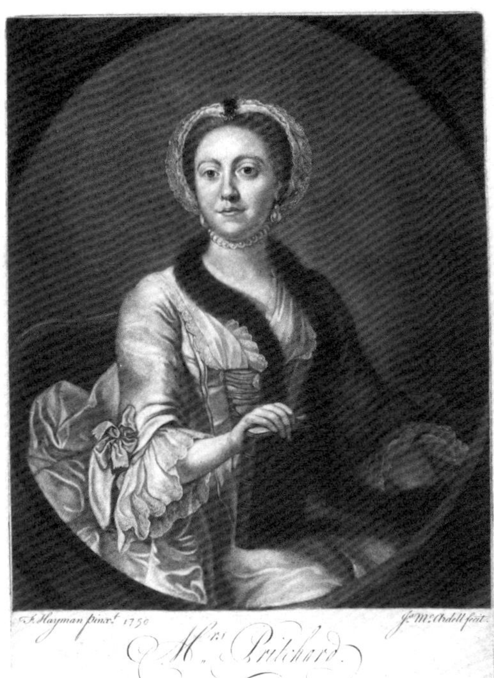

by 1765, or possibly later, when Sayer gained possession of the print, the sitter would have been at least fifty-four years old. There was clearly a need to change the plate and to make the sitter look older.

The print is not listed in Sayer's 1766 catalogue and it is likely that he published the altered plate only after Mrs Pritchard's death in 1768. If this conclusion is correct and McArdell was only responsible for the first state, the publication date scratched on the fourth state, '*25 April 1762*', must have been added after his death in 1765 and so cannot even represent the date at which the plate was published by Sayer. Sayer may have been attempting to mislead the public into believing that McArdell was responsible for the re-worked print; the omission of Sayer's name from the publication line would have contributed to the deliberate confusion.

It seems that Hannah Pritchard's reputation declined after her death: she was not included in any of the major illustrated theatre series published between 1775 and 1781, and although this print was listed in Sayer & Bennett's catalogue of 1775 as 'Mrs Pritchard the comedian', it was not included in Laurie & Whittle's 1795 catalogue.

Hannah Vaughan was born in 1709 and at an early age married a poor actor called Pritchard. In 1733 she appeared at Bartholomew's Fair, where she met with considerable success. She played an extremely wide variety of parts in her first season in London and remained at Drury Lane until 1741, playing chiefly comic characters. She then moved to Covent Garden where she stayed for three years, returning to Drury Lane when Garrick became patentee.

In the season 1761–2 she played eighteen major parts, dominating the stage. Gibbon commented on her versatility:

> [she] rehearsed, almost at the same time, the part of a furious Queen in the Green Room, and that of a Coquette on the Stage, and passed several times from one to another with the utmost ease and happiness.[2]

Even at the end of her career she had the ability to play youthful parts; her 'easy manner in speaking, and disengaged action, supplied the want of an elegant form and youthful countenance'.[3] She was the original Fanny in Garrick and Colman's *Clandestine Marriage*, and was also successful as the Queen in *Hamlet*.

During the season 1767–8 she gave a series of farewell performances, her last appearance being on 24 April 1768 as Lady Macbeth, when she spoke an epilogue written by Garrick. She retired, and died in Bath the following August.

Although Dr Johnson considered her a 'vulgar idiot' in real life, he conceded that, 'when she appeared upon the stage, [she] seemed to be inspired by gentility and understanding ... '.[4]

[1] Allen, p. 173, no. 39.
[2] Gibbon, Edward *Journal* for 26 November 1762.
[3] Davies, II, p. 189.
[4] Boswell *Life of Johnson* for 27 October 1783.

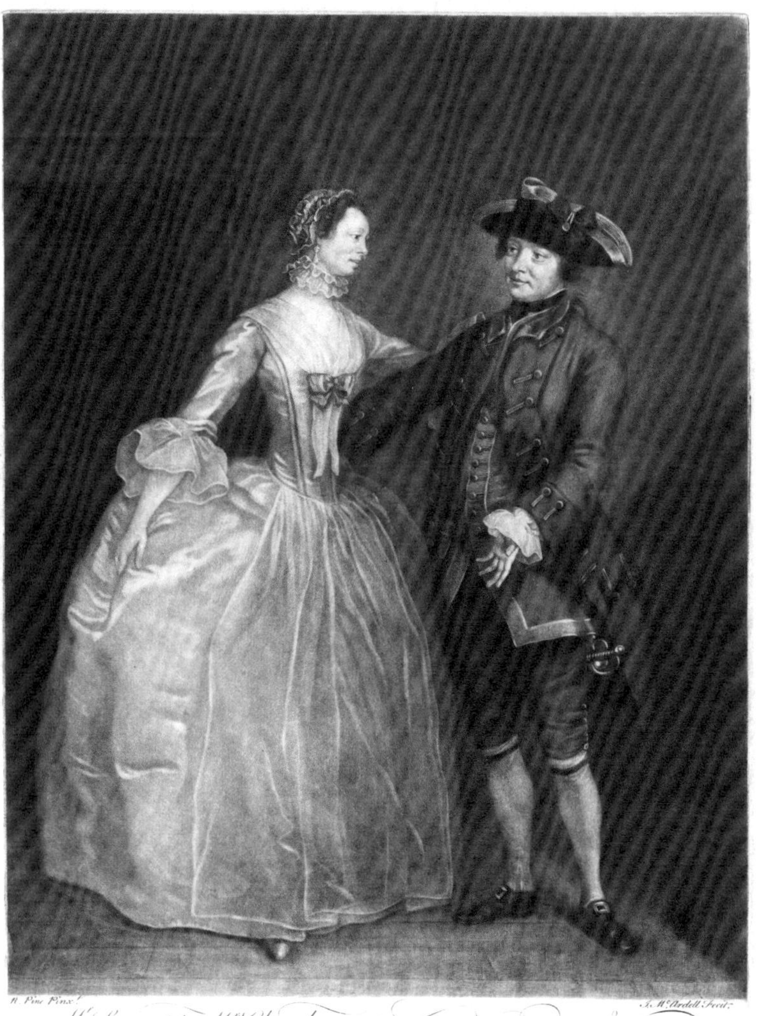

9 Mr Lowe and Mrs Chambers in the Characters of Capt Macheath and Polly

Engraved by James McArdell
after Robert Edge Pine

Published by Robert Edge Pine [June] 1752

395 x 297 I; 428 x 297 Pl.

References: CS 122; G 26; O'D (Lowe) 1; Hall (Lowe) 1

1. With the engraved inscription: "*R. Pine Pinx!* *** *J. McArdell Fecit. | Mr Lowe and Mrs Chambers in the Characters of Capt Macheath and Polly. | Fondly let me loll! &c.* Act. I. Scene. XIII.".
Impressions: BM; TM.

2. With the publication line added: " ***
Publish'd according to Act of Parliament. 1752 Price 3s.".
Impressions: CLB P17,023 (impression exhibited); BM; TM; H.

This print launched Robert Pine's career as a theatrical painter, although he had already been described as an 'eminent painter' by *The Universal Magazine* in 1748. He published his own prints, presumably in order to advertise his considerable abilities and encourage further patronage. By the end of the decade this role had been increasingly taken on by engravers, many of whom had also established themselves as printsellers. When in 1764 Zoffany and McArdell published '*Venice Preserv'd*', Zoffany took the subscriptions but McArdell distributed the prints. The publication of this print was advertised in *The London Evening Post* 11–13 June, 1752 (see over).

Walter Shropshire listed a 'fine & rare' impression of this print in his catalogue for 1774 at 7s 6d. In the Hope[1] sale in 1813[2], a 'scarce and fine' impression made 16s.

John Gay's play was considered to be thoroughly amoral, with a 'pernicious tendency to destroy morality in the lower class of the community'. Governments repeatedly tried to suppress it. Despite this between 1747 and 1776 it was performed well over two hundred times at Covent Garden and nearly half as many times at Drury Lane, making it the most popular stage entertainment of the century. Productions of the play were being performed at both

☞ In *The Beggar's Opera* by John Gay, the principal characters are Peachum, a receiver of stolen goods, who also makes a living by informing against his clients; his wife and his pretty daughter, Polly; Lockit, warder of Newgate and his daughter Lucy, and Captain Macheath, a highwayman and cad. Polly falls desperately in love with Macheath, who marries her. Her father, furious at her folly, denounces Macheath who is arrested and sent to Newgate. Here, Lucy falls in love with him, which results in a spirited conflict between her and Polly. In spite of her jealousy, Lucy procures Macheath's escape.

This Day was publish'd,

A Metzotinto Print, done by Mr. MAC ARDELL, from a Picture painted by Mr. Robert Pine, of Mr. LOWE and Mrs. CHAMBERS, in the Characters of Captain Macheath and Polly.

N. B. To be sold at Mr. Pine's, opposite New-street in St. Martin's lane, and by the Printsellers of London and Westminster.

patent houses when this print was published, and Covent Garden staged this particular production nineteen times in the 1751–2 season.

In a bitter twist of fate, the immense popular appeal of the play and its corrupting influence had a tragic consequence for one poor individual. It was reported in *The London Chronicle* for Guy Fawkes Day 1773 that:

> Thomas Bowen[3], of Red-Lion-street, Clerkenwell, in the county of Middlesex, England, and Israel Pottinger of the same parish, Bookseller, make oath and say, that they were present … when … William Cox, who was executed on Wednesday the 27th October last, had confessed that *The Beggar's Opera* was not only the first occasion of his ruin, but that he had frequently committed robberies to raise money to see that Play, or word to the like effect.[4]

The bad press and general condemnation that the play received can only have strengthened its hold on the repertory; with reviews stating that it was 'inflammatory with humour and vulgar with elegance; in short … one of those bewitching evils …',[5] who would want to miss it? One commentator observed that there was never a performance 'represented on the stage without creating an additional number of real thieves', whilst another put it more strongly:

> It must be confessed that although *The Beggar's Opera* abounds with wit, humour, and the most poignant satire, it is notwithstanding very ill calculated to mend the morals of the common people. *The Beggar's Opera* is, in truth, the Thief's Creed and Common Prayer Book, in which he fortifies himself in the most atrocious wickedness … .[6]

Thomas Lowe is depicted in this print in the part of Captain Macheath, a role that was often played by a leading actress in the company. He first appeared at Drury Lane Theatre in September 1740 in *The Devil to Pay* and rose to fame by singing the first public performance of 'Rule Britannia' in the same year. When his main rival John Beard returned to Drury Lane after a five year absence, Lowe, then a favourite singer at Vauxhall Gardens, decided to move to Covent Garden, where he appeared as Macheath in September 1748.

In the 1752–3 season Beard played Macheath in the rival production at Drury Lane eclipsing Lowe. Lowe's voice was described as, '… more happy [than Beard's], but his expression less characteristic, and his speaking, if possible, worse'.[7] Charles Dibdin, on the other hand, felt his voice to be more even and mellow than Beard's, although 'in love songs, when little more than mere utterance was necessary, he might be said to have exceeded him … Lowe lost himself beyond the namby-pamby poetry of Vauxhall; Beard was at home everywhere'.[8]

In 1763 Lowe left the stage to become manager of Marylebone Gardens for five years. While at first prosperous, he was ruined by the wet summer of 1769. He was engaged to sing at Sadler's Wells in April 1772 where he remained until his death in March 1783.

Little is known of Elizabeth Chambers, who made her anonymous debut as Polly at Covent Garden on 27 September 1751 'to great applause' and remained with the company for another seven years.

---

[1] Probably Henry Philip Hope, brother of Thomas Hope the virtuoso.

[2] *A Catalogue of the Valuable Collection of Prints and Drawings of Henry P. Hope Esq.*, Leigh and Sotheby, March 18–26 1813.

[3] Possibly the printseller who published small prints of the theatre in the 1770s.

[4] *The London Chronicle*, 5 Nov. 1773.

[5] Gentleman, I, p. 130.

[6] *The Gentleman's Magazine*, 15 Sept. 1773.

[7] Gentleman, I, p. 127.

[8] *The History of the Stage*, 1742, V, p. 364.

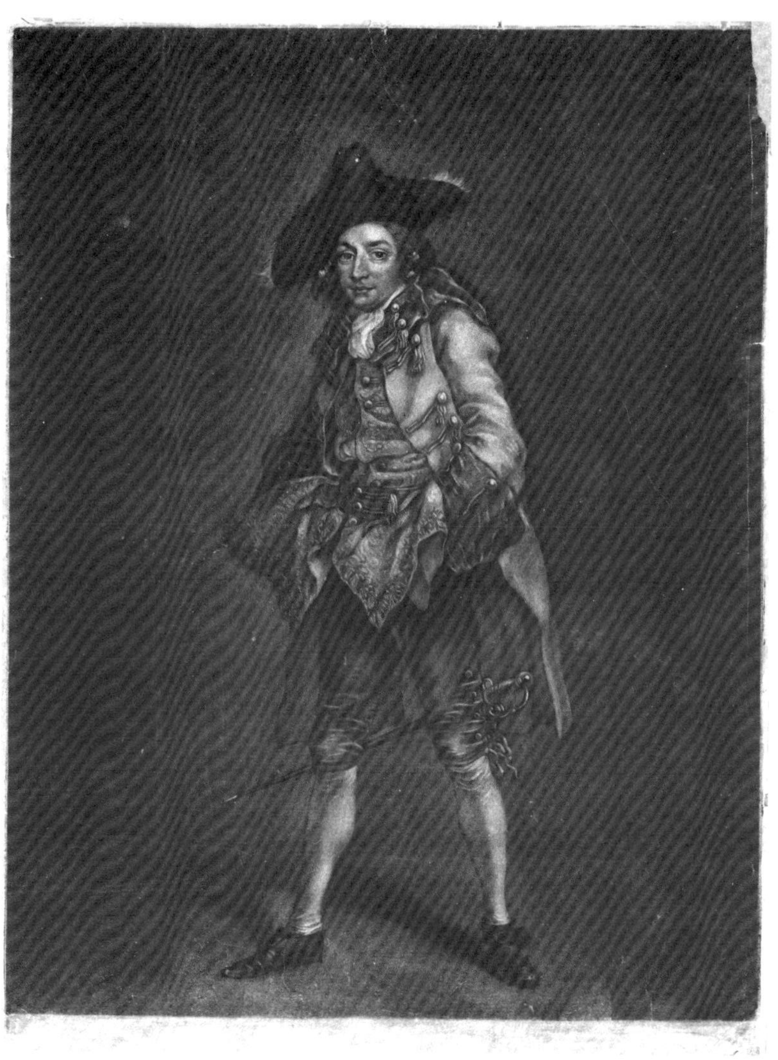

10 M.ͬ Woodwarde in the Character of yᵉ Fine Gentleman, in Lethe

Engraved by James McArdell
after Francis Hayman

[Published] sold by Elizabeth Griffin [1749–53]

Re-published by John Ryall and Robert Withy [1755–8]

330 x 250 I; 352 x 251 Pl.

References: CS 189; G 183; O'D 2; Hall 1

1. Progress proof before all letters showing the figure only. Before the sword-sling and additional white highlights.
Impressions: CLB P14,674 touched in crayon (impression exhibited).

2. With the engraved inscription: "*F. Hayman Delin. *** J,, M.ͨ, Ardell Fecit | M.ͬ, Woodwarde | in the Character of* yᵉ Fine *Gentleman, in LETHE.*

This print of Henry Woodward playing the part of the Fine Gentleman in *Lethe* is particularly interesting in that it derives from a single figure drawing rather than a fuller composition. The undated drawing by Hayman is now in the Fitzwilliam Museum, Cambridge. The same design was used for a Bow porcelain figure, an example of which was owned by Garrick who had great admiration for Woodward's performance in this part.

The progress proof exhibited here was printed merely as a guide to establish how the engraving was developing, and was not treated as a 'work of art'. Since it was for immediate use, it did not matter that a strong thumb-print appeared on the right hand side. The existence of the progress proof confirms Brian Allen's suggestion[1] that the drawing was a preparatory work by Hayman for McArdell. The progress proof reproduces the drawing exactly, even to the extent that the sword, lacking the sword-sling, hangs miraculously in mid-air.

In the finished state the background of the column, screen and window are added (see over). McArdell may have invented the background, since the initial design, which does not appear on the drawing, has been marked on the surface of the progress proof in crayon. After taking a proof McArdell could decide what further work he needed to complete. On this occasion, he marked the

*** Pr 1.* 6 / *** *** *Sold by E. Griffin next the Globe Tavern Fleet Street.".*
Impressions: CLB P36,001 (impression exhibited); H.

3. The plate worn and carefully re-worked.
Impressions: CLB.

4. Re-published by Ryall & Withy, the image re-worked overall and the publication line altered to: *"London Printed for I Ryall & R Withy, at Hogarth's Head in Fleet Street.".*
Impressions: BM; H.

proof to establish where to place the background in relation to the figure. When a progress proof is marked by the engraver or the artist in this manner it is known as a 'touched' proof. Touched proofs are widely sought after, firstly because they document the engraver's technique but also because they are extremely important records of changes to the plate.

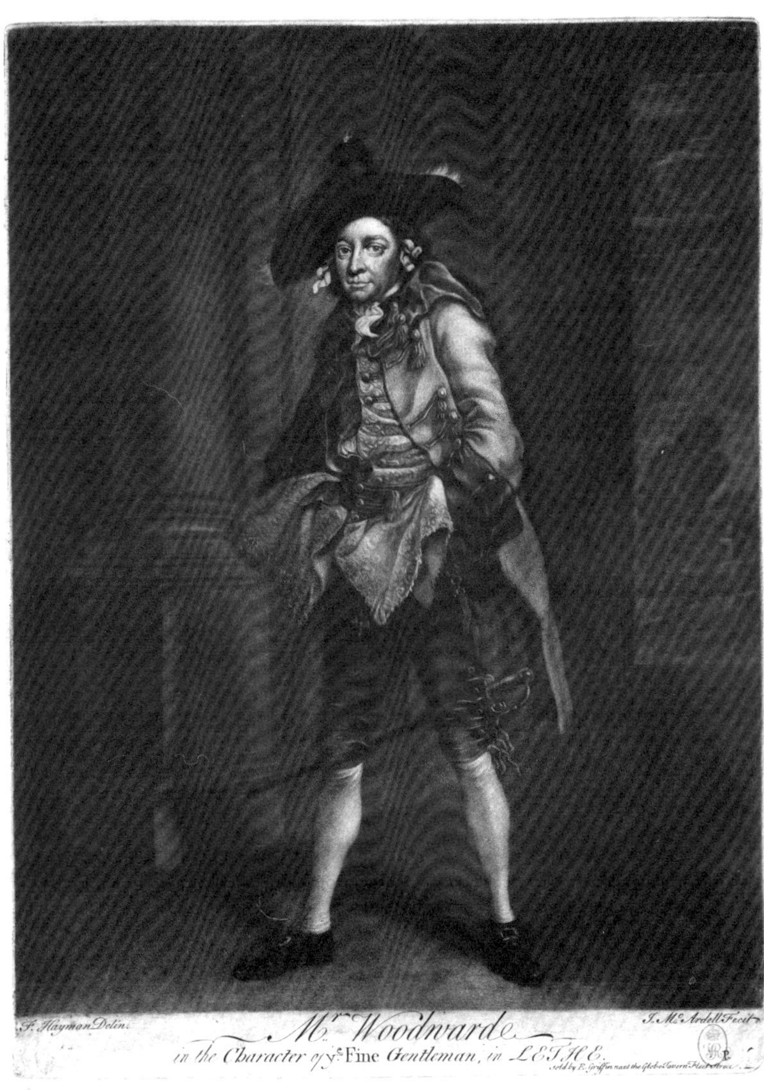

☞ The farce, *Lethe: or Æsop in the Shades*, a satirical after-piece written by David Garrick was first performed at Drury Lane in 1740. Described as a 'one act playlet of clearly defined episodic nature'[2], the action presented takes the form of a procession of characters or 'types' for the amusement of the audience. The setting is on a day of the year when Proserpine allows Aesop, the wise philosopher, to invite mortals to drink the waters of Lethe, the river of forgetfulness, and return to earth happy again. Ten characters appear, all of whom are opinionated, critical of life and more interested in presenting his or her personality than in taking the cure. The characters include: a 'Fine Gentleman' and 'Fine Lady', a lady writer, a Frenchman, a drunk, a poet, and Lord Chalkstone, a character added in 1756 and later developed into the character of Lord Ogleby for *The Clandestine Marriage*. The main targets of satire are the behaviour of theatre audiences and the problems of marriages of convenience, but many other topics such as foreign imports, landscape gardening, language, taste, the Methodist movement and the grand tour were also singled out.

Unfortunately the print is undated, but we know that the Bow porcelain figure was made in 1750. The print was issued [published] by Elizabeth Griffin, who had succeeded her husband Peter by at least late 1749 and continued to trade until 1753; assuming that she was the first printseller to issue this print, it is likely that it dates from this period. The publication of this print was probably prompted by the successful revival of *Lethe* in January 1749.

The evidence of considerable wear to the plate indicates that the print was extremely popular; an impression at Harvard is so worn that the figure has an almost ghostly appearance. The plate had already been re-worked before it was acquired by Ryall and Withy, who in their turn re-worked the plate in an attempt to prolong its life.

Frequently adapted with new and topical satire, the play enjoyed its greatest success whilst the two outstanding comedians, Woodward and Kitty Clive performed together. The 'exquisite ridicule' with which Clive played the part of the Fine Lady was amongst the elements that secured its lasting popularity. A Bow figure of her in this role appeared in 1750 as a pair to Woodward as the Fine Gentleman. The play also enabled Garrick to perform a variety of parts. It seems that the audience, as in so many other instances, went to see Garrick, as Neville recorded: '... Had no intention of going to the play, but seeing Garrick was to play Lord Chalkstone ... stood in ye same disagreeable situation ...'.

The part of the Fine Gentleman was originally written to satirise the behaviour of a wealthy group of theatre-goers. For many years it had been the tradition to allow some 'gentlemen', particularly at benefits, to be seated on benches at the rear of the stage. These members of the audience would often interfere with the progress of the players. As the Fine Gentleman boasts in the play:

> I dress in the Evening, and go generally behind the scenes of both Playhouses; not ... to be diverted with the play, but to intrigue, and show myself – I stand upon the Stage, talk loud, and stare about – which confounds the Actors, and disturbs the Audience ...

Like all such pieces that rely on topicality for their satire, *Lethe* is now forgotten. To coincide with the January 1749 revival of the play, Paul Vailliant published the first authorised edition;[3] by 1762 the sixth edition had been printed, which included the part of Lord Chalkstone. The interest in Garrick and the play were combined in Reeve and Dodd's *A Letter to Mr. GK, relative to his treble capacity of manager, actor and author; with some remarks on Lethe* which was advertised at the same time.

There can be no greater evidence of its contemporary popularity however, than the number of prints that showed the cast. In addition to the mezzotint of Woodward, an etching of similar size by Charles Mosley of Kitty Clive as 'the Fine Lady' was published in 1750. The following year this was followed by an anonymous etching of Ned Shuter as 'the Old Man', and finally in 1756 Garrick himself was etched by Gabriel Smith as 'Lord Chalkstone', a more recent addition to the cast. As late as 1771 smaller prints of Garrick in this role were being produced. As well as these prints, a printed cotton hanging was engraved in which a number of the members of the cast can be easily identified. All were produced after the extensive revision of the piece in 1749, in which year a command performance was given for the Prince and Princess of Wales, the cast including Clive, Blakes and Woodward. Further revivals took place in 1750–1 and in 1766–7 when there was another command performance.

In 1788 John Young, a pupil of John Raphael Smith, engraved a mezzotint depicting Robert Bransby, William Parsons and Watkins as Aesop, the Old Man and Servant in *Lethe* from a painting by Zoffany. This was probably designed as a companion piece to Finlayson's three mezzotints after Zoffany.

---

[1] Allen, p. 127.

[2] Stone & Kahrl, p. 204.

[3] There is an edition in the BL with an MS date of 1745, which was presumably an unauthorised version.

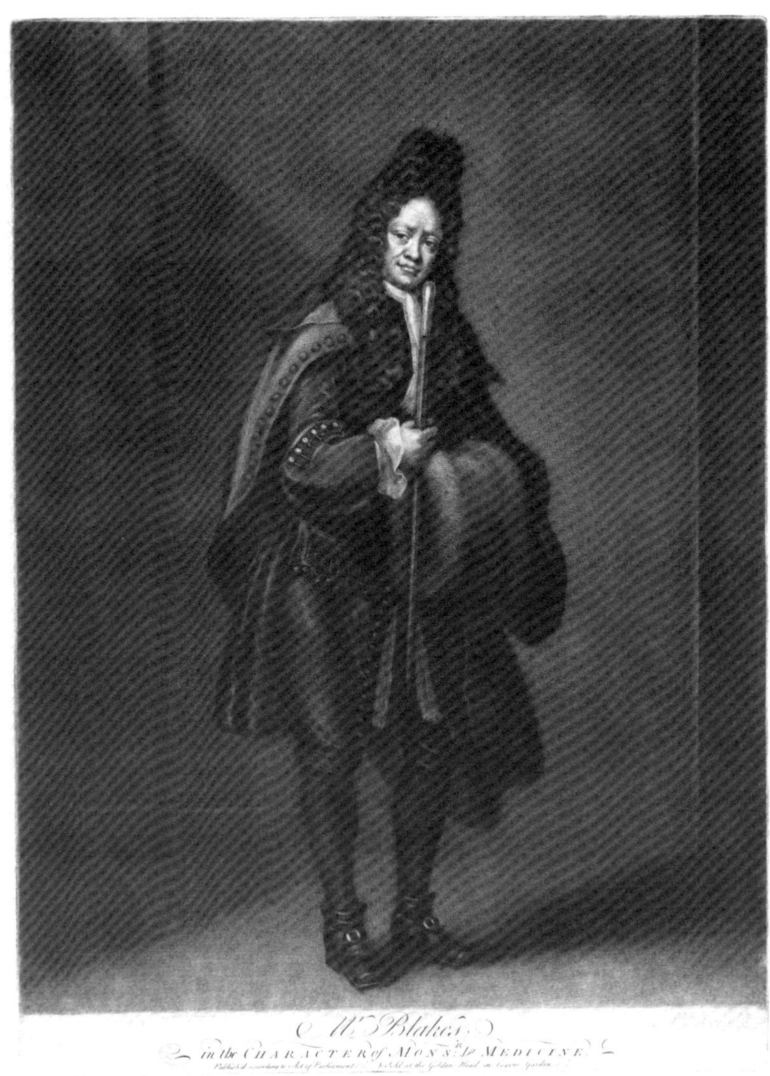

11 M.ʳ Blakes in the Character of Mons.ʳ la Medecine

Drawn and engraved by James McArdell

Published by James McArdell [c. 1754]

Re-published by Robert Sayer [after 1768]

334 x 252 I; 355 x 252 Pl.

References: CS 22; G 167; O'D 1; Hall 1

1. With the engraved inscription: "*M.ʳ Blakes | in the CHARACTER of MONS.ᴿ la MEDECINE. | Publiʃh'd according to Act of Parliament   & Sold at the Golden Head in Covent Garden.*".
Impressions: BM; TM.

2. With the inscription re-touched: *La* crudely altered to *Le* and *Publiʃh'd* altered to *Publish'd*. – "*M.ʳ Blakes | in the CHARACTER of MONS.ᴿ le MEDECINE. | Publish'd according to Act of Parliament .   & Sold at the Golden Head in Covent Garden.*".
Impressions: CLB P37,918 (impression exhibited); H.

This print is one of McArdell's earlier works. Like the portrait of '*Quin as Falstaff*', it seems to have been both drawn and engraved by McArdell, although this was not indicated on the print until it was republished by Sayer. McArdell's addition of the corpse, coffin and chair to the background was probably to enhance sales of this print. With these changes it was no longer just a single figure portrait but it now illustrated an extremely amusing scene in a popular farce, as well as commemorating the performance of a popular actor (see over). The styling of the address and the fact that the print was not listed in Sayer's 1766 catalogue indicates that Sayer republished the print in 1768 or a little later. It was characteristic of Sayer to attempt to enhance the desirability of the print by emphasising that it was an original work by McArdell (see page 8).

It is interesting to compare the faces in the two states: there is little evidence of wear during the ten years of the plate's existence. Any re-working was, like the alterations, dictated by the need to make the plate more commercial in the late 1760s.

The print was listed in Sayer & Bennett's catalogue for 1775, priced at 1s. In his catalogue for February 1799, the portrait specialist William Richardson listed another 'fine impression, before this man, &c. was introduced'. It is unusual for a state to be identi-

3. The background altered by the addition of a corpse rising from a coffin and a chair.
Impressions: BM.

4. Re-published by Robert Sayer. The figure of Blakes and the head of the corpse slightly re-worked: "*J,, M,,Ardell delin. et fecit. | M,, Blakes | in the CHARACTER of MONS.R le MEDICINE. | London, Printed for* Rob.! Sayer, *Map & Printseller, at N,.º 53 in Fleet Street.*".
Impressions: CLB P30,599 (impression exhibited); BM.

☞ The plot of the farce centres around Mr Gerald and his son, who unknown to each other are both courting Angelique, the daughter of Monsieur La Médecine, a French doctor. The Doctor supports the father's suit, but this is opposed by the Doctor's wife. Angelique loves Young Gerald, whose servant Crispin is in love with Beatrice, the Doctor's maid. When Crispin manages to meet with Beatrice in the laboratory, they are disturbed by the Doctor. Beatrice quickly pretends that her admirer is a newly hanged corpse that has been sent for dissection. The Doctor hurriedly prepares to cut the young man up, but Beatrice tells him that he is urgently needed at a rich lord's death-bed. In an attempt to win Angelique, Old Gerald tries to bribe Beatrice, but she uses this to extort jewels from him for Angelique. They even persuade the love-sick old man to play the corpse. At this moment Crispin arrives disguised as the Doctor and attended by Young Gerald. After they have tried to cut up Old Gerald, he jumps up and meets the real Doctor. He then accuses Angelique and Beatrice of cheating him of a fortune in jewels. Angelique returns with Young Gerald and announces their marriage. Monsieur La Médecine forgives them and tries to persuade Old Gerald to do the same.

---

[1] *An Essay upon the State of the Theatre … 1760,* quoted in the TDB.
[2] Bartholomew Fair was a fair which took place in Smithfield, London until 1835. Among the booths were a number of small theatres.

fied thus at this date; it is clear that Richardson wished to indicate that his print was an early state.

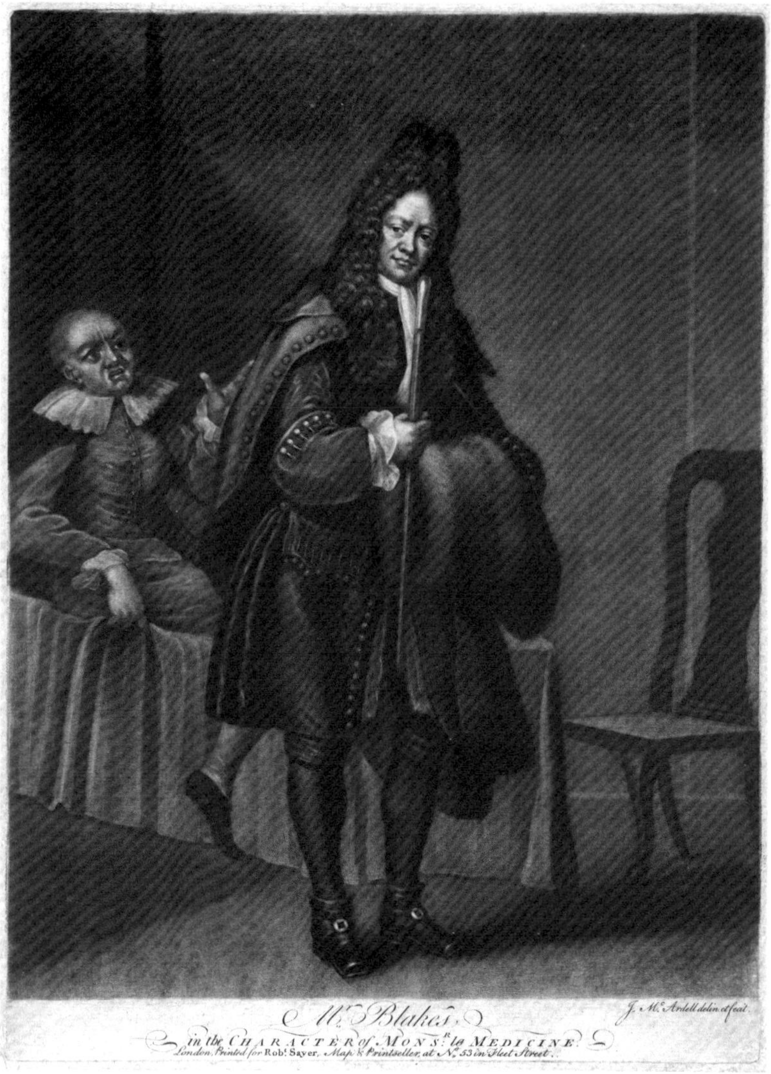

The print shows Charles Blakes caricaturing a Frenchman in Edward Ravenscroft's popular after-piece, *The Anatomist, or Sham Doctor,* a role he first played on 18 November 1743; the play subsequently ran for seventeen nights. He occasionally played tragic roles but was better suited to comedy, farce and pantomime, his speciality being Frenchmen. His Monsieur la Médecine was especially famous and he usually spoke the epilogue riding on an ass, a spectacle which he first performed on his benefit night on 21 April 1756. Parts such as this appealed to the popular prejudices of the time, for the Seven Years War with France broke out in 1756, but some critics did not appreciate the humour: 'Mr Blakes is reckoned a good mimick of a Frenchman … by such as have not been much conversant among Frenchmen'.[1]

Blakes first appeared at the Haymarket in May 1736 and was on the stage every year for twenty-seven years. In the summer of 1741 he appeared at Turbutt's booth at Bartholomew Fair[2] (see page 2) and then at Lincoln's Inn Fields, occasionally playing at Drury Lane. Charles Blakes died in Castle Street, Leicester Square in May 1763.

26

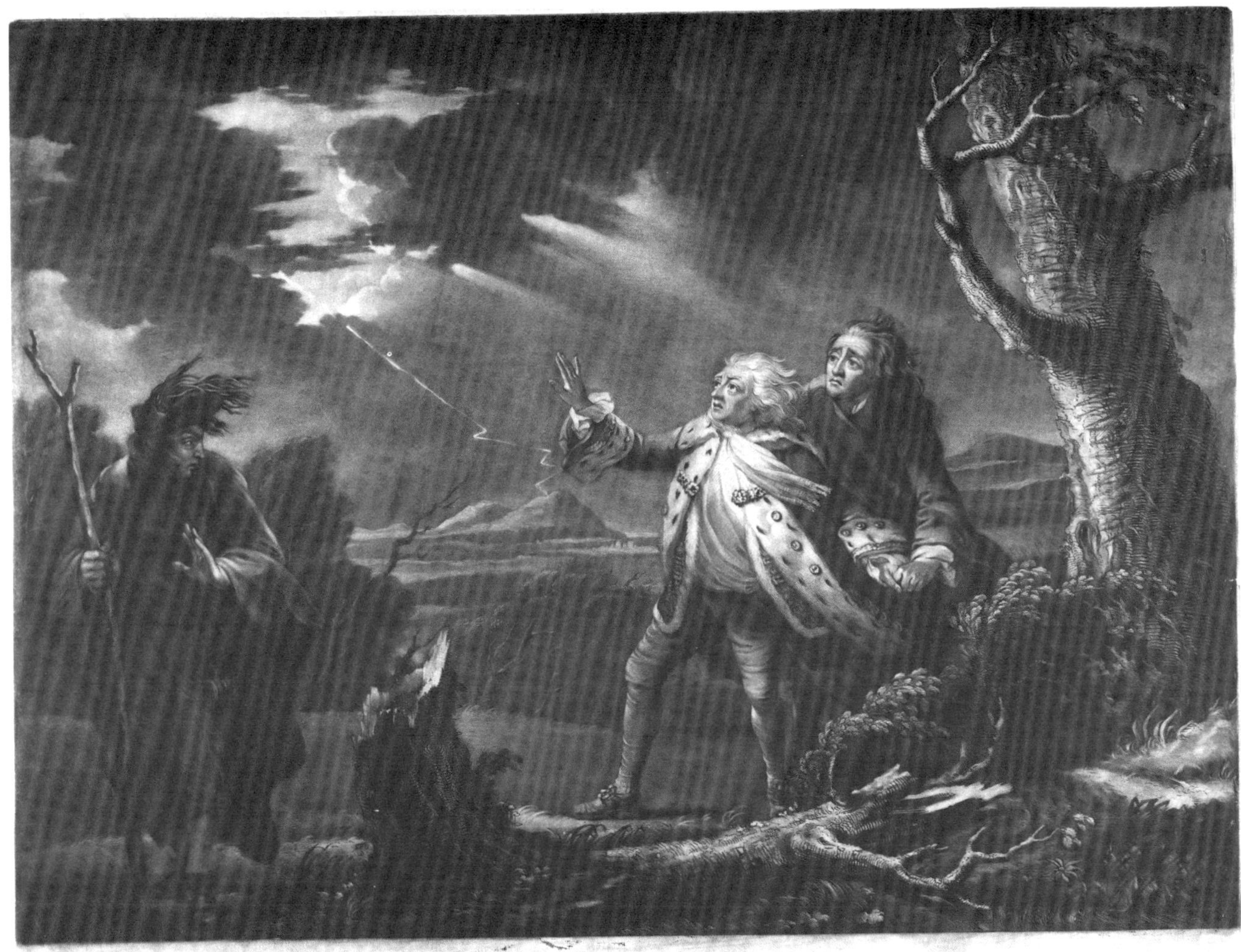

12 Mr Garrick in the Character of King Lear

Engraved by James McArdell
after Benjamin Wilson

Published by James McArdell [16 May] 1761

386 x 515 I; 412 x 515 Pl.

References: CS 79; R 79; G 85; O'D 126; Hall 214

1. Finished proof before all letters.
Impressions: CLB P8,488 (impression exhibited)

2. With scratched inscription.
Impressions: said to be at Harvard.

3. With the engraved inscription: *"B: Wilson Pinx.^t *** J.^s Mc Ardell fecit. / Mr Garrick in the* Character *of* King Lear. / *Act 3.^d Scene 1.st / Done from ye Original Picture in the Collection of Henry Hoare Esqr — *** Publish'd accord.^g to Act of Parliament; 1761. & fold at the Golden Head in Cov.^t Garden."*.
Impressions: CLB; BM; TM; H.

The original painting, once in the possession of Henry Hoare, is now lost. Although McArdell had already produced his splendid engraving of *Garrick as Hamlet* (see page 52) and two line engravings of *Romeo and Juliet* had been published[1], this is the first large scale, landscape-format mezzotint of a theatrical scene. The high chiaroscuro of the wild storm scene – most effectively rendered in this medium – anticipates the splendid run of theatrical mezzotints after Johann Zoffany, who had been employed as a background painter in Wilson's studio.

A touched proof of the print was exhibited at the Society of Artists in 1761 as 'Mr Garrick in the Character of King Lear drawn upon with Indian ink by Mr Wilson, from whose original picture it was taken'. The smaller piracy, published by John Ryall in 1761, seems to have been available by 7 March 1761, before McArdell's plate was finished, since he warned the public in an advertisement placed in *The Public Advertiser* on that day (see over). McArdell's mezzotint was presumably not completed and printed until 16 May when he advertised its publication in the same paper (see over). If the plate had been completed earlier, a finished impression would have been exhibited at the Society of Artists in the first week of May.

After McArdell's death in 1765, this plate was acquired by Robert Sayer and was listed in Sayer & Bennett's 1775 catalogue

TO prevent Impoſition, Mr. Mac Ardell thinks proper to inform the Public, that he propoſes very ſhortly to publiſh, from the original Picture of Mr. B. Wilſon, a Metzotinto of Garrick in King Lear, of which a ſpurious Print has lately appeared. The Size of the Plate is 21 Inches by 16; being the ſame with that of Romeo.

This Day is publiſhed, Price 7 s. 6d. A Metzotinto Print of Mr. GARRICK in the Character of King LEAR. Done by J. M'ARDELL from the Original Picture painted by B. WILSON, and ſold at the Golden-Head in Covent-Garden.

☞ The play presents Lear, King of Britain, a petulant and foolish old man, who has three daughters: Goneril, wife of the Duke of Albany; Regan, wife of the Duke of Cornwall and Cordelia, for whom the King of France and the Duke of Burgundy are suitors. Intending to divide his kingdom between his daughters according to their affection for him, he bids them say which loves him most. Goneril and Regan profess extreme affection but Cordelia, self-willed and disgusted at their hollow words, refuses to flatter. Infuriated by her reply, Lear divides her share between his other daughters, with the condition that he and one hundred knights shall be maintained by each daughter in turn. In this scene, Goneril and Regan have revealed their true colours and turned their father out into the storm; on a storm-blasted heath, his wits begin to turn. He is in the company of Gloucester's son Edgar, disguised as 'Poor Tom', and his loyal servant Kent, whom Lear had earlier banished, also in disguise; Garrick is portrayed in the print with Edgar, played by William Havard, and Kent (probably Astley Brandsby).

priced at 7s 6d. By 1795 Laurie & Whittle had raised the price of impressions of this print in their catalogue to 10s 6d. To judge by the prices charged by dealers, fine impressions of McArdell's print were either rare or held in high esteem. In the 1770s fine and rare proofs were offered at prices between one and two guineas, even fetching such prices at auction, but by 1813 the auction price for two impressions, 'Proofs and letters, Brilliant', had fallen to 11s.[3]

Garrick was obviously pleased with this print since he ordered impressions to be sent to him for distribution in Paris in 1764 (see page 52).

Garrick first appeared as Lear in Nahum Tate's 1681 version of the play and he continued to play the part regularly between 1742 and 1766. In 1756 he restored much of the original dialogue which had been dispensed with by Tate, although the tragic ending of the play was still not reinstated; it was considered to be too disturbing for English taste. The omission of the Fool from this print was explained by Davies:

It was once in contemplation with Mr Garrick to restore the part of the Fool, which he designed for Woodward, who promised to be very chaste in his colouring and not counteract the agonies of Lear: but the manager would not hazard so bold an attempt; he feared, Mr Colman, that the feelings of Lear would derive no advantage from the buffooneries of the parti-coloured jester.[4]

Garrick and Spranger Barry competed as Lear, playing it simultaneously in the 1756–7 season, and Wilson's painting was possibly commissioned to celebrate Garrick's acknowledged triumph in the part in which Fanny Burney considered him to be '… exquisitely great – every idea which I had formed of his talents, although I have ever idolised him, was exceeded'.[5] Horace Walpole, however, was not so impressed: 'as I told him, I was more shocked at the rest of the company than pleased with him … to give greater brilliancy to his own setting he had selected the very worst performers of his troop'.[6]

The storm scene held the greatest visual potential of the play and proved to be particularly affecting:

'Tis an odd Effect of a laugh to produce Tears; but I believe there was hardly a dry eye in the House on his executing that first absolute Act of Madness in the Character [of Lear].[7]

The portrayal of the inner tempest in the king's mind was also especially remembered by Murphy who wrote in 1801 that 'it was in Lear's madness that Garrick's genius was remarkably distinguished.'[8] It was said that Garrick had based his interpretation of this scene on personal observation of a man who had been driven mad as a result of having accidentally caused his young daughter's death.

Of the many parts that Garrick played in his career, the role of Lear was considered to be the one in which Garrick was best able to display the full range of his acting prowess. Thomas Wilkes was transfixed:

I never see him coming down from one corner of the Stage, with his old grey hair standing, as it were, erect upon his head, his face filled with horror and attention, his hands expanded and his whole frame actuated by a dreadful solemnity, but I

am astounded and share in all his distresses … it is here that
the power of his eye, corresponding with an attitude peculiar
to his own judgement and proper to the situation, is of force
sufficient to thrill through the veins and pierce the hardest
bosom.[9]

[1] '*Mr Garrick and Mrs Ann Bellamy in the
Characters of Romeo and Juliet*' by Simon
Ravenet after Wilson and '*Mr Barry and Miss
Nossiter in the Characters of Romeo and Juliet*'
William Elliot after Robert Pyle.

[2] Presumably Ravenet's engraving which is near
this size, rather than McArdell's mezzotint.

[3] Lot 538, *A Catalogue of the Valuable Collection of
Prints and Drawings of Henry P. Hope, Esq.*,
18–26 March, 1813.

[4] *Dramatic Miscellanies*, II, pp. 266–7.

[5] Troide, Lars E. *ed. The Early Journals and
Letters of Fanny Burney*, I, p. 242, after seeing a
performance 19 February 1773.

[6] Horace Walpole quoted in the DNB.

[7] Dr John Hill quoted in *The London Daily
Advertiser*, 27 February 1752.

[8] Murphy, I, p. 27.

[9] Wilkes, Thomas *A General View of the Stage*,
1759, p. 234.

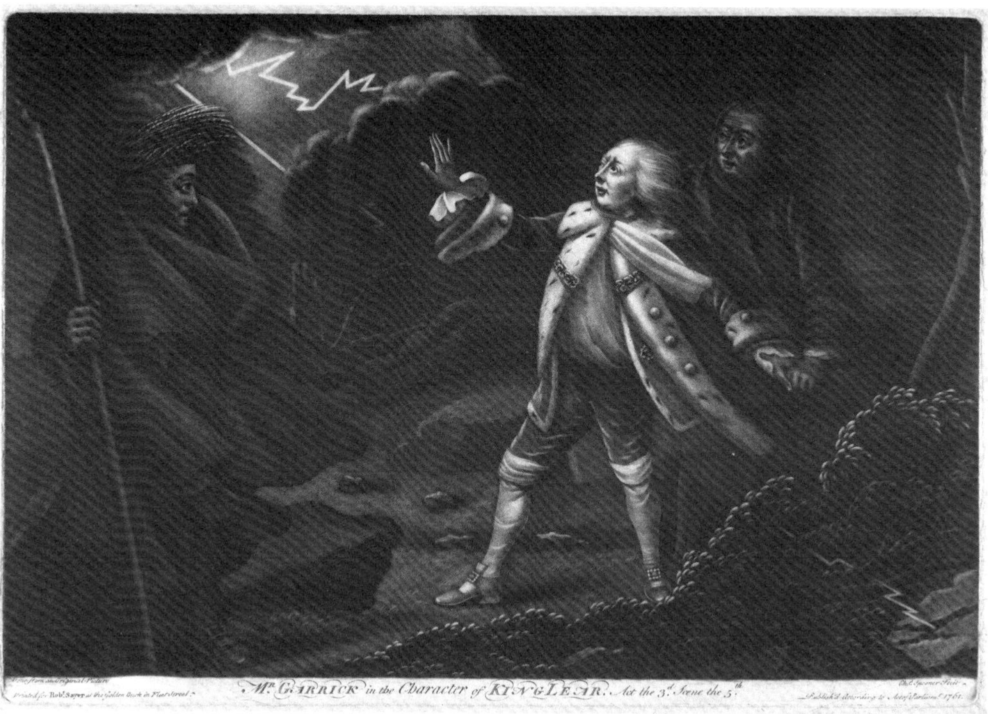

13 MR Garrick in the Character of King Lear, Act the 3.^d Scene the 5th

Engraved by Charles Spooner from drawing after the original [Benjamin Wilson] by Richard Houston

Published by John Ryall 1761

Re-published by Robert Sayer [before 1768]

243 x 356 I; 253 x 356 Pl.

References: CS p. 1339; O'D 127; Hall 216 & 217

1. With the engraved inscription: *"R.,^d Houston delin.^t ab Originali. *** C,, Spooner Fecit, / MR GARRICK in the CHARACTER of KING LEAR. / ACT the 3,^d Scene the 5th / Publish'd accord^g to Act of Parliament 1761 pr 2^s *** London printed for John Ryall in Fleet Street.".*
Impressions: CLB P37,980 (impression exhibited); H.

2. With the price altered to '1s'.
Impressions: CLB.

---

3. The plate apparently reduced to 240 x 349 I; 251 x 351 Pl. and extensively re-worked; the inscription altered: *"Done from an Original Picture *** Chas Spooner Fecit~ / MR GARRICK in the Character of KING LEAR, Act the 3.^d Scene the 5.th / Printed for Robt Sayer at the Golden Buck in Fleet Street. *** Publish'd according to Act of Parliam.^t 1761.".*
Impressions: CLB; H.

This is the first mezzotint piracy of a theatrical scene and is probably the 'spurious Print' referred to by McArdell in his advertisement of 7 March 1760 (see page 27). There may be two or more plates of this print: Sayer's plates appear to be smaller than Ryall's[1] and the last two Sayer states are radically different from the earliest. It is not possible to compare different states for in the early Ryall states the mezzotint ground is laid heavily, thereby effectively camouflaging the underlying etched lines. Thus it is impossible to see if they are proportionate to the measurements of the plates or if they even correspond. In the final three states, the underlying etching differs. What can be readily seen in the third state has disappeared in the fourth, but no perceptible differences can be found in the inscriptions, except for the heavy wear in the later state.

In the last two states the plate was extensively re-worked: many details have been altered, but two key changes, a tree added in the foreground and the re-alignment of Edgar's left foot, suggest that when Sayer owned McArdell's plate, he altered Spooner's piracy to resemble it more closely. This small piracy, measuring 10 x 14 inches, was sold by Sayer for 1s uncoloured; the McArdell plate, measuring 21 x 16 inches, would have cost 7s 6d. The smaller plate was listed again in Sayer & Bennett's 1775 catalogue at the same price, but perhaps because either memories of Garrick had faded or the plate was beyond printing, it was dropped from Laurie & Whittle's 1795 catalogue (see page 32).

If Sayer acquired Ryall's plate, it was before he obtained McArdell's plate, for only the former is listed in his 1766 catalogue. The partnership of Ryall & Withy seems to have ended in 1758–59, a fire destroying Withy's premises in Sweeting's Alley on 10 November 1759.[2] After the dissolution of the partnership each of the partners traded alone; Withy later abandoned printselling altogether to become a 'stockbroker' dealing in everything from soap to property.

4. The plate extensively re-worked. The face, background and l. foot of Edgar re-worked and a branch added to foreground.
Impressions: CLB.

5. With the number '*166*' added.
Impressions: BM.

The chiaroscuro of the painting helps to obscure the weak draughtsmanship of this piracy; in later examples, like that of *She Stoops to Conquer* (see page 79), the engraver could not disguise his draughtsmanship in this manner and as a result the engraving is finer. A piracy such as this however was not aimed at an art-loving audience, but probably sold in hundreds to people who had seen the performance and wanted to prolong the memory; this is perhaps best understood in the context of a more modern practice, the purchase of a souvenir programme. Thomas Davies reveals this print purchasing public when he reminded his readers that:

> They, who have had the exquisite pleasure to see Garrick in *King Lear*, will most unfeignedly wish that his action and elocution could have been perpetuated. A Reynolds could have faithfully transcribed a look and an attitude; but alas! this would have been but an imperfect representation. The wonders of his voice and multiplied expression could not have been preserved![3]

By 1795 Garrick had been dead for over fifteen years, and there was no longer a call for the smaller, cheaper and cruder version. The expensive plate of course still had a market, both as a prized work by McArdell and as one that showed Garrick in one of his greatest roles.

William Havard, who played Edgar to Garrick's Lear, was born in 1710 in Dublin and achieved 'respectable mediocrity' both as an actor and a dramatist. He appeared at Drury Lane on the first night that the theatre opened with Garrick as manager, in September 1747, and played a wide variety of mainly secondary characters.

The 'jealous' actor Charles Adams[4] was not impressed by his acting and after seeing a performance of King Lear complained in a letter that Havard,

> who is esteem'd the third Man in the Theatre did Edgar last Saturday so execrebly [sic] Spiritless, I would whip a Boy of ten years old who, with a Month's study, did not perform it better ... so very insipid – Some Masterly Strokes indeed he had, but they were so uncouth in him ...[5]

However, the general consensus was that Havard's Edgar was one of his most memorable performances and in *The Anti-Rosciad* it was declared:

> Havard, 'tis true does seldom play with fire,
> Which Havard's parts but rarely do require.
> But who can say his strain unvary'd floes,
> That sees him counterfeit brave Edgar's woes?

Undoubtedly, the management of both patent theatres now depended heavily upon the unsung players who appeared year after year, dependably, patiently and tirelessly, acting in supporting roles while the stars, Garrick, Barry, Weston, Foote and others took the finest parts. It was this integrity that Davies singled out in Havard, who he felt

> deserved to be remembered, not so much for his stage abilities, which were indeed far from contemptible, as for his probity, the gentleness of his manners, and the benevolence of his disposition.[6]

Havard died in 1778, and his close friend Paul Whitehead the satirist wrote verses for his tombstone which summarise his career: 'Views of ambition ne'er his hopes employ'd, / Yet honest fame he courted and enjoy'd …'.[7]

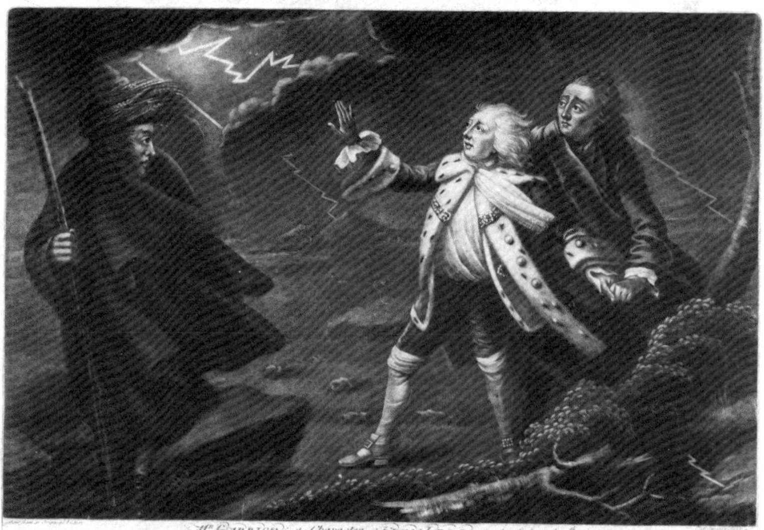

[1] Engravings are printed on wetted paper, which needs to be wetter in later states. Drying can cause a shrinkage of up to three per cent.

[2] *The Gentleman's Magazine*, 10 Nov. 1759: 'About five o'clock in the morning a dreadful fire broke out at Hamlin's coffee-house in Sweeting's Alley, near the Royal Exchange, which consumed that and the New York Coffee-house adjoining to it …'. Withy's premises and twelve others, all in the front of Cornhill, were ruined. The premises of another printseller, Thomas Bakewell, was still standing.

[3] *Dramatic Miscellanies*, II, p. 319.

[4] (fl. c. 1745–51).

[5] TDB.

[6] Davies, II, p. 195.

[7] *ibid.*, p. 211.

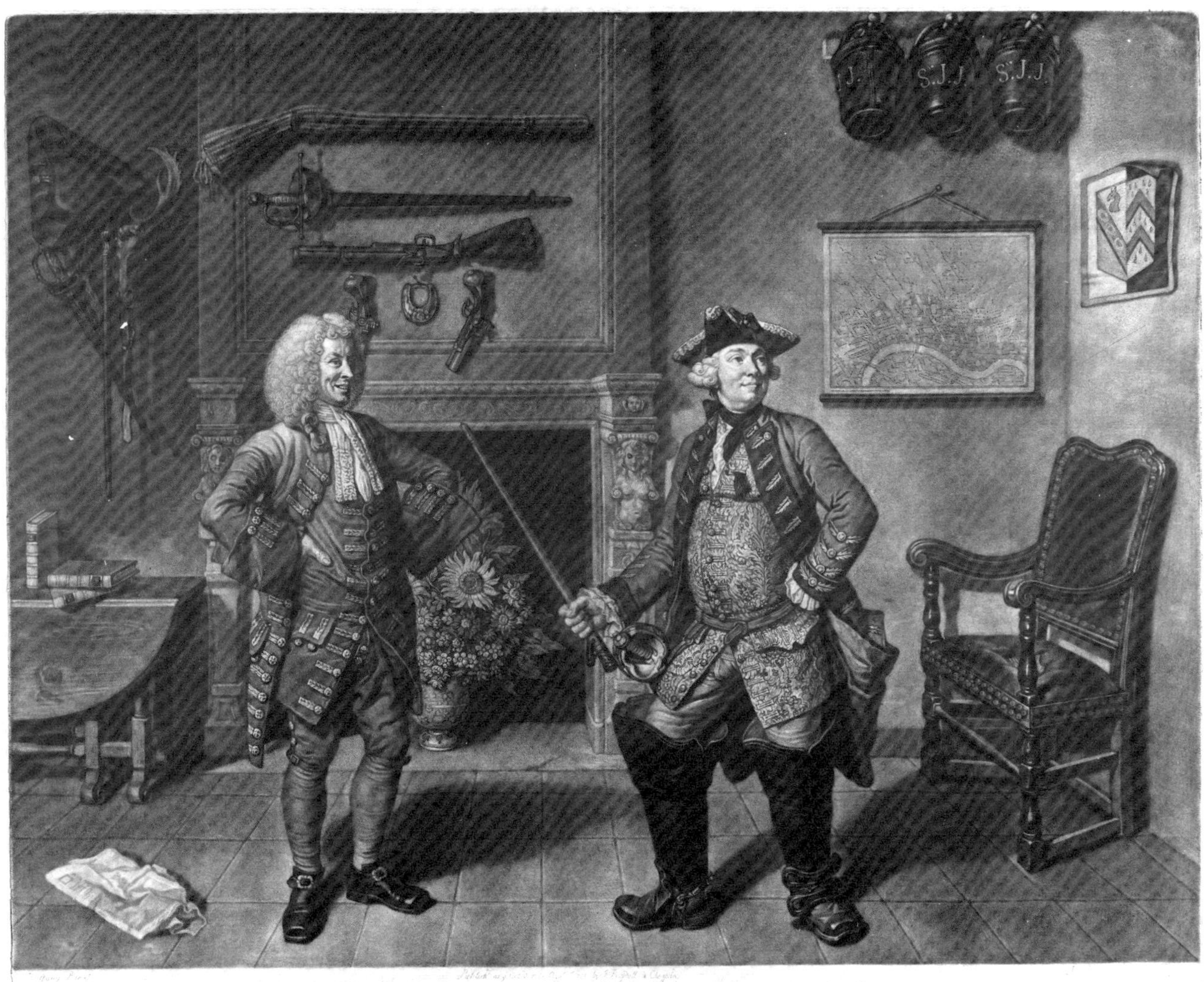

14 Mr. Foote in the Character of Major Sturgeon, in the Mayor of Garrat

Engraved by Johann Gottfried Haid
after Johann Zoffany

Published by John Boydell 14 August 1765

404 x 506 I; 430 x 506 Pl.

References: CS 2; O'D 17

1. Finished proof before all letters.
Impressions: BM.

2. Finished proof with the scratched inscription: "*Zoffany Pinx.*, *** *J. G. Haid fecit / Publish.ᵈ as ye Act directs Aug.ˢᵗ 1ˢᵗ 1765 by J. Boydell in Cheapside*".
Impressions: CLB P30,377 (impression exhibited); BM; TM; H.

3. With the engraved inscription: "J. Boydell

The painting by Johann Zoffany was presumably commissioned by Samuel Foote, who left it in his will[1] to William Fitzherbert, one of his executors. The picture was in George Colman's possession shortly afterwards and was sold after he died in 1795; it was subsequently in the collection of the Earl of Carlisle. Garrick left for the continent in 1763 and it is likely that Foote decided to take advantage of his absence with a well-timed piece of self-publicity. An entry in Foote's account held with Drummonds for 25 October reads: 'To cash paid for Jn. Zoffany £42', which may be a prepayment for this painting. Boydell listed the plate in his catalogue for 1773 at 7s 6d and in the following year Shropshire was selling a 'very fine proof before letters' for 15s. The plate was eventually sold in 1818 after Josiah Boydell's death; it was purchased by 'Walker' for sixteen guineas, together with the plates to '*Garrick and Miss Bellamy in Romeo and Juliet*' and '*Garrick and Mrs Pritchard in Macbeth*'.

Johann Gottfried Haid came from a family of mezzotint engravers at Augsburg. Before coming to England in about 1764 to work for John Boydell, he produced slightly wooden and naive mezzotint portraits. Whilst in England his work became softer and

Excud.ᵗ / *Zoffanij Pinxit* *** *J. G. Haid fecit.* / *M*ᴿ
FOOTE in the Character of MAJOR STURGEON,
/ *in the Mayor of Garrat.* / Publiſhed according
to Act of Parliament Auguſt 14ᵗʰ 1765. by *JOHN
BOYDELL*, Engraver in Cheapſide,
LONDON.".
Impressions: CLB; BM; H.

☞ Samuel Foote's *Mayor of Garratt* is set in
Garratt, a hamlet in Wandsworth, on the day of
the mock election of the Mayor of Garratt. Jerry
Sneak, the hen-pecked son-in-law of Sir John
Jollop, the landowner of Garratt, gets elected.
The humour derives from the principal charac-
ters: Mrs Sneak, who objects to her husband's
election; the Mob of Electors, and Major
Sturgeon of the recently disbanded Middlesex
Militia, a fish-broker who lives at Brentford,
who talks of training manoeuvres as 'Actions'.
The franchise for the election at Garratt is said
by Caulfield, in his Blackguardiana, to be open
to all who have had 'carnal congress' with a
woman in the open air on Wandsworth
Common.

far more subtle, possibly due to the fact that English copper was
softer. This effect can also be seen in the handful of works by his
brother Johann Jacob which were engraved for Boydell at the same
time. Haid also engraved another fine theatrical print after
Zoffany, '*Mr Garrick in the Farmer's Return*'. He moved to Vienna
and remained there for the rest of his life.

The Haid family were perhaps the best of the Augsburg school
of mezzotint engravers. In their hands mezzotint suddenly blos-
somed in Germany, where previously it had been a medium used
for the quick production of cheap portraits. Under the Haids' influence, mezzotint engravers followed the English improvements and
by exploiting all the advantages of the technique they started to
produce fine quality prints.

Foote's play, a comic after-piece, was first performed on 20 June
1763 and met with considerable success, being performed thirty-
seven times in that year alone. Much of the play's immediate
success lay in its topicality; the Peace of Paris had just concluded
the Seven Years' War and Foote's play was designed to ridicule
the Militia, which had been raised for home defence. The plot
centres around Sturgeon, a Citizen and Fishmonger, who as a
Major in the militia attempts to come to terms with his 'new position' in society, that of an Officer and Gentleman.

---

[1] The will was proved 22 October 1777.

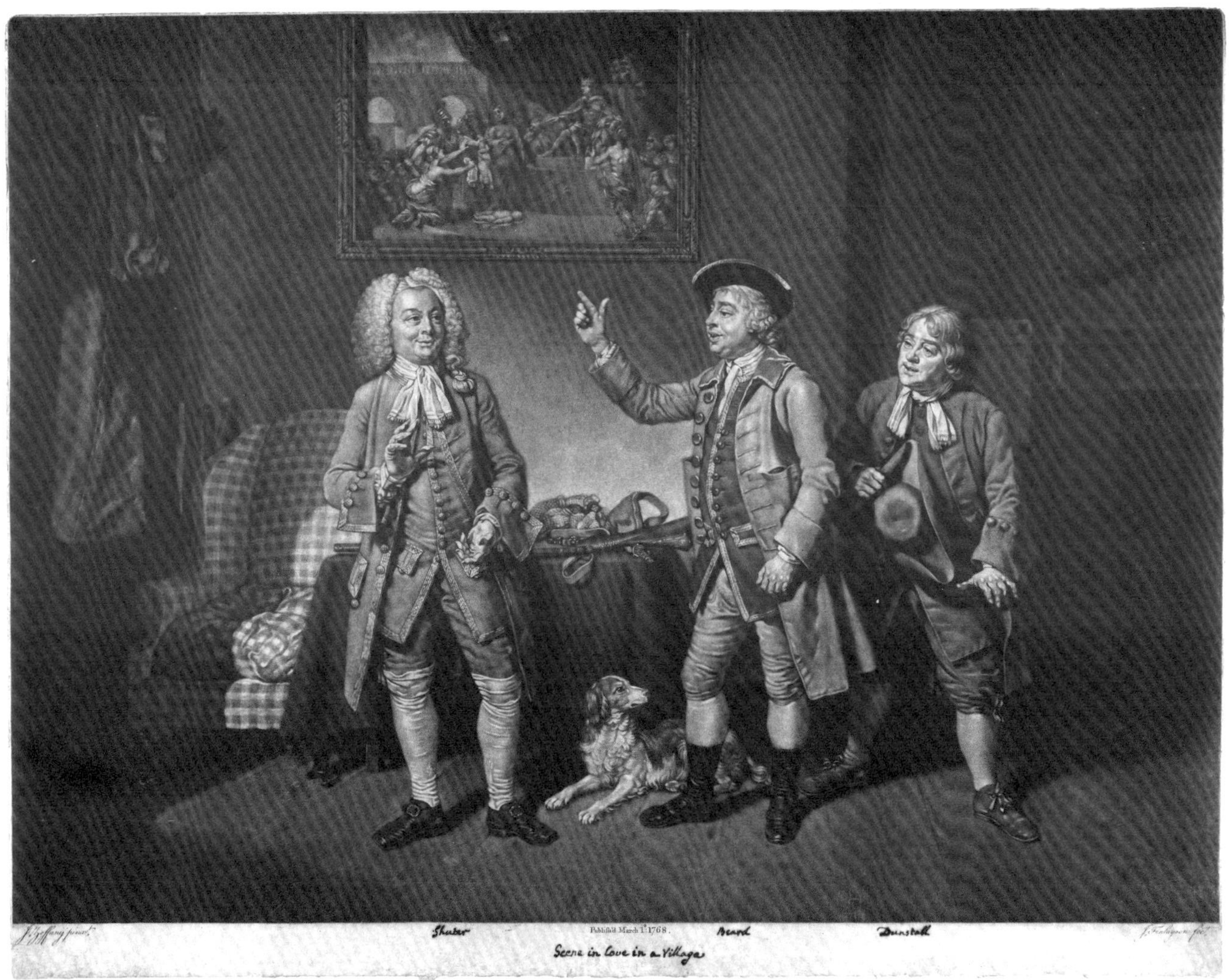

15 M.r Shuter, M.r Beard & M.r Dunstall, in the Characters of Justice Woodcock, Hawthorn & Hodge

Engraved by John Finlayson
after Johann Zoffany

Published 1 March 1768

[Re-published by] Sold by John Zoffany, John Finlayson and Henry Parker

417 x 555 I; 455 x 555 Pl.

References: CS 14; O'D groups p. 29

1. Finished proof with the engraved inscription at the base of the image: "Publiſh'd March 1.ft 1768. / J,, *Zoffanij pinx.,* *** J,, *Finlayson fec.,*".
Impressions: CLB P12,244 (impression exhibited); BM.

Now in the Detroit Institute of Art, the painting by Johann Zoffany was exhibited at the Society of Artists in May 1767. Of the three versions that exist, two have the picture of the Judgement of Solomon in the background and the third, van Dyck's portrait of the Children of Charles I. It is possible that the painting commemorated the retirement of John Beard, who last appeared as Hawthorn on 9 April 1767. The mezzotint was exhibited at the Society of Artists in May 1768; in September it was exhibited again, together with the painting, in a special exhibition for the King of Denmark. Initially the print was jointly published by the painter and the engraver but it was re-published with the additional involvement of Henry Parker[1], as were the two other prints engraved by Finlayson after Zoffany, '*The Provok'd Wife*' (see page 37) and '*The Devil on Two Sticks*' (see page 65).

Parker is said to have retired from printselling when he purchased the office of Clerk of the Chamber, Guildhall in 1774; he was then in a position to sell his share in the plates. This was the year that John Finlayson died and Finlayson's wife Olive, being the sole executrix, could then have sold her share to Sayer. The plates were listed in Sayer & Bennett's 1775 catalogue and all three remained with Sayer and his successors until at least 1795. At

2. With the added engraved inscription:
"Publifh'd March 1.ᶠᵗ 1768. / J,, Zoffanij pinx,!, *** J,, Finlayson fec!,/ Mᴿ SHUTER, Mᴿ BEARD & Mᴿ DUNSTALL, in the Characters of JUSTICE WOODCOCK, HAWTHORN & HODGE. / Love in a Village Act 1ˢᵗ Scene, 6.ᵗʰ / Sold by M,ᵣ Zoffanij in Lincoln's Inn Fields, M,ᵣ Finlayson in Berwick Street, Soho. and M,ᵣ Parker at N,º 82, in Cornhill."
Impressions: CLB.

☞ In Bickerstaffe and Carey's *Love in a Village*, Rosetta has fled an arranged marriage and, disguised as a servant, hides in the household of Justice Woodcock, whose daughter Lucinda is unhappy, despite a promising romance with Mr Eustace. Rosetta advises Lucinda to elope (she later follows this advice) and they discuss the handsome new gardener who, unbeknown to them, is the sole heir of one William Meadows. Young Meadows is in disguise, to avoid his proposed bride, little knowing that she is in fact Lucinda, with whom he has fallen in love. Matters are complicated by Rosetta's disdain towards him, despite her own growing passion, and her evasion of two other suits: that of Woodcock, whose failure is constantly and humorously chided by Hawthorn, and that of Hodge, Lucinda's servant, who is himself pursued. To this must be added the relentless sleuthing of Woodcock's sister, in her increasingly desperate and farcical attempts to foil Lucinda's plans; it is she who is finally ridiculed when all is eventually resolved.

[1] Henry Parker (d. 1809), print and book seller, stationer.
[2] Richard Holmes Laurie (d.1758) succeeded father as Whittle's partner 1812, sole proprietor 1818.
[3] Gentleman, I, p. 168.
[4] *Dramatic Miscellanies*, III, p. 375.
[5] Gentleman, I, p. 127.

a later date Boydell gained possession of the plates, which were sold after the death of Josiah Boydell in 1818, together with the remaining proofs and the prints from their stock. The catalogue for the 1818 Boydell sale indicates that only two of the three shares in the plates were to be sold; this suggests that the last share could have been retained by Zoffany's wife, Zoffany having died in 1810, or by Richard Holmes Laurie[2] who succeeded to the business in 1818. The plates were sold for £2 12s 6d.

Several suggestions can be put forward to explain the use of just a publication date in the first state, instead of the more usual type of publication line which records the formal involvement of those who distributed the prints. All three prints were exhibited at the Society of Artists between 1768–70 and the omission of any involvement of a major printseller may have been to avoid the taint of commercialism. Alternatively, the artist and engraver could have printed off a number of fine early impressions which they could sell themselves, with Parker's name added at a later date. A further explanation is that Parker purchased a third share in the publication of all three prints after November 1769 and it was then that his publication details were added.

'*Love in a Village*' shows the cast of the original production acting together for the last time during the 1766–7 season. After *The Beggar's Opera* and *Romeo and Juliet*, *Love in a Village* was the most popular theatrical piece of its time, being staged one hundred and eighty-three times at Covent Garden alone before 1776.

The performances of these three actors were highly acclaimed by Francis Gentleman: 'The part of Woodcock was clearly designed for Mr Shuter, and I presume it will be admitted that no author ever judged an actor's capacity better … as he [Hawthorn] lived, so we may say he died, with that truly great intelligent English singer, Mr Beard'[3]; Dunstall also deserved a 'great deal of praise'. Davies was critical of the play itself: 'this piece is nothing more than showy base metal, flavoured with a very indulgent stamp of public favour'[4]; Lichtenberg felt it was marred by Shuter's constant exaggeration.

John Beard was born in about 1716, sang in the King's Chapel from an early age, and first appeared in drama in 1737 at Drury Lane in *The Devil to Pay*. He was happily married to Lady Henrietta Herbert, but she died young in 1753 and he subsequently married Charlotte Rich, daughter of the Covent Garden manager. In 1761 Beard took control of the theatre after his father-in-law's death. He was very popular, especially in his favourite part of Macheath, and was praised for his strength of character. He retired from the stage in May 1767 and died at Hampton in 1791.

Dibdin considered Beard to be 'the best English singer'; his voice was 'sound, male, powerful, and extensive. His tones were natural, and he had flexibility enough to execute any passages, however difficult'. One critic complained that 'his speaking was intolerable and he appeared too much of the gentleman.'[5]

John Dunstall, a Londoner, was born in 1717. His first appearance was as Driver in *Oroonoko* in 1740. Over a long and varied career he played numerous roles, dying a few days short of his sixty-first birthday. He was a pleasant man and had few vices, with the exception of acknowledging his friends when on stage.

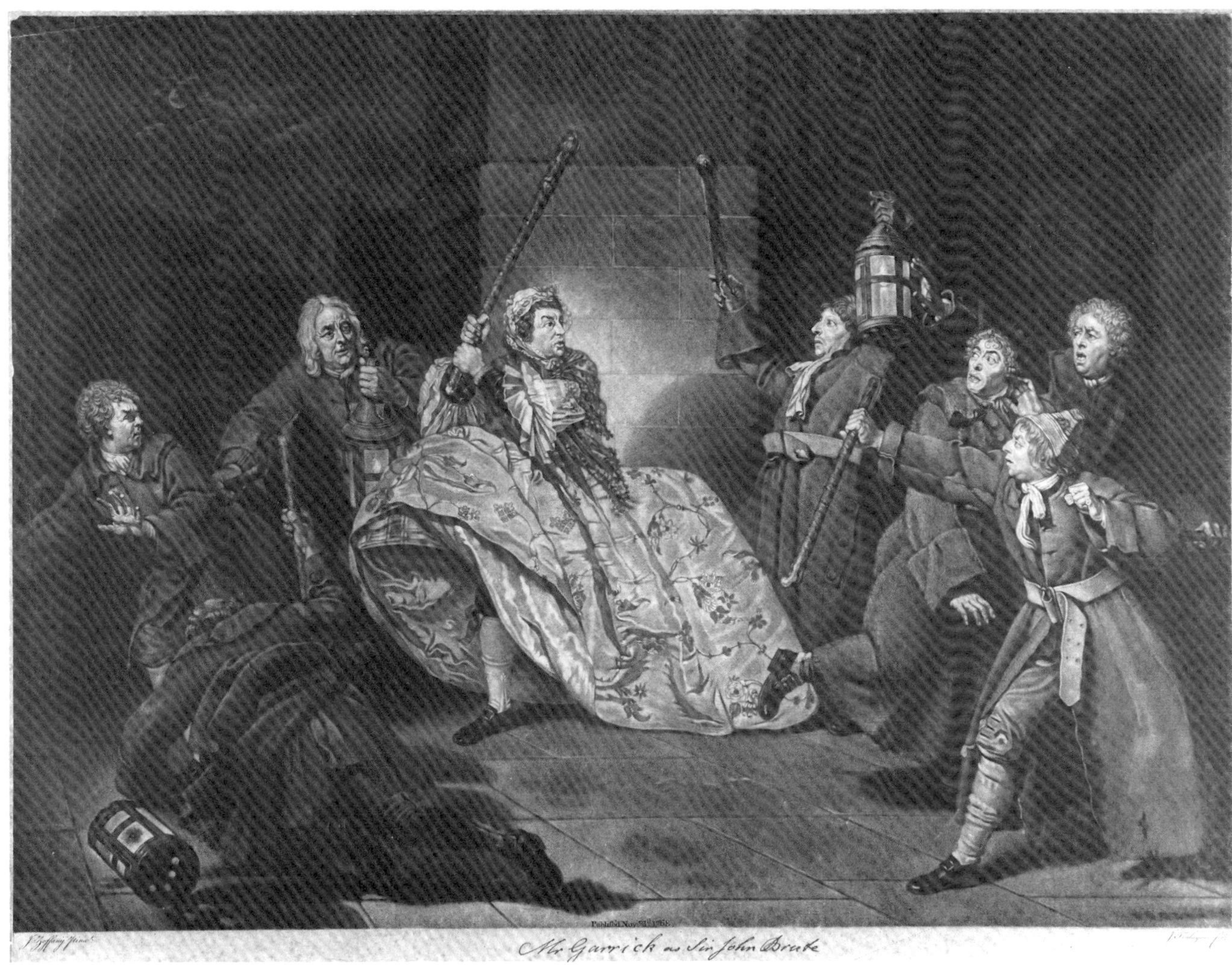

16 Mr Garrick in the Character of Sr John Brute

Engraved by John Finlayson
after Johann Zoffany

Published 1 November 1768

[Re-published by] Sold by John Zoffany,
John Finlayson and Henry Parker

418 x 553 I; 455 x 555 Pl.

References: CS 28; O'D groups p. 29

1. With the engraved inscription: In c. at the
base of the image "Publifh'd Novr 1^{ft} 1768.". In
the inscription space below "*J: Zoffanij Pinx.!***
J,, Finlayson fec,!*".
Impressions: CLB P8,487 (impression exhibited); BM;
TM.

2. With the added engraved inscription: "*M^R
GARRICK* in the Character of *S^R JOHN
BRUTE, M.! Vaughan, M.! Hallet, M.! Clough, M.!
Parsons, M.! Watkins, & M.! Phillips, in the
Characters of the Watchmen.* | THE PROVOK'D

Garrick commissioned Zoffany's painting for his villa at Hampton;
it was exhibited at the Society of Artists in 1765 and Garrick left it
to his brother George on his death. The print, which was initially
published by Zoffany and Finlayson, was acquired by Robert
Sayer and subsequently by John Boydell, together with two other
plates after Zoffany; this is discussed under the first of these three
prints, '*Love in a Village*' (see page 35). The mezzotint was exhibited at the Society of Artists in 1769.

This print shows the cast of 18 April 1763. Garrick played Sir
John Brute in every season but two during his career, a total of one
hundred and five performances. He even played the part in his
final season, when new topical details had been added.

Lichtenberg described in detail the way in which Garrick
brought the character to life:

Sir John Brute is not merely a dissolute fellow, but Garrick
makes him an old fop also … Mr Garrick plays … in such a
way that I should certainly have known him to be a most
remarkable man, even if I had never heard anything of him
and had seen him in one scene only in this play. Then he
comes home excessively drunk … His waistcoat is open from
top to bottom, his stockings full of wrinkles, with the garters
hanging down, and, moreover – which is vastly strange – two

WIFE. ACT IV, SCENE I. / *Sold by M.ʳ Zoffanij, in Lincoln's Inn Fields, M.ʳ Finlayson, in Berwick Street, Soho; & M.ʳ Parker, N.º 82, in Cornhill.".*
Impressions: BM; TM; H.

☞ In Vanbrugh's *The Provoked Wife*, Sir John Brute, a churlish gentleman and coward, mistreats his wife. She is wooed by Constant, but remains faithful to her husband. Constant's friend, Heartfree, who prides himself on his indifference to women, falls in love with her niece Belinda. The two ladies, for a frolic, invite Constant and Heartfree to meet them in Spring Gardens. Here Lady Brute is about to yield to the ardent addresses of Constant, when they are interrupted. The two couples return to Lady Brute's house and sit down to cards, confident that Sir John will not return from his drinking-bout for some hours. Sir John, however, has been arrested by the watch for brawling in the streets disguised in a lady's short cloak and gown, in an amusing scene depicted in this print: 'Sirrah, I am Bonduca, Queen of the Welchmen; and with a leek as long as my pedigree, I will destroy your Roman legions in an instant. Britons, Strike home.'. Dismissed by the magistrate, he comes home and finds the two men, but refuses the duel offered him by Constant. The presence of the men is attributed to the proposed marriage of Heartfree and Belinda, and all ends happily.

kinds of garters; one would hardly be surprised, indeed, if he had picked up odd shoes.[1]

Quin's portrayal of Sir John Brute was of a coarse and vulgar man, detested particularly by the ladies of the audience. Garrick, on the other hand, presented him as a wickedly appealing man who was essentially a gentleman; people could not help but be seduced by him:

> Sir John Brute is Garrick's favourite part, although people have often attacked him on account of this play, turning against him the very zeal with which he maintains it on the stage, and saying openly that his own character could be little better than Sir John Brute's … the play is in part most lewd, but highly entertaining on account of Sir John's character, which is represented so amazingly by Garrick.[2]

Of the watchmen, only William Parsons had a distinguished career (see page 47).

[1] Lichtenberg, p. 18.
[2] *ibid.*, p. 71.

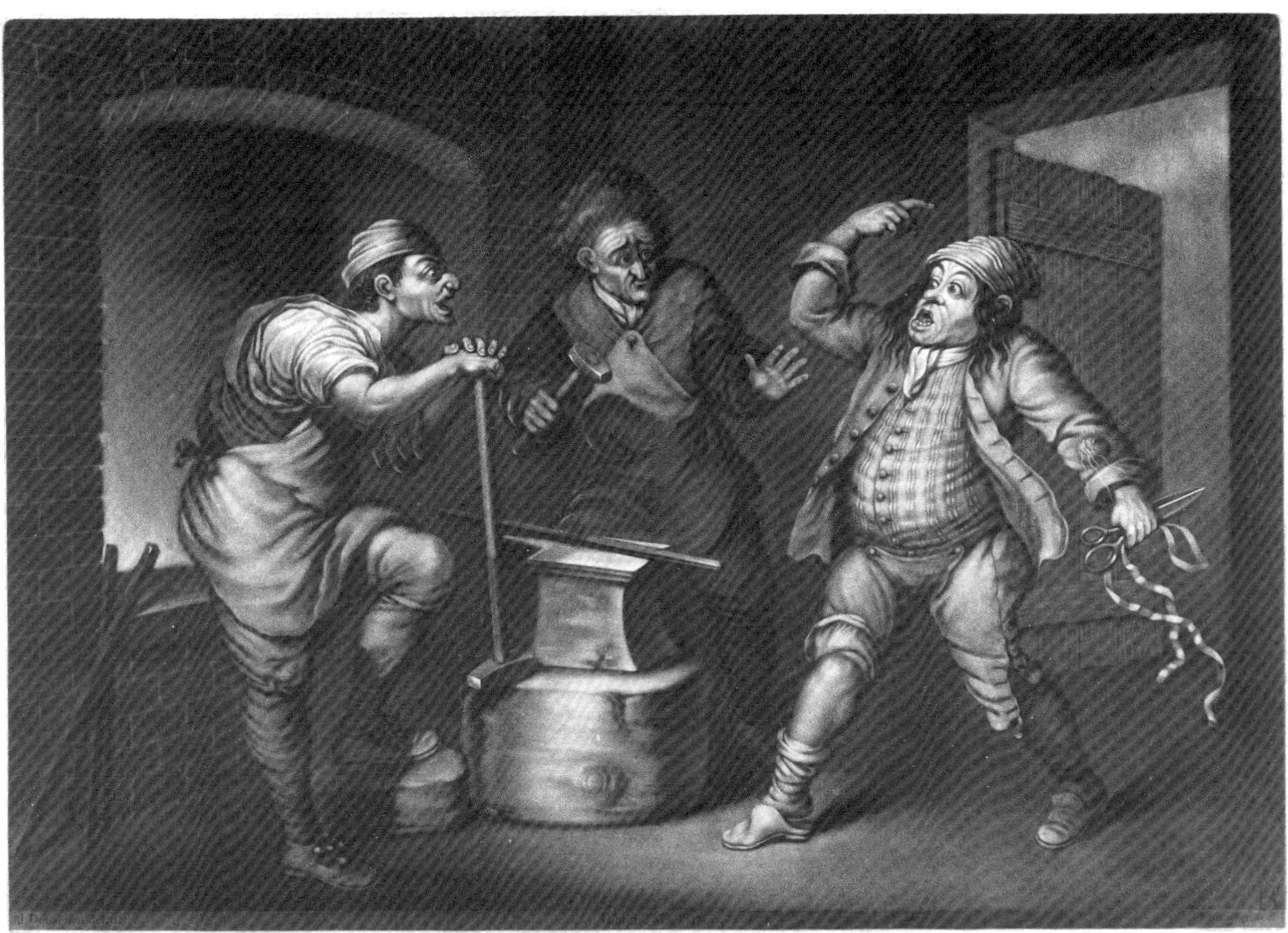

17 The Newsmongers

Engraved by John Finlayson
after John Donaldson

Published by John Finlayson 1 May 1769

325 x 452 I; 327 x 453 Pl.

Previously unrecorded print

1. With the engraved inscription at the base of the image: "J. Donaldſon delinᵗ *** Publiſh'd May 1ſᵗ 1769. *** J. Finlayſon fecᵗ". Impressions: CLB P13,132 ex. coll. Thomas Blaydes, *Lugt* 2442 (impression exhibited).

2. With the added engraved inscription below the image: "The Newſmongers, / I ſaw a ſmith ſtand with his hammer, thus, The whilſt his iron did on the anvil cool, With open mouth ſwallowing a taylor's news; *King* John *Act 4ᵗʰ Scene 2ᵈ* / Sold by Mʳ. Finlayſon, in Berwick Street, Soho.". Impressions: CLB.

This print illustrates a scene from a play, but not actors in part. The treatment of the figures and the composition as a whole belongs to the genre of mezzotint caricature. Little is known about the painter, John Donaldson, who was born in Edinburgh and became a miniaturist, ending his career as a porcelain painter.

The engraver, John Finlayson, was born in about 1730. Like Donaldson, he painted miniatures on enamel and in watercolour, exhibiting his work at the Free Society of Artists between 1762–3 and at the Society of Artists in 1768. The latter awarded him a premium in 1764 for an enamel painting as well as a gold palette and thirty guineas for a mezzotint in 1773. Two years after the engraver's death in 1774,[1] the auctioneer Langford advertised the sale of his stock-in-trade (see over). No precise date is known for this sale, which was advertised[2] as due to take place in February 1776, and there is no recorded survival of a copy of the sale catalogue.

The small group of copper-plates mentioned in the advertisement includes this print and a print after Murillo, 'Tinker', which was published in 1770. It is surprising that there is no mention of any of the better known plates that Finlayson engraved after paintings by Zoffany; this is probably because Finlayson's share in the three plates was sold privately to Robert Sayer. Walter Shropshire listed a 'proof' impression of '*The Newsmongers*' in his catalogue for

39

1770 at 3s. The plate passed into the hands of John Boydell and was sold in 1818, together with twenty six proofs, as part of a lot which included three other plates.

The print illustrates a scene from Act IV, Scene II of Shakespeare's *King John* (see page 69) in which Hubert reports to John the news that he is suspected of Arthur's murder:

'... Young Arthur's death is common in their mouths:
When they talk of him, they shake their heads
And whisper one another in the ear;
And he that speaks doth gripe the hearer's wrist,
Whilst he that hears makes fearful action
With wrinkled brows, with nods, with rolling eyes,
I saw a smith stand with his hammer, thus,
The whilst his iron did on the anvil cool,
With open mouth swallowing a tailor's news ...'

Edward Penny painted the same scene which, when exhibited at the Royal Academy in 1769, was the centre of attention. His picture was engraved by Richard Houston and published by Sayer in 1771[3] (see below). Penny's approach was that of a serious history painter and is more influenced by Italian art than by Zoffany's theatre histories.

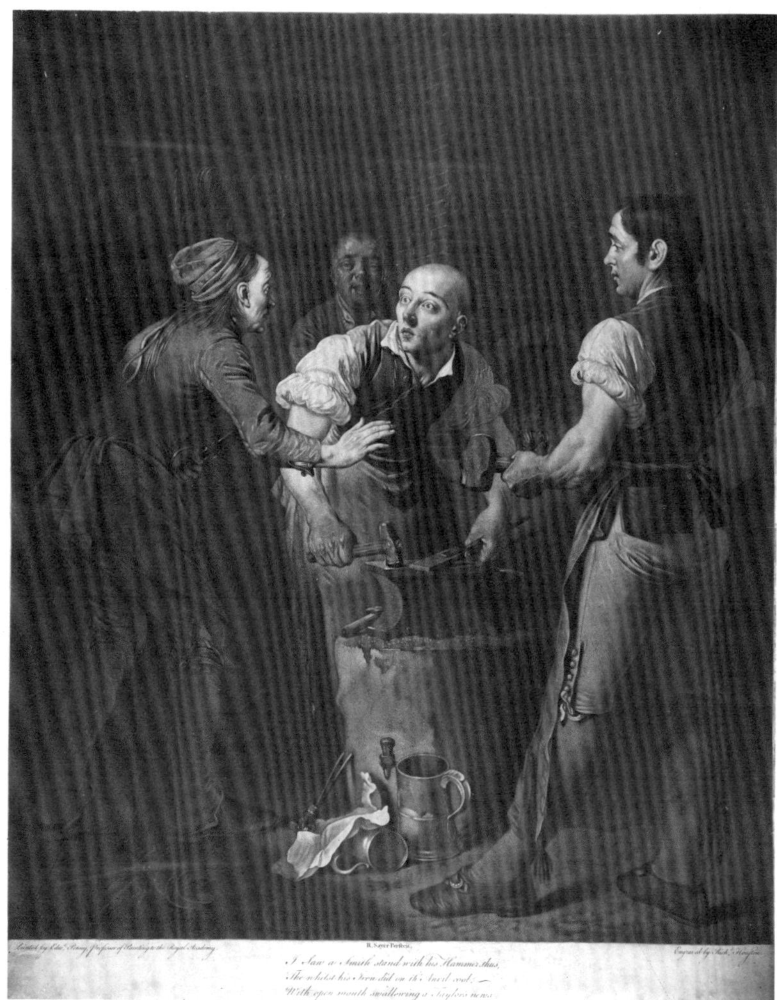

¹ P.R.O. Will Prob. 11–995. sig. 47, proved Feb. 1774 in which he describes himself as a miniature painter.
² *The Morning Post and Daily Advertiser*, 27 Jan. 1776.
³ Sayer & Bennett in their catalogue for 1775 indicate that the pair to this print, the same size 24 x 18 ins, was Richard Earlom's '*The Porter and Hare*' which Sayer first published in March 1774.

40

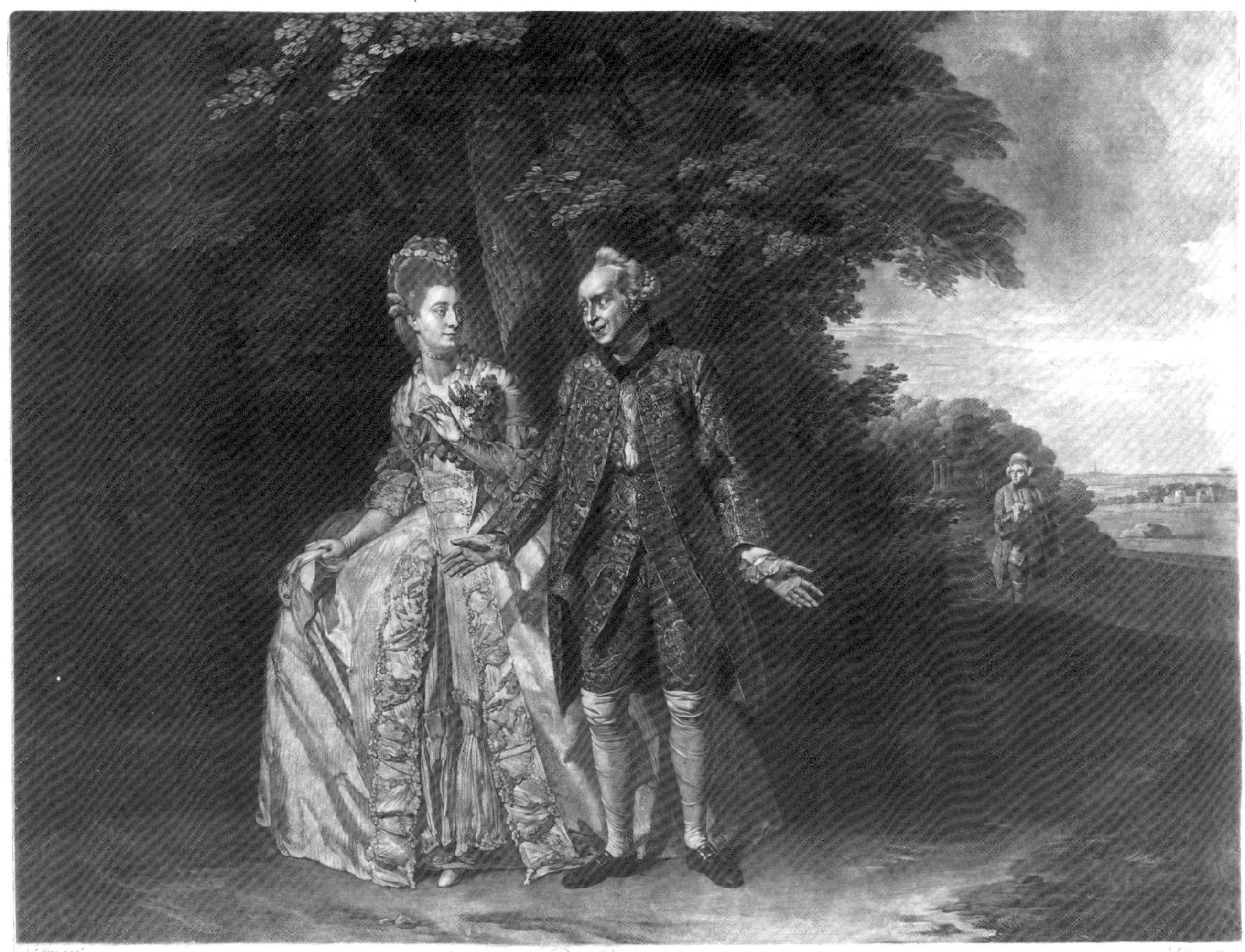

18 M.r King and M.rs Baddeley in the Characters of Lord Ogleby, and Miss Fanny Sterling

Engraved by Richard Earlom
after Johann Zoffany

Published by Robert Sayer 1 November 1772

429 x 559 I; 465 x 559 Pl.

References: CS 26; O'D (T. King) 7

1. Finished proof with the scratched inscription: "J Zoffany pinx.t *** R Sayer excudit *** R.d Earlom sculp.st 1772 / Publish'd November 1.st. 1772 by R Sayer, N.o 53, Fleet Street".
Impressions: BM; TM.

2. With the engraved inscription: "*J. Zoffany pinx!* *** *R. Earlom sculp!* / *M.r KING and M.rs BADDELEY* in the Characters of *LORD OGLEBY, and Mifs FANNY STERLING.* / O

At a Command Performance of *The Clandestine Marriage* on 24 October 1771, the King was so delighted by Mrs Baddeley's coyness in the scene depicted here that he requested Zoffany to paint her. The scene was particularly humorous because Canton (Mr Baddeley) encourages Lord Ogleby (Thomas King) to make love to his wife (Mrs Baddeley); it was said that the Baddeleys were on such bad terms that they never uttered a word to each other 'except when the utterance was dramatic'.[1] She was reputed to have had numerous affairs which were tolerated by her husband, himself a philanderer, who merely insisted that she contribute to his expenses. The painting, now in the Garrick Club, was never exhibited. The mezzotint was listed in Sayer & Bennett's catalogue for 1775 at 10s 6d and in Laurie & Whittle's catalogue for 1795, but by then the price had been reduced to 7s 6d.

This is the only theatrical print engraved by Richard Earlom, one of the most distinguished mezzotint engravers of his generation. His output was dominated by large plates of large and complex paintings, including Indian genre scenes after Zoffany. Unlike other engravers of his stature he did not publish his own prints, but instead worked for the major printsellers, Sayer,

41

thou amiable Creature command my Heart for it is vanquifh'd. *** CLANDESTINE MARRIAGE. Act IV. | *Publish'd as the Act directs, Nov.ʳ 1.ˢᵗ 1772, by* Rob.ᵗ Sayer, N.º 53 *in Fleet Street*, London.".
Impressions: CLB P23,989 (impression exhibited); BM; H.

☞ In *The Clandestine Marriage*, Mr Sterling's clerk, Lovewell, has secretly married his employer's younger daughter Fanny, but dares not risk her father's anger by revealing this. The socially ambitious father has arranged a marriage between his elder daughter and Sir John Melvil, Lord Ogleby's nephew. Ogleby and Melvil arrive at Sterling's house to make the final arrangements, when Melvil suddenly admits his preference for Fanny. She rejects his advances but still cannot bring herself to reveal her own marriage. Melvil tries to bribe Sterling to gain permission to court Fanny. However, Mrs Heidelberg, Sterling's wealthy and vulgar sister, resents this as an affront to her family, and demands that Fanny is turned out of the house. In the scene depicted here, Fanny in despair speaks to Lord Ogleby, an amorous old beau, who mistakes her confession as a declaration of love and announces that he will marry her himself: 'O thou amiable Creature, command my Heart for it is vanquish'd'. This causes further confusion but finally Lovewell is discovered in Fanny's bedroom by the whole household. Lord Ogleby good-naturedly intervenes, and all is resolved.

Boydell and later Benjamin Beale Evans. He was originally taught stipple engraving by G. B. Cipriani[2] and was one of the first mezzotint engravers to etch the outline and darkest passages on the plate before laying the ground. Many of these etched proofs survive, particularly those for his plates of Hogarth's *Marriage à la Mode*.

The play, written by Garrick and Colman, was first performed at Drury Lane on 20 February 1766. Mrs Baddeley took over the part of Fanny for the first time in 1768 and continued to play it until 1771 when, after falling out with Garrick in a dispute about her salary and other benefits, she left the stage for two years. In a letter to Samuel Foote, Garrick admonishes him for giving Mrs Baddeley airs above her station:

> You have so puff'd up that Lady's vanity by ye great Compliment You made her in the Maid of Bath, that she has sent us word, that unless we will give her three pounds a Week more, than she is Articled for (her articles not being yet out) with other conditions, about her not playing in Farces, the time of her Benefit & half a score more impudences, she would not come to her business . . .[3]

Thomas King was born in 1730 in Mayfair, where his father was a tradesman. He was articled to a solicitor, but ran away with Shuter to join a travelling company in 1747. He played at various booths and fairs where he was seen by Garrick, who on Yates's recommendation engaged him at Drury Lane. He began with tragic characters, first appearing in a minor role in *King Lear*, but was only successful in humorous parts. Lord Ogleby was his most acclaimed comic role, his performance reputedly equalling Garrick's success as Hamlet. He was also the original Sir Peter Teazle in the first performance of *The School for Scandal* on 8 May 1777, in which part he was engraved by Robert Laurie.

At the beginning of his career King played many major roles with Mrs Pritchard in Bristol to some acclaim, and he also played at Bath for a season. In October 1759 he returned to London where he was given leading parts and became a mainstay of Drury Lane, although he occasionally appeared elsewhere. In 1766 he married Miss Baker, a hornpipe dancer.

King also wrote his own pieces, particularly farces. In 1769 he bought William Powell's share in the King Street Theatre, where he was manager and actor for two seasons. He also acquired a share of Sadler's Wells Theatre where he undertook a number of reforms; one of these was the introduction of horse patrols to escort visitors to and from the theatre, which was then in the outer suburbs. In 1787–8 Sheridan persuaded King to take on the role of acting manager at Drury Lane, a job which he found extremely vexing. He died on 11 December 1805, impoverished by his gambling losses.

Few actors managed to play as many new parts as King did during his fifty-five years on stage and although like a great many other players of this period he is now comparatively unknown, his contribution was considerable. He was described as one of the most intelligent actors of the century and it was said that he, 'sensibly confined a talent which could have succeeded to some degree in any walk of performance to those few lines of comedy where he was supreme'.[4] Dibdin, whom King had first engaged at Sadler's

Wells, described him as 'a performer who has thrown novelty into old characters, consequence into new, and nature into all'.[10]

Garrick, as co-author of *The Clandestine Marriage*, felt that although King had great merit in his interpretation of the part, it was not as he had intended. Despite this, Davies attests to the success of King's portrayal of the character:

> Lord Ogleby ... is most certainly as much an original, and as much a child of laughter, as any character on the stage – harmlessly vain, pleasantly odd, commendably generous; a coxcomb not void of sense, a master full of whim, a lover full of false fire, yet a valuable friend; possessed of delicate feelings and nice honour: the peculiarities of this difficult part are supported with eminent abilities by that most excellent comedian, Mr King, who here strikes out in the water colour painting of life, a most beautiful and striking caricature, conceived with some degree of poetical extravagance, yet so much meliorated by his execution, that thousands who have never seen such a human being as Lord Ogleby must ... allow, nay wish there may be such a man whose foibles are so inoffensive.[6]

As late as 1820 William Hazlitt reminisced in his London Memoirs, '... there was King, whose acting left a taste on the palate, sharp and sweet like quince; with an old, hard, withered face, like a John-apple, puckered up into a thousand wrinkles ...'.

---

[1] TDB.

[2] Giovanni Battista Cipriani R.A. (1727–85), decorative painter and etcher.

[3] *Letters*, no. 653, 24 Sept. [1771].

[4] TDB.

[5] Genest, V, p. 348.

[6] *Dramatic Miscellanies*, I, p. 251.

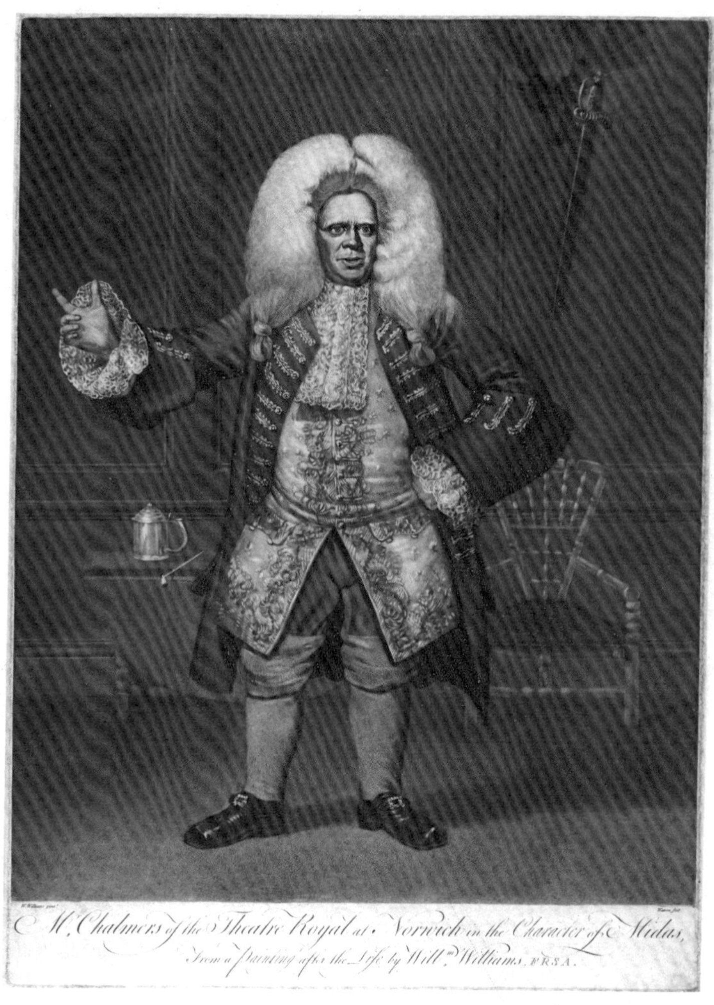

19 M.r Chalmers of the Theatre Royal at Norwich in the Character of Midas

Engraved by James Watson
after William Williams

[Published by William Williams
9 September 1769]

460 x 352 I; 502 x 353 Pl.

References: CS 28; G 35; O'D 1; Hall 1

1. Finished proof before all letters. The inscription space grounded and the dark areas very strong, particularly the inside of the coat tails and shadows on the face.
Impressions: H.

2. With the engraved inscription: "W. *Williams pinx! *** Watson fecit. | M.r, Chalmers of the Theatre Royal at Norwich in the Character of Midas, | From a Painting after the Life by Will.m Williams. F R S A.".*
Impressions: CLB P17,682 (impression exhibited); BM; H.

This is the only provincially published mezzotint of an actor in this period. This rare print was never handled by any of the major London publishers of the time, although there are numerous instances of London printsellers listing their provincial counterparts as distributors for their prints; Benjamin Jagger of Norwich, for example, was one of several provincial printsellers listed by Walter Shropshire in advertisements for his catalogues. Norwich was the right size and distance from the capital to have a cultural life of its own; a short sea voyage to London – or Amsterdam – brought a metropolitan culture within reach. London painters visited regularly; the engraver John Raphael Smith held an exhibition of his prints and drawings there on 7 August 1784. In this print the combination of a provincial player and a provincial painter result in a picture that appears twenty years out of date; it looks as if Chalmers is about to declaim, as Quin and his predecessors had.

William Williams had arrived in Norwich by 1767 and in the following year moved into the house previously occupied by Thomas Bardwell, Norwich's most distinguished resident artist and the first man to paint Garrick as Richard III (see page 67). Here Williams held an exhibition consisting of a number of history paintings, portraits and landscapes to demonstrate his talent and range of abilities. Here too, he established an academy 'for the Instruction of young Gentlemen in Drawing on the true Principles of Perspective and Anatomy'.[1]

☞ The play tells of a time when Apollo, expelled from the heavens for rebellion, falls to earth 'with a rude shock'. He finds employment in the house of Squire Midas, a county magnate – 'Churchwarden, Knight O' the Shire, and Custos Rotulorum' – who, although already married, is courting Nysa, a peasant maid; Apollo in the meantime flirts with her friend Daphne. All goes well until Midas has to choose between the musical talents of the god Pan, who has become a drunken bagpiper, and his shepherd, Poll, who is in fact Apollo. When Midas chooses Pan, Apollo reveals his identity, knocks Midas' wig off and changes his ears into the ears of an ass. He then departs heavenwards.

[1] *Norwich Mercury*, 25 June 1769.

[2] *Norwich Mercury*, 10 June 1769.

[3] *Norfolk Chronicle*, 9 Sept. 1769.

[4] Clarke, H.G. *The Story of English Glass Prints*, London 1928.

[5] *Norfolk and Norwich Notes & Queries*, I, p. 256.

It is possible that theatrical scene painting gave Williams his greatest employment; in April 1770 he left Norwich for York, Newcastle and Hull to paint scenery at the theatres, although he proposed to return to Norwich now and then to execute commissions that were taken in by his wife. Tate Wilkinson held his abilities as a scene painter in high regard and apparently ordered £500 worth of scenery as early as 1765. Williams was painting pantomime scenery in Norwich in 1768 when he advertised his proposal to publish a mezzotint of James Chalmers in the role of Midas.

In April he exhibited the painting at the Society of Artists and subsequently in Norwich. In June another advertisement was placed in *The Norwich Mercury*,[2] in which the engraver of the print was named as being Mr. [James] Watson. By September the plate had been completed and printed.[3]

It is extremely interesting that Williams advertises copies of this print 'correctly colour'd after the Painting': few mezzotints of this size (20 x 14 inches) survive with contemporary hand colouring. Being large, they would most likely have been framed, often unglazed, destroying their chance of survival. The smaller 'posture' mezzotints, either in portrait or landscape format measuring 10 x 14 inches, and prints measuring 6 x 4½ inches, often of the same subjects, are more commonly found coloured. A number of glass prints – mezzotints laid on glass and coloured from behind – have survived, but they are always difficult to date precisely and few large examples survive.[4]

Kane O'Hara's *Midas, a Musical Burletta*, was the most successful of several pieces of this sort, for which there had been a brief vogue in the early 1760s. Said to have 'exemplified the rise of the burlesque masque …', it was first staged in Dublin in 1762 and was introduced to London in February 1764 at Covent Garden. There it enjoyed one hundred and thirty performances before 1776 and continued to be revived amazingly often for a piece of its kind until about 1824.

Very little is known about James Chalmers, who is usually confused with his son, whose career on the London stage was considerably more successful. Chalmers senior and his wife Sarah both played with the Norwich company, which was one of the most important provincial companies of its time and seems to have been one that toured, albeit locally. Neither acted on the London stage; a letter written by a Mr Ives of Yarmouth sheds a little light on the reason for this: 'Our players are just come …', he writes in November 1770,

> I was there on Friday evening. We have got some new ones, but they are poor wretches. Indeed, I think the company is at the lowest I ever knew. Chalmers is here but is not suffered to appear on the stage. Elated with the thought of preferment in London, the last night he played at Norwich he spoke an epilogue riding upon an ass; and in very plain terms bid the audience do a very unmannerly thing. Quarrelling afterwards with Foote, he threw up his London engagement, came down to Norwich and offered to make satisfaction for his public affront, which was not accepted, and he was forbid the stage.[5]

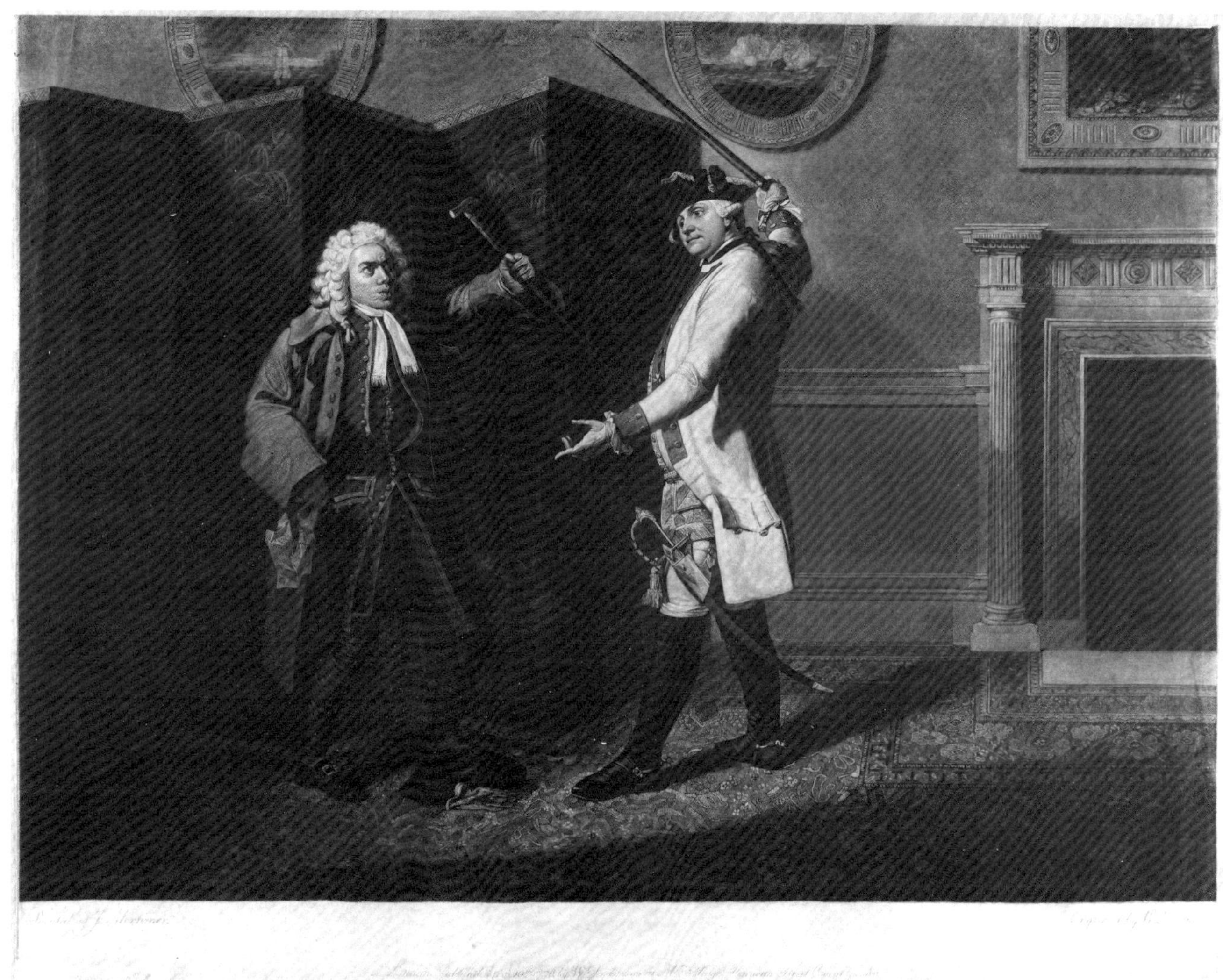

20 Mr. Parsons and Mr. Moody in the Characters of Varland and Major O'Flaherty in the West Indian

Engraved by William Dickinson
after John Hamilton Mortimer

[Issued by 1774]

[Re-published?] by William Dickinson
and Thomas Watson 10 April 1776

418 x 552 I; 460 x 552 Pl.

References: CS 57; O'D 13; Hall 6

1. Finished proof before all letters.
Impressions: BM.

2. [Finished proof with the scratched inscription: *"Painted by J,, Mortimer. ***
Engrav'd by W, Dickinson,, / London. Publiſh'd*

John Hamilton Mortimer's The West Indian was one of the first paintings made of a play in its opening season. Hopkins,[1] the seasoned prompter, recorded that it was, 'receiv'd with the greatest applause imaginable particularly Mr Moody's part. He play'd finely – it will have a great run'. Indeed the comedy, first performed at Drury Lane on 19 January 1771, was a great success and ran for twenty-eight consecutive nights. It is likely that Mortimer commenced his painting almost immediately, since it was completed in time to be exhibited at the Society of Artists that May. William Dickinson exhibited his mezzotint of the painting there five years later. On 13 May, shortly after the exhibition commenced, the print was advertised for the first time in *The Morning Chronicle* (see page 48).

An impression of this print had been listed in Thane's[2] catalogue for May 1774 at 10s 6d, the price advertised by Watson & Dickinson, indicates that it had been available, perhaps only privately and in proof state, at least two years before it was exhibited at the Society of Artists and before its publication was announced in the newspapers.

It is interesting to note that when Dickinson advertised this print he was still selling his prints from Mrs [Sarah] Sledge's establishment, an arrangement that is first recorded in July 1774. In *The*

Feby 20th 1776 by W. Dickinson at Mrs Sledge's Henrietta Street Covent Garden". (CS)].

3. With the publication date altered: *"London. Publiſh'd April 10,th 1776.".*

Impressions: CLB P37,947 (impression exhibited).

4. With the engraved inscription: *"Painted by J. Mortimer. *** Engraved by W,, Dickinson. / Mr PARSONS and Mr MOODY in the Characters of VARLAND and MAJOR O'FLAHERTY in the West Indian. / Therefore give it me without more words and ſave yourſelf a beating; do now you had beſt. Act IV. Scene 9. / London. Publiſh'd April the 10,th 1776: by Dickinson at Mrs Sledge's Henrietta Street Covent Garden.".*

Impressions: TM.

5. With the added inscription: *", and Tho,^s Watſon N,^o 142 New Bond Street.".*

Impressions: CLB; BM.

6. The plate damaged. A sizeable area of damage behind the figure of Moody consisting of vertical scratches with no attempt at repair.

Impressions: H.

☞ In Richard Cumberland's comedy, Stockwell has secretly married the daughter of his rich employer, old Belcour. Their son, having been passed off on Old Belcour as a foundling, has been brought up by him and inherited all his property. This 'young Belcour' returns home to his real father, but Stockwell delays recognising him as his son until he has tested his character. The generous but foolish Young Belcour falls in love at first sight with Louisa and follows her to where she lives with her father, the impecunious Captain Dudley, and her brother Charles. There he is tricked into thinking that she is Charles's mistress. Charles, however, is in love with Charlotte, step-daughter of his avaricious aunt Lady Rusport, but will not admit his love although it is reciprocated. Belcour generously helps Captain Dudley in his needs, but is rude to Louisa, under a mistaken idea of her character which leads to grave complications and a duel with Charles. Lady Rusport has an admirer, the extremely amiable Major O'Flaherty, who detects her suborning her father's lawyer to destroy a will that cuts her out of his fortune, giving it to young Dudley. Snatching the will – the scene shown in the print – the Major takes it to Stockwell. Here, the confusion is cleared up by Charlotte; Belcour is forgiven by Louisa and obtains her hand, while Charles marries Charlotte.

Morning Chronicle Mrs Sledge advertised herself as a printseller and profilist,[3] but little else is known about her business; it is possible that several of the family were active in Henrietta Street from about 1771 until 1794. The publishing arrangements between Sledge and Dickinson are not clear but they seem to have run until November 1778 when Dickinson took over Walter Shropshire's shop in New Bond Street. By January 1779 the engraver John Jacobé, said to have been Dickinson's pupil, had started publishing from Sledge's premises, as had Joseph Saunders between 1778–9.

When Watson died prematurely in October 1781, Dickinson seems to have retained control of the copper-plate, which was sold for four guineas in 1794, after he had been bankrupted.[4] Goodwin notes that Dickinson is known to have taken over McArdell's business in Covent Garden.

Criticism was divided: Sylas Neville considered the play to be an admirable comedy and the best that had been produced since *The Clandestine Marriage* and Benjamin Victor thought that its success, 'succeeded that of any comedy in the memory of the oldest man living', but another reviewer was less taken:

> the West Indian is of itself no extraordinary instance of dramatic excellence, altho' it has many recommendatory allurements about it. Even venison served up in a hash will not do for a public entertainment, the West Indian is only mutton tolerably well favoured.[5]

Nevertheless the play maintained a prominent place in the repertory of Drury Lane for several seasons, with much of its success due to Moody's portrayal of Major O'Flaherty, a 'burlesque Irish character'. Although Garrick had apparently considered giving the part to Barry initially, he wrote to Moody: 'I have read a Comedy yesterday of great merit – a charming character for you – Major O'Flarty the Frisk of a play'.[6] In this role it was said that Moody's '... judgement and masterly execution' succeeded in making 'a subordinate character (tho' not the hero of the fable) the hero of the audience ... he is become at Drury Lane, what Shuter is at Covent Garden; with this difference, that Moody is the favourite of the boxes, as well as the galleries.'

William Parsons, another member of the original cast, was born in 1736 in Cheapside. He became the pupil of Sir Henry Cheere, the sculptor, and exhibited paintings at the Society of Artists between 1763 and 1773. He took part in amateur theatricals with Charles Holland and William Powell, with his professional debut apparently taking place in York in the mid-1750s. Parsons and his wife appeared in *The Beggar's Opera* at Drury Lane in the autumn of 1762, as Filch and Polly respectively. He remained associated with Drury Lane for the next thirty-two seasons, also acting regularly at the Haymarket.[7]

By the mid-1770s, although only in his late thirties, his forte had become old men and country clowns. He had expert comic skills and was prone to buffoonery, enjoying practical jokes even to the extent of whispering to fellow actors during a performance to make them laugh: '... who can be grave when Parsons either looks or speaks?'[8]

Unfortunately he suffered acute asthma attacks throughout his life and for years he, 'gasped through all his characters'. Ill and worn out, he was forced to sit down for most of his last appearance, in *The Critic* in January 1795, when he was applauded with 'pity and regret'. He died the following month and was described in Colman's play *New Hay at the Old Market* as

> one of the comicalest fellows I ever did see [and] one of the honestest … When an individual has combined private worth and public talent, he quits the bustling scene of life with twofold applause, and we doubly deplore his exit.

This day is published, Price 10s. 6d.

A MEZZOTINTO PRINT, engraved by W. Dickenson, of Mr. Moody and Mr. Parsons, in the Characters of Major O'Flaherty, and Valint, in the West Indian, from an original picture, painted by Mr. Mortimer.

Likewise, Price 7s. 6d.

Lady Charles Spencer, from Sir Joshua Reynolds.

In a few days will be published, Price 7s. 6d.

A Lady, in the character of St. Cecilia, from Sir Joshua Reynolds.

Published and sold by W. Dickinson, at Mrs. Sledge's, Henrietta-street, Covent-garden; and Thomas Watlin, No. 142, New Bond-street.

FOR THE FIRST TIME

At the Theatre Royal in DRURY-LANE

This present Saturday, Jan. 19, 1771,

Will be Presented a NEW COMEDY, call'd

The WEST INDIAN

The PRINCIPAL CHARACTERS by

Mr. KING,

Mr. AICKIN, Mr. MOODY,

Mr. PACKER, Mr. CAUTHERLEY

Mr. PARSONS, Mr. BADDELEY,

Mr. J. AICKIN, Mr. WRIGHT

Mr. WHEELER, Mr. WATKINS,

Mrs. BADDELEY,

Mrs. HOPKINS, Mrs. EGERTON

Mrs. LOVE, Mrs. BRADSHAW,

AND

Mrs. ABINGTON.

WITH A

Prologue to be spoken by Mr. REDDISH

And Epilogue by Mrs. ABINGTON.

NEW SCENES, DRESSES, and DECORATIONS.

To which will be added

DAPHNE and AMINTOR.

Amintor by Mr. DAVIES,

Mindora by Mrs. SCOTT,

Daphne by Miss RADLEY.

With DANCES by

Signor Giorgi, Mr. Atkins, Mrs. King, Miss Tetley, Miss Rogers, Miss Gollett, &c.

The Fifth Night of ALMIDA will be on Wednesday next.

[1] William Hopkins (d. 1780), Drury Lane prompter.

[2] John Thane (1748–1818), medallist and drawing collector.

[3] *The Morning Chronicle*, 3 May 1774.

[4] Certified bankrupt 29 June 1793.

[5] *The London Chronicle*, 13 April 1774.

[6] *Letters*, no. 592, 25 June 1770.

[7] Opened 1720. In 1766 a new theatre was erected on the same site by Samuel Foote.

[8] *Dramatic Miscellanies*, I, p. 308.

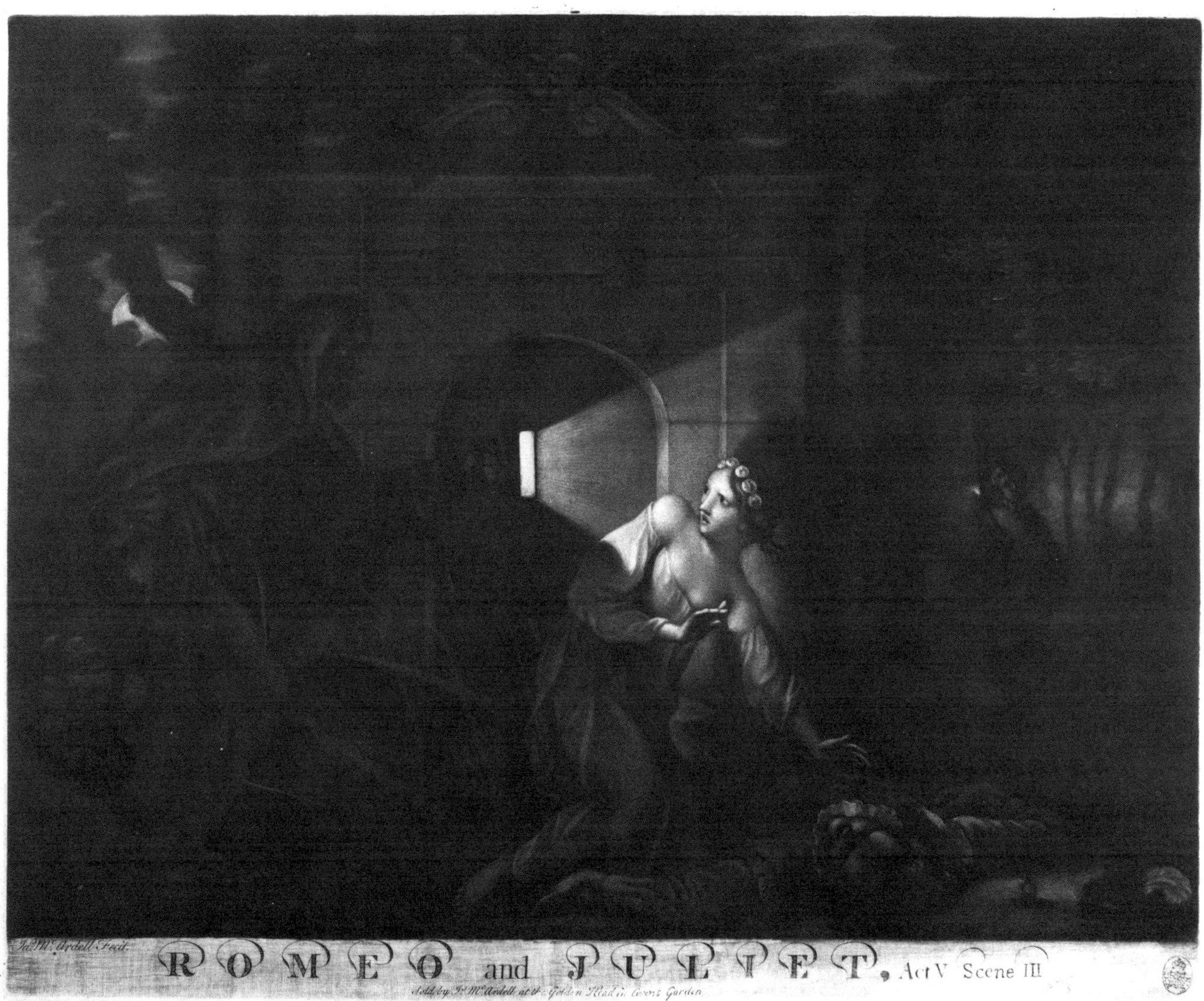

21 Romeo and Juliet, Act V Scene III

Engraved by James McArdell
[after Benjamin Wilson]

[Published by] Sold by James McArdell

355 x 454 I; 380 x 456 Pl.

Previously unrecorded print.

1. With the engraved inscription: *"Ja.*
M.ͨArdell Fecit. | ROMEO and JULIET, Act V
Scene III | Sold by J.ͨ M.ͨArdell at the Golden Head
*in Covent Garden * * * P*ͬ5ˢ*"*.
Impressions: CLB P26,087 ex. coll. Dresden Print
Room, *Lugt* 1647 & 1618 (impression exhibited).

No reference to this print has been found except for the note of an impression that was sold from the collection of Henry P. Hope in March 1813, priced at 6s 6d. Another mezzotint of the same subject, attributed to 'Wilson', was engraved by Richard Houston for Robert Sayer. This suggests that McArdell's print was also from a painting by Benjamin Wilson, although no original design is known. McArdell's print, although undated, would seem to be the earlier publication; Houston's print was published by Robert Sayer in the late 1760s.

After McArdell's death in 1765, the plate was not added to Sayer's stock, unlike so many others by McArdell, or to that of any other printseller, and it is consequently extremely rare. It seems that Sayer, aware of the popularity of the play and the success of Ravenet's engraving, which was soon to be acquired by John Boydell (in 1765), set Houston to copy McArdell's mezzotint. Since attribution of this print to McArdell was out of the question, he may have tried to make a link to Wilson.

It is important to contrast McArdell's print with the better known image after Wilson engraved by Simon François Ravenet, which depicts Garrick and George Anne Bellamy inside the tomb.

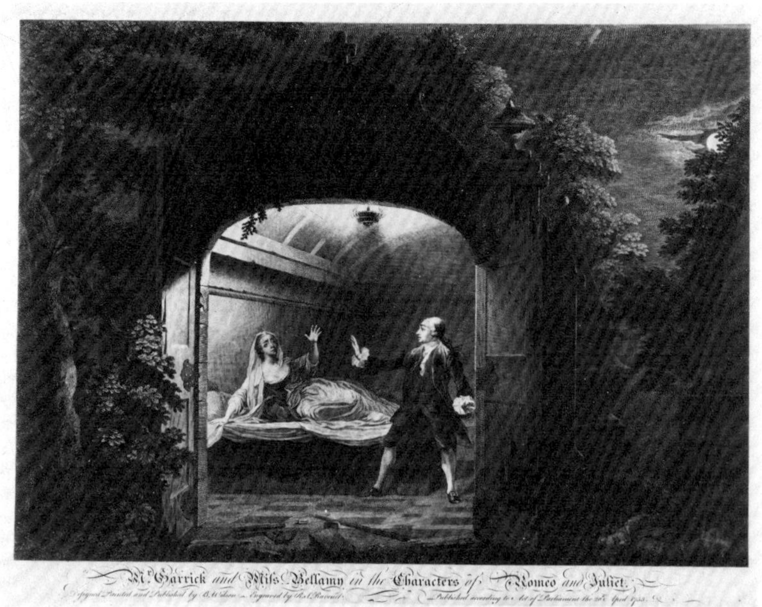

Ravenet's print, which portrays Garrick in one of his favourite parts, was published by subscription in the spring of 1753. Wilson chose to paint the scene from Garrick's sentimental version of the play in which seventy-five lines were added to the dying sequence. This allows Juliet to wake whilst Romeo is still alive and the lovers have a final passionate exchange before they both die.

McArdell's image shows the moment outside the tomb when, hearing the watchman, Juliet snatches up Romeo's dagger in order to stab herself. This image could also represent Shakespeare's original ending in which after a last kiss on Juliet's lips, Romeo drinks the poison he has brought with him and dies. Juliet awakes to find Romeo dead by her side, the cup still in his hand, and realising that he has drunk the poison she stabs herself. Whereas the interior scene shows actual players as if they were on the stage, McArdell's exterior version does not. As a result the image becomes a mere illustration to the play. It is surprising that whoever produced the original design did not capitalise on the depiction of a popular play by recording a specific performance. Whether this design was Wilson's or McArdell's may never be known.

Garrick, having initially employed Zoffany to paint group portraits of his family and friends at Hampton, became aware that Zoffany's more realistic style of painting was better suited to publicise his acting than that of Wilson, the leading exponent of the 'Rembrandtesque'. Zoffany had been employed by Wilson as his drapery painter and it was here that Garrick first met him. The contrast between the two painters is best seen in the comparison between Ravenet's engraving and McArdell's mezzotint of Zoffany's 'Venice Preserv'd' (see page 55).

Shakespeare's *Romeo and Juliet* had been revived by Theophilus Cibber at the Haymarket in 1744 after an absence from the stage of nearly a century. Four years later Garrick's revived and adapted version, first performed on 29 November, established the acting text for the rest of the century. His alterations appealed to the sentimentality of the eighteenth-century audience and were much acclaimed; even one of Garrick's opponents was prepared to admit that: 'Nothing was ever better calculated to draw tears from an audience ... The circumstance of Juliet's awaking ... is perhaps the finest touch of nature in any tragedy ancient or modern'.[1]

Initially, Spranger Barry and Mrs Cibber took the leading roles and enjoyed great success, playing twenty performances in the course of the season. However, the play was not revived the following year; attributing this decision to envy on Garrick's part, Barry crossed over to Covent Garden together with his leading lady. From 29 September 1750 the two houses staged the play in direct competition. After twelve nights Garrick and George Ann Bellamy at Drury Lane were victorious when ill-health prevented Mrs Cibber from acting the part again.[2] Garrick gloated over Drury Lane's apparent triumph: 'Ye Battle is at last Ended, & in our favour ... our Antagonists yielded last thursday Night ...'.[3] Garrick's delight was reinforced by the furtive appearance of both Barry and Mrs Cibber in his audience on the final night. Garrick went on to play Romeo on no less than sixty occasions throughout his career, very occasionally taking the part of Mercutio when he did not play the lead. The play's popularity was second only to that of *The Beggar's Opera*.

Opinions seem to have been split as to which was the superior performance; some of the audience even watched Barry's first scenes and then hurried over to Drury Lane to see the final scenes played by Garrick. Meanwhile the theatre-going public became aggrieved at the lack of variety that was on offer, prompting a complaint which appeared in *The Daily Advertiser* on 12 October:

Well – what tonight, says angry Ned,
As up from bed he rouses,
Romeo again! and shakes his head,
Ah! Pox on both your houses!

The rivalry between the two houses and the public participation in the duel induced many to comment on the relative attributes and failings of the two Romeos and their stage lovers; one or two critics even resorted to studying the text again, to discover which portrayal was as Shakespeare had intended. Was it the tender passion of Barry's fond lover or the impulsiveness and violence of Garrick's passionate young man? Francis Gentleman considered that Barry had the better figure and that 'the superior grace of Mr Garrick's attitudes, the vivacity of his countenance, and the fire of his expression' meant that Garrick 'commanded most applause – Mr Barry most tears ...'.[4]

Despite the obvious success of her partnership with Barry, Mrs Cibber seems to have preferred Garrick as a stage lover, although an admirer of Barry remarked wistfully:

Had I been Juliet to Garrick's Romeo, – so ardent and impassioned was he, I should have expected he would have come up to me in the balcony; but had I been Juliet to Barry's Romeo, – so tender, so eloquent, and so seductive was he, that I should have gone down to him![5]

[1] [Morgan, MacNamara] A Letter to Miss Nossiter 1753, pp. 50–56.
[2] *The Beggar's Opera* was staged instead.
[3] *Letters*, no. 96, 13 Oct. 1750.
[4] Gentleman, I, pp. 189–90.
[5] TDB.

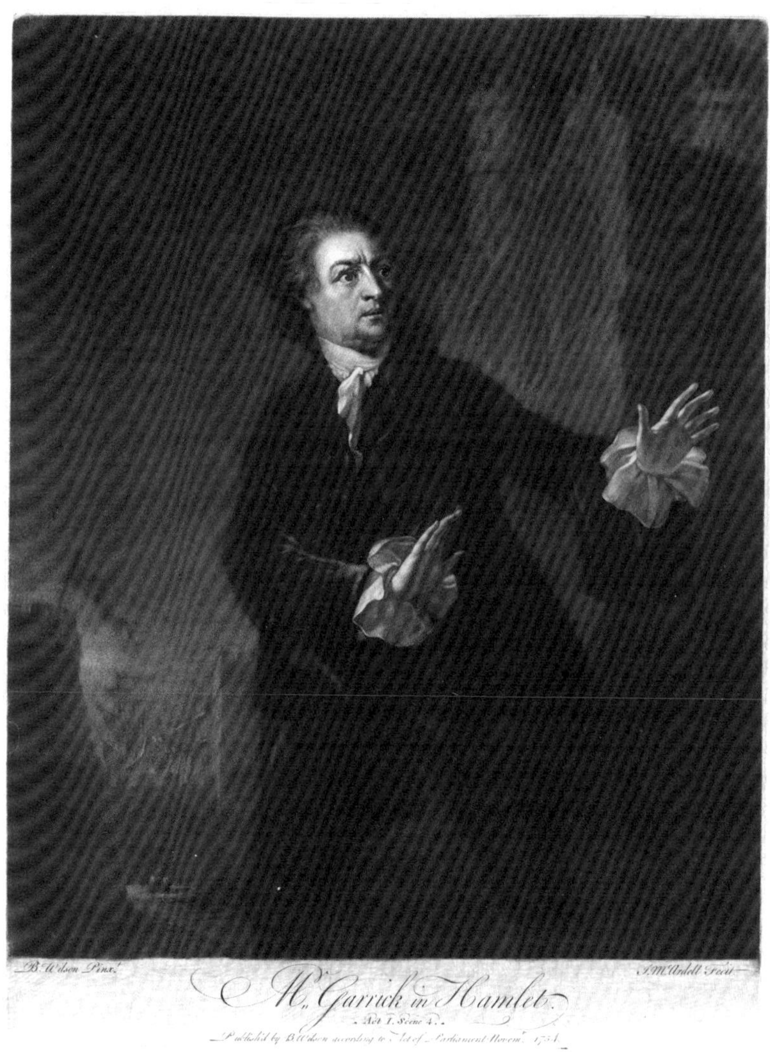

22 M.r Garrick in Hamlet

Engraved by James McArdell
after Benjamin Wilson

Published by Benjamin Wilson
1 November 1754

Re-published by Richard Holmes Laurie
[after 1818]

419 x 320 I; 459 x 333 Pl.

References: CS 78; R 78; G 34; O'D 134;
Hall 202

**1. With engraved inscription, before the day
of the month or the price was added:** "*B.
Wilson Pinx.t, *** J., M.cArdell Fecit. | M.r Garrick
in Hamlet. | Act 1. Scene 4. | Publish'd by B. Wilson
according to Act of Parliament Novem.r 1754.*".
Impressions: CLB P26,089 (impression exhibited).

**2. With engraved inscription, the price '5s'
added, but before the day of the month.**
Impressions: CLB.

Although this print was published by Benjamin Wilson, as it had to be in order to secure him the copyright, an advertisement shows that it was being distributed by McArdell by mid-January 1755:[1]

> *This Day was publish'd, Price 5 s.*
> A PRINT of Mr. GARRICK, in the Character of Hamlet, done from a Painting of B. Wilson's, by James McArdell.
> To be had at the Golden Head in Covent-Garden, and at the Print-Shops.

After McArdell's death the plate was acquired by Robert Sayer and it was listed in Sayer & Bennett's catalogue for 1775 at 5s. The plate subsequently passed into the hands of Sayer's successors, Laurie & Whittle, who listed it in their catalogue for 1795. It was republished by Laurie's son after he took over the business in 1818. In 1771 Shropshire listed an impression at 15s; this must have been a remarkably fine proof to merit a price that was three times that of readily available impressions from Sayer's shop.

Unlike some other McArdell plates acquired by Sayer, this print has not been seen bearing Sayer's publication line; this is perhaps because Benjamin Wilson owned the copyright. Given Sayer's

3. With the day of the month added: "*Novem.,*
1.ˢᵗ 1754.".
Impressions: CLB; BM.

4. Re-published by Richard Holmes Laurie:
"*Published by* R.H. Laurie, *53 Fleet Street,
London.*".
Impressions: H.

Paris Nov.ʳ 20 1764

I am so plagu'd here
for my Prints or rather Prints of Me that
I must desire You to send me by Yᵉ first
opportunity six prints from Reynold's
picture, You may apply to Yᵉ Engraver he
lives in Leicester field & his name is Fisher,
he will give you good ones, if he knows they
are for Me – You must likewise send me
a King Lear by Wilson, Hamlet dᵒ
Jaffier & Belv[idera] by Zoffanij, speak to
him for two or 3, & what Else he may have done
of Me – Ther is likewise a print of
Me, as I am, from Lotard's picture
Scrap'd by MacArdel, send me
2 or 3 of them, speak to MacArdel,
*   & any other prints of*
Me, if tolerable, that I can't remember.

propensity to tamper with publication dates, it is possible that the price and the date were added by him when he re-published the plate, rather than by McArdell. The publication of this print in 1754 may have been partly in response to the fact that Barry had left Garrick's company and was playing Hamlet in opposition at Covent Garden.

The print illustrates the moment when Garrick is confronted by the ghost of his dead father, the noble king of Denmark, who was murdered by his brother Claudius; the latter then married 'with indecent haste' the dead king's widow. The ghost has returned to relate the circumstances of the murder and demand vengeance. Although Garrick himself played this part no more than twice a season, it was the most frequently revived play during his career, only exceeded in number of performances by *Romeo and Juliet*. Garrick regarded his interpretation of the scene depicted in the print as one of his greatest achievements, frequently representing it for the benefit of friends and acquaintances, including the great French actress Mme Clairon. In 1764 he ordered supplies of the print to be sent to Paris for distribution amongst the people he had met.

The same chilling scene is described by Lichtenberg in minute detail, after seeing one of Garrick's spell-binding performances:

Hamlet appears in a black dress, the only one in the whole court, alas! still worn for his poor father, who has been dead scarce a couple of months. Horatio and Marcellus, in uniform, are with him, and they are waiting for the ghost; Hamlet has folded his arms under his cloak and pulled his hat down over his eyes; it is a cold night and just twelve o'clock; the theatre is darkened, and the whole audience of some thousands are as

By His MAJESTY's Company of Comedians,
AT THE

THEATRE ROYAL
In *DRURY-LANE*,

This prefent *Tuefday*, being the 16th of *October*,

Will be prefented the TRAGEDY, of

HAMLET.

Hamlet by Mr. GARRICK,

The *King* by Mr. DAVIES,
The *Ghoft* by Mr. BERRY,
Horatio by Mr. HAVARD,
Polonius by Mr. TASWELL,
Laertes by Mr. BLAKES,
Oftrick by Mr. WOODWARD,

Rofencraus Mr. *Simfon*, | Player *King* Mr. *Burton*,
Guildenftern Mr. *Scrafe*, | Player *Queen* Mrs. *Bennet*.

The *Gravediggers* by Mr. YATES, and Mr. *Vaughan*,

Ophelia by Mrs. CIBBER,
Queen by Mrs. PRITCHARD.

To which will be added a *FARCE*, call'd

The ANATOMIST.

Monf. Le Medecin by Mr. BLAKES,
Crifpin by Mr. YATES,
Old Gerald by Mr. CLOUGH,
Beatrice by Mrs. BENNET.

Boxes 5s. Pit 3s. Firft Gallery 2s. Upper Gallery 1s.
PLACES for the Boxes to be had of Mr. VARNEY, at the Stage-door of the Theatre.
To begin exactly at Six o'Clock.   *Vivat* REX.

To-morrow, the *Carelefs Husband*, and the Entertainment of QUEEN MAB.

---

quiet, and their faces are motionless, as though they were painted on the walls of the theatre; even from the furthest end of the playhouse one could hear a pin drop. Suddenly, as Hamlet moves towards the back of the stage slightly to the left and turns his back on the audience, Horatio starts, and saying: 'Look my lord, it comes', points to the right, where the ghost has already appeared and stands motionless, before any one is aware of him. At these words Garrick turns sharply and at the same moment staggers back two or three paces with his knees giving way under him; his hat falls to the ground and both his arms, especially the left, are stretched out nearly to their full length, with hands as high as his head, the right arm more bent and the hand lower, and fingers apart; his mouth is open; thus he stands rooted to the spot, with legs apart, but no loss of dignity, ... His whole demeanour is so expressive of terror that it made my flesh creep even before he began to speak. The almost terror-struck silence of the audience, which preceded this appearance and filled one with a sense of insecurity, probably did much to enhance this effect.[4]

Garrick may have heightened the sense of terror in this scene even further by contriving to make his hair stand on end with the assistance of a mechanical wig.[5] Whatever his means, the effect was extraordinary and prompted Henry Fielding's admiration: '... if that little man there upon the stage is not frightened, I never saw a man frightened in my life'.[6]

From the time of his first performance in this role in Ireland in 1742, Garrick gradually revised his own interpretation and tinkered with the text of the play. In 1763, whilst Garrick was abroad in France, George Colman, then manager of Drury Lane, decided to publish Garrick's acting text. Nine years later, using the 1747 Hughs-Wilks edition of the text, Garrick altered the play, restoring over six hundred lines of Shakespeare's text and adding only eleven lines of his own. He wrote proudly to Morellet[7]:

> I have play'd the Devil this Winter, I have dar'd to alter Hamlet, I have thrown away the gravedigger, & all ye 5th Act, & not withstanding the Galleries were fond of them, I have met with more applause than I did at five & twenty – there is a great revolution in our theatrical history, & for wch 20 years ago instead of Shouts of approbation, I should have had ye benches thrown at my head.[8]

Sylas Neville was amongst those who did not appreciate these alterations, observing that: 'Several parts of Y^e play, as it is in Shakespeare, are omitted rather improperly'.

Along with his textual alterations, Garrick seems to have made another innovation that was still being commented on twenty years later: performing in contemporary dress. 'W', writing in *The Morning Chronicle* in February 1773, makes the rather disparaging comments:

> 'Twas cruel of him [Garrick] to disrobe Hamlet of the elegant drapery ... the new dressed Hamlet is made so very jemmy, and his skirts so docked and trimmed, that I think he deserves to be dignified with the title of the Macaroni Hamlet.[9]

It is said that Garrick was eventually buried with a copy of the text of *Hamlet*.[10]

[1] *The London Evening Post*, 23–25 Jan.

[2] *Letters*, no. 343, 20 Nov. 1764.

[3] It has been suggested that the acute observations made by Lichtenberg to his correspondents could well have been assisted by engravings, which he used as *aide memoires*.

[4] Lichtenberg, pp. 9–10.

[5] Burnim, K.A. *Eighteenth century Theatrical Illustrations in the Light of Contemporary Documents*, Theatre Notebook 1959, XIV.2.

[6] Fielding, Henry *Tom Jones*, 1749, Bk. XVI, Ch. V.

[7] Abbé André Morellet.

[8] *Letters*, no. 730, 4 [Jan.] 1773.

[9] *The Morning Chronicle*, 15 Feb. 1773.

[10] *Dramatic Miscellanies*, II, p. 328.

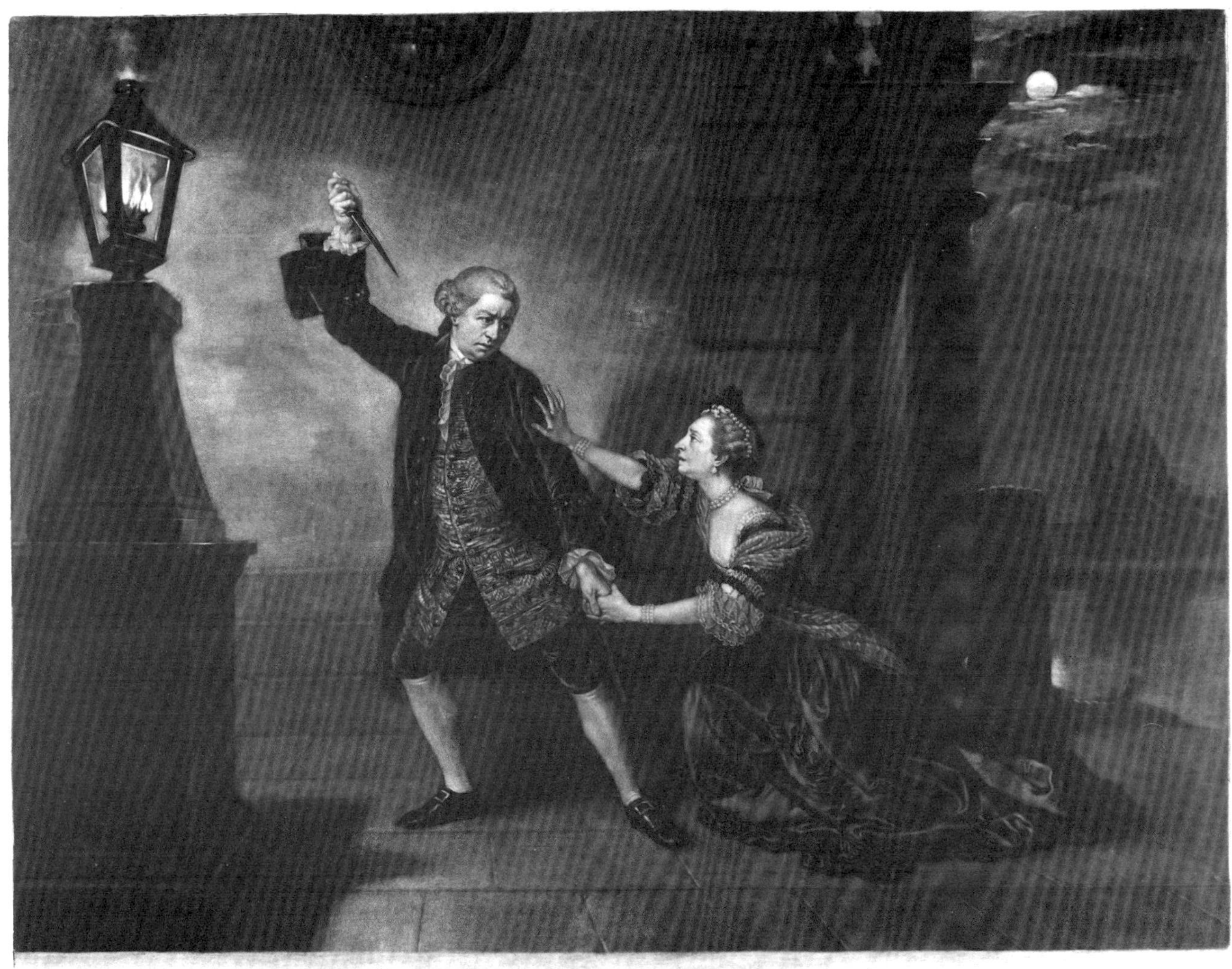

23 Mr Garrick and Mrs Cibber in the Characters of Jaffier and Belvidera

Engraved by James McArdell
after Johann Zoffany

[Published by] sold by James McArdell
on 25 March 1764

434 x 554 I; 457 x 555 Pl.

References: CS 80; G 104; O'D (Garrick) 144; Hall (Garrick) 212

1. Finished proof before all letters.
Impressions: CLB P15,510 (impression exhibited); BM; H.

2. With the engraved inscription: "*Zoffanij Pinx! *** Ja,ˢ Mᶜ,Ardell fecit. / Mr Garrick and Mrs Cibber in the Characters of Jaffier and Belvidera. / Venice Preserved Act 4. Scene 2ᵈ / Publish'd March 25. 1764. according to Act of*

This was McArdell's last great theatrical plate and the first major theatrical image to be published after an original painting by Zoffany. The painting, now in the collection of Lord Lambton, was possibly commissioned by Garrick to celebrate his last performance as Jaffeir, one of his favourite parts, on 20 October 1762. It was exhibited at the Society of Artists in 1763, although the print was not exhibited. This mezzotint was one of the images chosen by Garrick to distribute among his friends in Paris.[1]

The advertisements indicate that although Zoffany took in the subscriptions and exhibited the painting to stimulate interest, he left the advertising and the distribution of the print to the engraver. Some time after McArdell's death in 1765, the plate was acquired by Robert Sayer, who re-worked and re-published it. The soft and subtle technique used by McArdell is replaced by a severe and brassy reworking. Every conceivable highlight is enhanced: the lantern in the upper left corner flares alarmingly; Jaffeir's buttons, originally velvet, glitter like diamonds and any subtlety is burnished off. The re-engraved plate bears all the hallmarks of Robert Laurie (see over). If the re-working was by Laurie, the plate must have been re-published by Sayer after 1770 when Laurie began his apprenticeship; even then it is safe to assume

*Parliament *** Sold by J,, M.°Ardell, at the Corner of Henrietta Street in Covent Garden."*.
Impressions: CLB; BM; TM; H.

3. The plate entirely re-worked. [Re-issued by Sayer & Bennett].
Impressions: H.

January 1763.
PROPOSALS for Publishing by SUBSCRIPTION,
A PRINT in Metzotinto by Mr.
M'ARDELL, from an original Painting of Mr. ZAFFANIJ,
Representing,
Mr. GARRICK and Mrs. CIBBER
In the Characters of
JAFFIER and BELVIDERA,
In the last Scene of the Fourth Act of VENICE PRESERV'D.
The Price Half a Guinea ; Five Shillings to be paid at the Time of Subscribing, and the Remainer on the Delivery of the Print, which will be in the Beginning of May next.
Subscriptions to be taken in at Mr. Zaffanij's, in the Great Piazza, Covent Garden ; and the Original Picture to be seen there till the Middle of February.

The Public Advertiser, 11 January 1763

Saturday next will be published, Price 10s. 6d
A Metzotieto Print of Mr.
GARRICK and Mrs. CIBBER, in the Characters of Jaffier and Belvidera, Venice Preserved, Act IV. Scene II. Done from the original Painting of Mr. ZOFFANI.
By J. M'ARDELL.
And sold at the Corner of Henrietta-street, next to Southampton-street, Covent Garden ; where the Prints are delivered to the Subscribers.

The Public Advertiser, 12 April 1764

that only after several years' experience would he have been allowed to tamper with such an important and commercial plate.

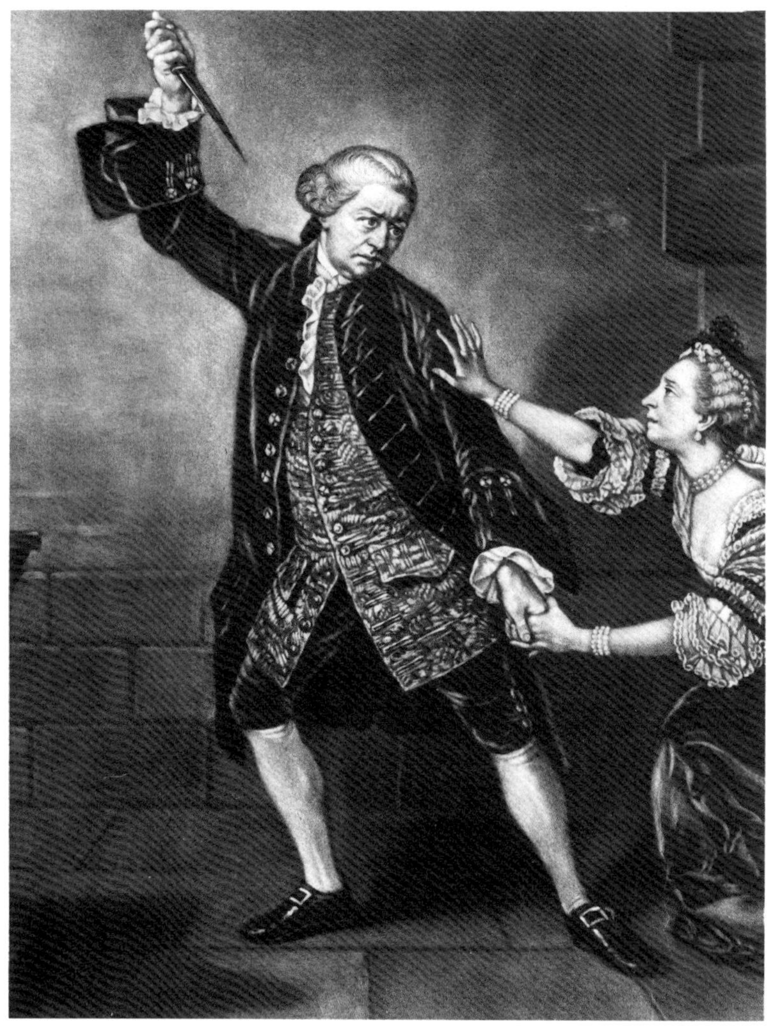

In 1771 Walter Shropshire was selling what must have been a remarkably fine impression at 1 guinea. Sayer & Bennett listed the print in their 1775 catalogue at 10s 6d. The plate was sold to Laurie & Whittle, together with the rest of Sayer's stock, after his death and was listed in their catalogue for 1795. Although this was thirty-one years after it was first published, it was still available at the original price of 10s 6d. There are also an octavo mezzotint engraved by [James] Wilson and published by Robert Sayer and a larger etching by Stayner, after this print.

Venice Preserv'd, first performed on 7 February 1682, was considered to be one of the most exciting plays of the eighteenth-century. Arthur Murphy thought it the finest example of tragedy since the days of Shakespeare.

Susannah Cibber had played the part of Belvidera since 1736,[3] but the dynamic partnership with Garrick did not begin until 1748. It was a point of discussion whether Mrs Cibber or Mrs Barry excelled as Belvidera: Aaron Hill praised the former's superb voice and her features which 'succeed best on stage', although Dr Johnson considered that she had probably 'got more reputation

56

☞ *Venice Preserv'd*, written by Thomas Otway, was based on The Spanish Conspiracy, or Bedimar's plot to overthrow the Venetian Republic in 1618. The dramatic story concerns the plot laid in Venice to overthrow the Senate by Pierre, a fictitious character, and others. Jaffeir, a friend of Pierre, is married to Belvidera, the daughter of Priuli, a Senator, but due to his impoverished status the couple have been disowned by Priuli and are now destitute. In his despair, Jaffeir joins the conspirators. Belvidera implores him to spare her father and to expose the plot. He does so, after a promise from the Senate that they will spare the conspirators. Pierre accuses Jaffeir of treachery, the Senate renege on their deal and, horrified by what he has done, Jaffeir threatens to kill Belvidera and himself. This tense moment is illustrated here: 'The affright poor Belvidera is thrown into by Jaffeir's drawing his dagger, is succeeded by the bell which announces the execution of Pierre; and makes a fine picture of pity, distress and terror!'.[2] Dissuaded by Belvidera, Jaffeir attempts to make her father relent. He does so, but the Senate remain firm. Jaffeir saves Pierre from the dishonour of a traitor's fate by killing him on the scaffold, then takes his own life. On hearing the news, Belvidera expires.

than she deserved, as she had a great sameness'. Gentleman also favoured Mrs Cibber since she had 'a countenance most exquisitely formed to express anguish and distraction [and] far surpassed her competitors in those scenes where deep and violent feelings occur'.[4]

Although Garrick had played Pierre in his first season at Goodman's Fields in 1742, it was not until 1748 that he took the part of Jaffeir. He and Spranger Barry vied for precedence:

> [Garrick] finds it very difficult to make the transition from anger to sorrow ... and in the same manner, Mr. Barry, whose natural tendency is to elegant distress, finds it as hard to pass from that to anger ... It is therefore these players succeed so happily in different parts of the same character ... nobody will ever be able to say, with justice, which of them performs it best.[5]

Hill suggested that, 'Mr Garrick and Mr Barry are both excellent in Jaffeir ...', but that, '... Mr Garrick's natural disposition is to dignity, and Mr Barry's to tenderness'.[6]

It was felt that Garrick and Cibber were: 'formed by nature for the illustration of each other's talents'.[7] Hill admired the combination, commenting that 'Garrick ... is as naturally violent as Mrs Cibber is melancholy ...'.[8]

---

[1] See page 52.
[2] *Dramatic Miscellanies*, III, p. 231.
[3] Genest, III, p. 490 ff.
[4] Gentleman, I, p. 335.
[5] Hill, p. 65.
[6] *ibid.*, p. 85.
[7] Gentleman, I, pp. 85–6.
[8] Hill, p. 65.

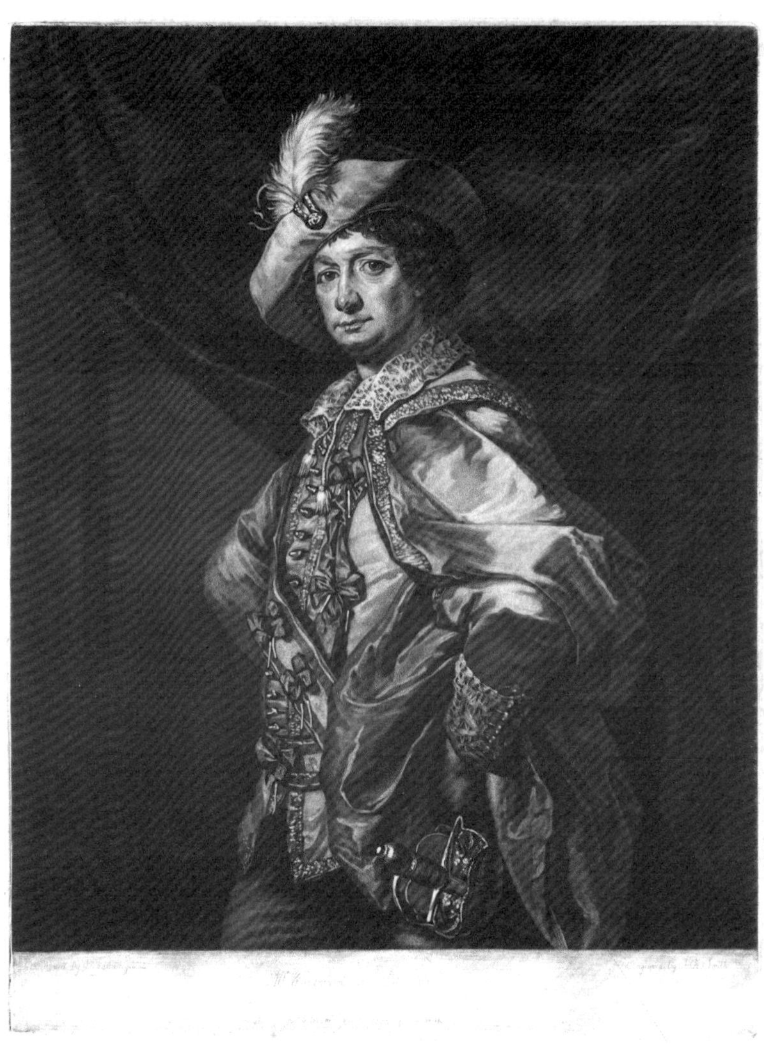

24 Mr Woodward in Petruchio

Engraved by John Raphael Smith
after Benjamin Vandergucht

Published by John Raphael Smith
10 September 1774

Re-published by John Raphael Smith and
William Humphrey 15 September 1774

Re-published by William Richardson [1791]

344 x 276 I; 376 x 277 Pl.

References: CS 177; F 380; O'D 3; Hall 21

1. Finished proof with the scratched inscription: "*Painted by B. Vandergucht *** Engraved by J.R. Smith / Mr Woodward in Petruchio / publish'd 10th* [sic] *September 1774 by J R Smith *** printed by J Gamble*".
Impressions: CLB P32,178 (impression exhibited); BM.

2. With the engraved inscription: "*Painted by B: Vandergucht. *** Engraved by J,,R,, Smith / *M.^R

The painting, now at the Yale Centre for British Art, was exhibited by Benjamin Vandergucht at the Royal Academy in 1774 together with three other theatrical subjects. A reviewer of the exhibition noted that: 'The Figure is spirited, easy and natural; the Drapery well cast, and painted with a Breadth and Freedom of pencilling; but the colouring is hard and dry.'

John Raphael Smith exhibited the mezzotint at the Society of Artists in 1775 and seems to have published some proofs himself, before selling a share in the plate to William Humphrey, a leading West End printseller. The plate was acquired by William Richardson, possibly by 1791 since an impression was listed in his catalogue for that year priced at 5s.

It is remarkably early for a rolling press printer to be acknowledged on a print at this date: they came into their own only when the larger mezzotints were printed in the second quarter of the nineteenth century. Little is known about Gamble, who was probably the James Gamble recorded as a printseller in 1779.[1]

Vandergucht was born in 1753 and after training at the Royal Academy, became a portrait painter. His theatrical paintings, for example, The Register Office, plagiarised the works of Zoffany. He drowned at Chiswick in 1794.

Three productions of *Catherine and Petruchio* were running in

WOODWARD *in the Character of*
PETRUCHIO. / *Publish'd 15,th Sept,: 1774, by*
J,,R,, Smith, N,º 4, Exeter Court, & W,, Humphry,
printseller, Gerrard Street, Soho. / [in scratched
letters] *printed by J Gamble *** price 4s"*.
Impressions: CLB; BM.

3. With the publication line altered: [Pubd by
W Richardson, Antient & Modern Print
Warehouse 174 Strand. (CS)].

**4. Re-published with the publication line
erased.**
Impressions: BM.

☞ Garrick's three act comedy *Catherine and
Petruchio* was an adaptation from Shakespeare's
The Taming of the Shrew. Petruchio, a gentleman
of Verona, a shrewd man of unqualified
patience, determines to marry Katharina, the
notoriously difficult elder daughter of Baptista
of Padua. He courts her, undeterred by her rude
rebuffs, pretending to find her courteous and
gentle. Her taming begins on her wedding day
when his contrived delays and scarecrow-like
appearance humiliate her; he goes on to abuse
the priest, refuse to attend the bridal feast and
then hurries his wife home on an old nag. When
they arrive he announces that neither bed nor
food is good enough for his new wife, refusing
therefore to let her either eat or sleep, and
driving her to distraction with other seemingly
mad schemes. After a number of other marriages have been arranged, there is a feast at
which a bet is made amongst the bridegrooms as
to which wife shall prove the most docile;
Petruchio wins triumphantly.

London in the mid eighteenth-century. Woodward first played
Petruchio, one of his most celebrated parts, at Drury Lane in 1754;
on this occasion he played opposite Hannah Pritchard at her
benefit. Davies considered that Woodward's representation of the
character was 'perhaps, more wild, extravagant, and fantastical,
than the author designed it should be; and he carried his acting of
it to an almost ridiculous excess …',[2] although he did agree with
Churchill's perceptive observation that Woodward 'excelled most
in parts where Nature had stretched her powers to a ridiculous
excess'.[3]

Several prints were engraved of Woodward in other roles: he
appears together with Ned Shuter as Captain Bobadil and Master
Stephen in *Every Man in his Humour*; as the Fine Gentleman in
Lethe (see page 22); as Mercutio in an etching published by
William Herbert in 1753, and as Harlequin in the *Theatrical Steel-
Yards of 1750*.

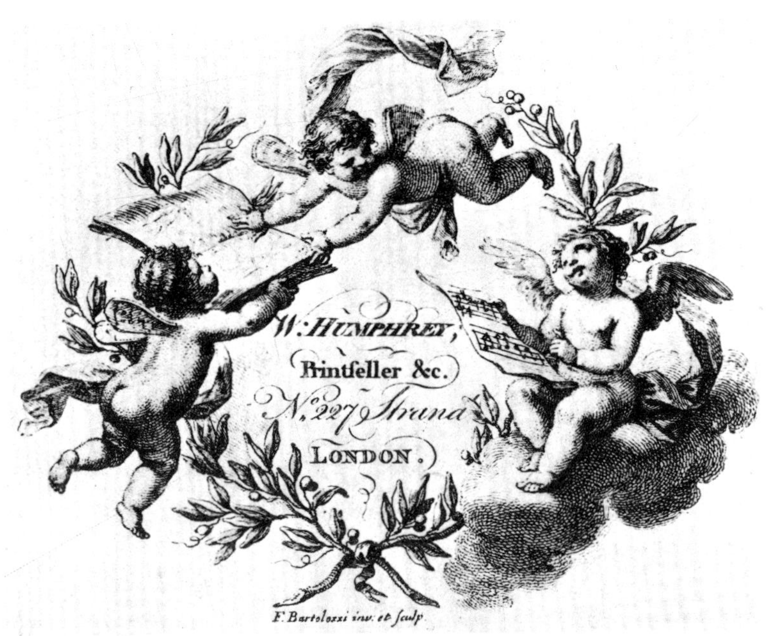

William Humphrey's trade card, altered from a benefit ticket for
Felice Giardini.

[1] Maxted, Ian *The British Book Trades 1775–87:
an index to insurance Policies*, Exeter 1992.
[2] Davies, I, p. 199.
[3] Churchill's *Rosciad* quoted in Davies, I, p. 191.

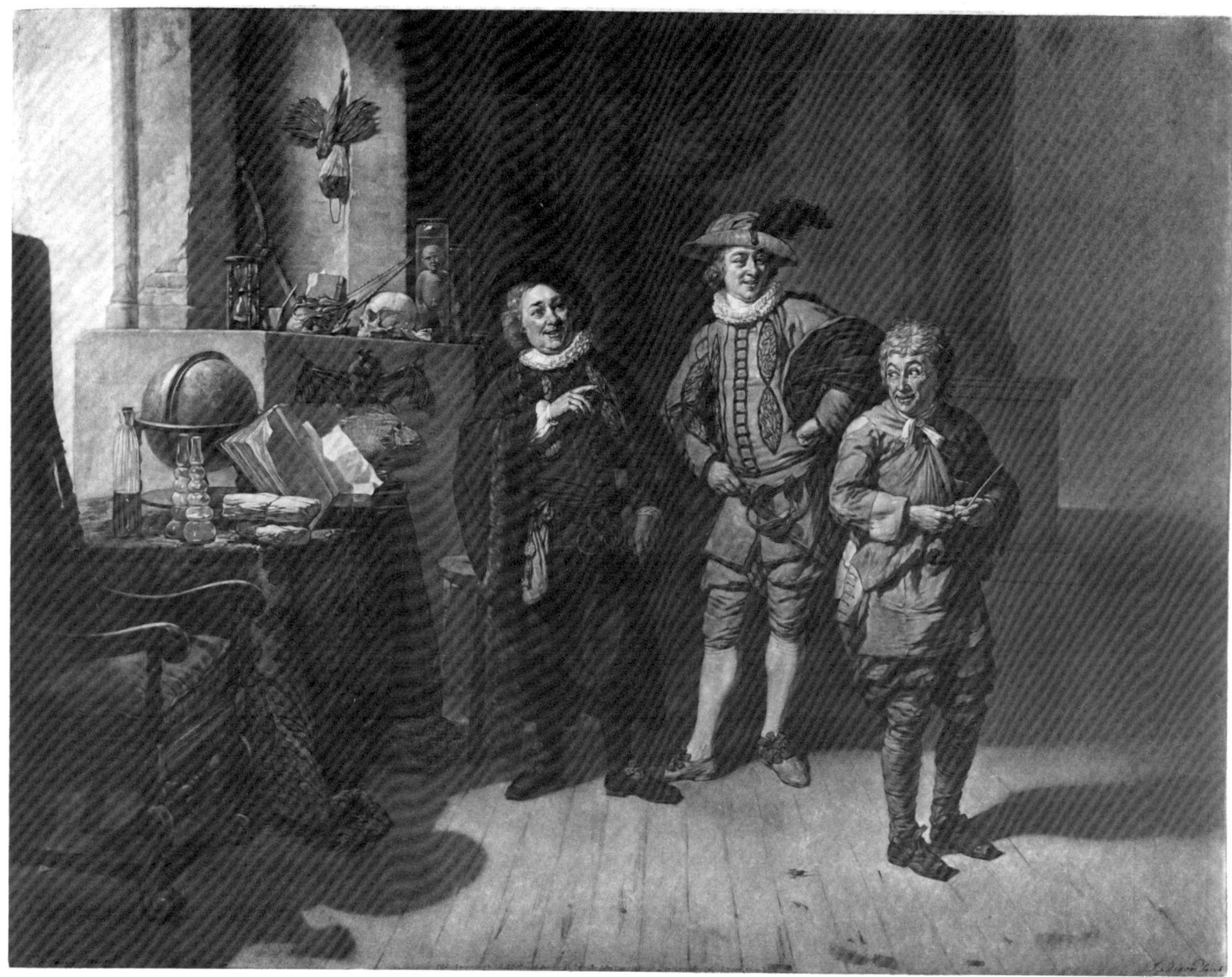

25 M.r Garrick in the Character of Abel Drugger, M.r Burton and M.r Palmer in the Characters of Subtle and Face.

Engraved by John Dixon after Johann Zoffany

Published by John Dixon 12 January 1771

Sold by Carington Bowles and John Boydell and Alfred Drury

480 x 603 I; 481 x 604 Pl.

References: CS 17; O'D groups p. 29

1. Finished proof before all letters.
Impressions: CLB.

2. With engraved publication line only at base of image: "Publish'd according to Act of Parliament January ye 12.th 1771, by John Dixon in Broad Street oppofite Poland Street Carnaby Market.".
Impressions: CLB P8,493 (impression exhibited); BM.

Zoffany's painting was exhibited at the Royal Academy in 1770 and was purchased by Sir Joshua Reynolds. The Earl of Carlisle is said to have then offered Reynolds twenty guineas above the one hundred pounds that he paid for the picture, which Reynolds accepted on condition that the difference went to Zoffany. Dixon exhibited his print at the Society of Artists the following year. Fine impressions seem to have been already in demand just three years later when Shropshire listed a copy in his sale catalogue[1] at 15s. In the same year, Sayer advertised a series of small portraits of French and English players, indicating that they were after 'De Fish' (Defesch)[2]; quite clearly a number of these images were copied from Zoffany and other painters. It is to these that Lichtenberg referred:

> An engraving has been made of this part of the scene [*The Beaux Stratagem*], and Sayer[3] has included a copy of it among his well-known little pictures … although there are in the same collection of pictures such excellent likenesses of him as Abel Drugger and Sir John Brute that they can scarce be surpassed.[4]

It is likely that Sayer & Bennett had purchased control of the large plate by 1776, enabling them to commission Dixon to engrave a single figure plate which was published in March of that

3. With the added inscription: "*M.ᴿ GARRICK in the CHARACTER of ABEL DRUGGER, M.ᴿ BURTON and M.ᴿ PALMER in the CHARAC-TERS of SUBTLE and FACE. Alchemist, Act 2, Scene 6.ᵗʰ I Zoffany Pinx.!* / Publish'd according to Act of Parliament January the 12.ᵗʰ 1771 by John Dixon in Kemps Row opposite Ranelagh Chelsea and Sold by A: Drury in Dukes Court S.ᵗ Martins Lane, Ca. Bowles in S.ʳ Pauls Church Yard and J. Boydel[sic] Cheapſide.".
Impressions: C.

4. With the added dedication to Earl of Carlisle, at bottom to r: "*To Fred.ᵏ Earl of Carlisle Vic.,̇ Morpeth. | *** This Plate is humbly inscribed by his Lordships obed.ᵗ Servt John Dixon*".
Impressions: BM; H.

year. This single figure plate was listed in Laurie & Whittle's catalogue of prints for 1795 priced at 5s, or 7s 6d for proofs, while the large plate was priced at 10s 6d. Samuel Reynolds also engraved a mezzotint copy of the single figure in 1825.

The print shows Garrick at the most widely acclaimed moment of his performance in Ben Jonson's *The Alchemist*, when he has just broken a phial in the Alchemist's house. This episode, added by Garrick for extra effect, was not in Jonson's play but originated from an accident that happened to Colley Cibber when playing the part.

The part of Abel Drugger was the epitome of low comedy even though the character appears on stage for only a short time and has few lines; in the hands of a master, a minor part like this could become a major role. Garrick's aim in his portrayal of the character was to create, 'the completest low picture of grotesque terror that can be imagined by a Dutch painter'.[5] Both Quin and Colley Cibber, actors of the earlier period, had been celebrated for their performances in this role but Garrick, who played the part for the first time on 21 March 1743, offered a new interpretation. He rejected Theophilus Cibber's '... absurd grimace and ridiculous tricks ...', and cast off all buffoonery, basing his portrayal upon an acute observation of the characteristics of a simpleton. As one critic observed: 'There is no twisting of Features, no Squinting, but all is correct as if a real Tobacco Boy were before us. It is really surprising how he ... can present us such a Face of Inanity'.[6]

Lichtenberg felt that Garrick added extraordinary details to the character which could not be surpassed:

> When the astrologers spell out from the stars the name Abel Drugger, henceforth to be great, the poor gullible creature says with heartfelt delight: 'That is my name'. Garrick makes him keep his joy to himself, for to blurt it out before everyone would be lacking in decency. So Garrick turns aside, hugging his delight to himself for a few moments, so that he actually gets those red rings round his eyes which often accompany great joy, at least, when violently suppressed, and says to himself; 'That is my name'. The effect of this judicious restraint is indescribable, for one did not see him as a simpleton being gulled, but as a much more ridiculous creature, with an air of secret triumph, thinking himself the slyest of rogues'.[7]

Whatever the production, it seems that the whole world came specifically to see Garrick, whose performance often rescued a poor cast or a weak play. This was the case with *The Alchemist*, one critic asserting that, 'nothing but his [Garrick's] singular excellence in Drugger, has kept the comedy on the stage for many years past. It bids very fair now to lie undisturbed upon the dramatic shelf ...'.[8] Members of the audience, such as Fanny Burney, found the performance excelled in showing, 'the extreme meanness, the vulgarity, the low wit, the vacancy of countenance, the appearance of unlicked nature in all his motions'.[9]

Garrick played Abel Drugger throughout his career, performing the role more than eighty times. When he first took the part he convinced those who had only previously seen him as Richard III or King Lear that there was 'nothing in human life that such a genius was not able to represent'.[10]

John Burton was born in about 1749 in London, the son of an actor. He first appeared on the stage as a boy in 1762. He continued to play young roles billed as 'Master Burton' until the 1767–8 season, when he began to be billed as 'J. Burton' and was given more mature parts. He played minor roles throughout his career, such as the grave-digger in *Hamlet* and one of the witches in *Macbeth*.

Burton was liked and respected, although Haslewood[11] remarked how disappointing it was that, having grown up in the theatre of Weston, Shuter and Garrick, he was not a comedian of high distinction but instead an 'inoffensive bottle muser', worthy only in little parts. Hopkins felt that he was a 'reliable utility actor' and 'a useful stop-gap'. He died 'in great distress' in Newgate prison in 1797.

John Palmer was born in about 1744, the son of a soldier. He became a bill-sticker and door-keeper at Drury Lane, but was encouraged by Garrick to join the army. Avoiding this, Palmer joined a printseller's shop in Ludgate Hill.

Palmer appeared on stage for the first time in April 1762, engaged by Foote who said that his 'tragedy was d——d bad' but that his 'comedy might do'. Although still not impressed by him, Garrick took on Palmer when he was dismissed by Foote in the middle of a season, but only for minor parts. He travelled for a time and on his return was engaged again by Garrick, with an increase in salary. Deaths of major actors of the company such as his namesake 'Gentleman' Palmer and Charles Holland meant that he was employed for the next four years. Palmer finally managed to gain Garrick's respect when he learned a part at extremely short notice.

While acting in the *Grecian Daughter* with Mrs Barry, Palmer was disabled for a few months when the spring in her stage dagger failed. After appearing all over the country, he began to build the Royal Theatre in Wellclose Square, near Goodman's Fields. He finished it, despite opposition, but it closed two years later in 1789 and Palmer was jailed for debt. In 1798, mourning the death of his wife, he went to Liverpool. His last performance was impressive for in the fourth act of the play he keeled over and died; the audience supposed, until his body was removed, that this was merely good acting.

[1] *Walter Shropshire's Catalogue of Prints, for the Year 1774. No. 158, three doors beyond Grafton-street, in New Bond-street. The sale to begin on Tuesday, March the 8th, …* [London, 1774].

[2] *THE DRAMATIC CHARACTERS OF the English, French, and Italian stages.* Advertised in *The Morning Chronicle*, 11 Feb. 1774.

[3] These small plates were available from Sayer for 6d, the wholesale price of 10s 6d for the set, or for 1 guinea 'beautifully coloured'.

[4] A letter of 30 Nov. 1775 in Lichtenberg, pp. 25–6.

[5] Garrick, p. 9.

[6] *The London Chronicle*, March 1757.

[7] A letter of 1 Oct. 1775 in Lichtenberg, pp. 3–4.

[8] *The Morning Post*, 12 April 1760.

[9] 1773.

[10] Genest, IV, for the years 1736–7.

[11] Haslewood, Joseph *The Secret History of the Green Room*, 1792.

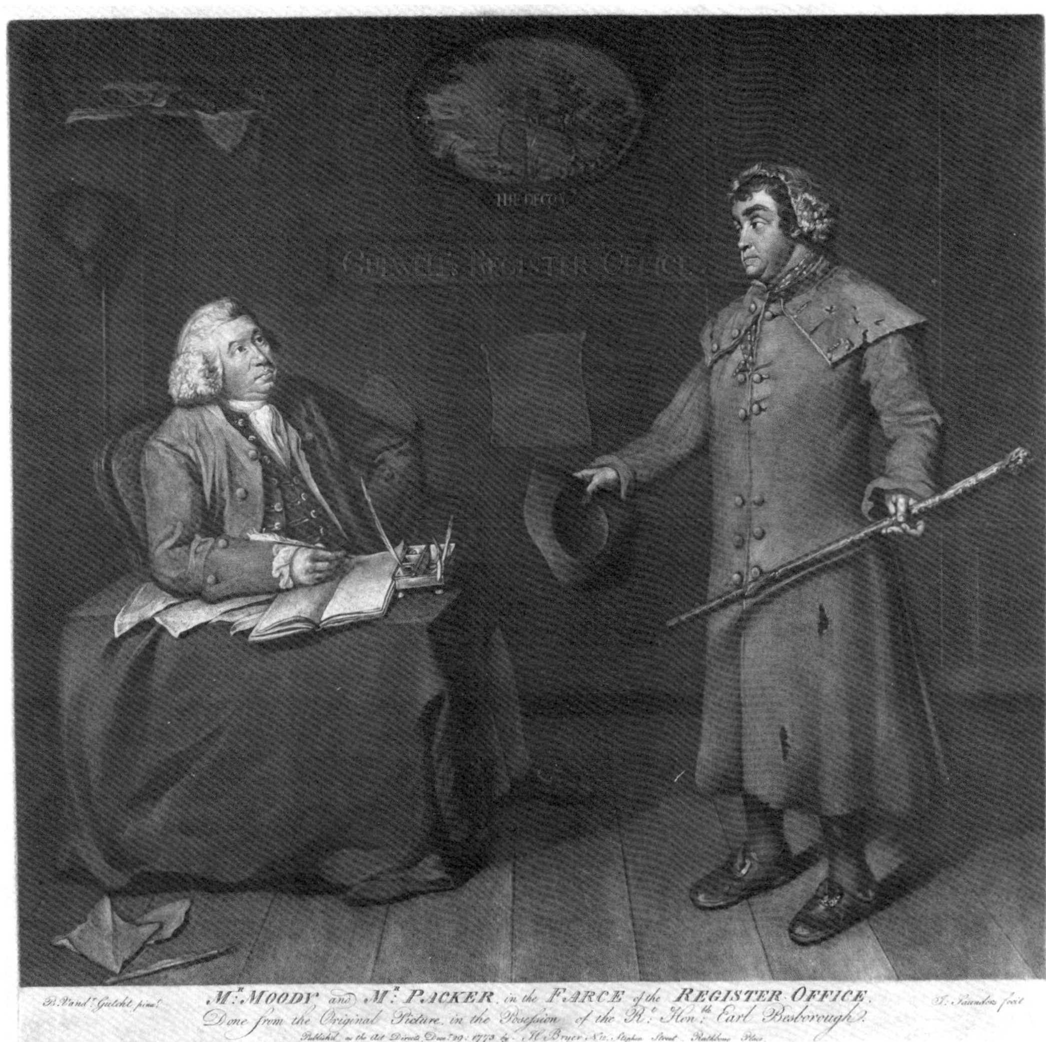

26 M^R. Moody and M^R. Packer, in the Farce of the Register Office

Engraved by Joseph Saunders
after Benjamin Vandergucht

Published by Joseph Saunders December 1773

Re-published by Henry Bryer
29 December 1773

Re-published by Sayer & Bennett June 1777

424 x 448 I; 450 x 448 Pl.

References: CS 9; R 9; O'D (Moody) 8; Hall (Moody) 6

1. [Proof before inscription].
Impressions: (said to be at Harvard)

2. Finished proof with the scratched inscription: *"B Vand! Gutcht Pinx! *** Saunders Fecit"*.
Impressions: BM.

Benjamin Vandergucht's painting, now at Leicester Museum and Art Gallery, was exhibited at the Royal Academy in 1773 together with his painting of Johnston as Gibby in the Wonder. Joseph Saunders published this print in December 1773, whilst he was a student at the Royal Academy schools. Saunders exhibited this print and the mezzotint '*Mr Johnston as Gibby in the Wonder*' at the Society of Artists exhibition in 1774, probably in the hope that they would be taken up and distributed by a printseller. If this was his aim, he seems to have been successful since both plates were acquired by Henry Bryer. Bryer's partnership with William Wynne Ryland had ended in bankruptcy the previous year. It is of interest to note that of the nine mezzotint portraits by Saunders recorded in Chaloner Smith, Bryer re-published four; two further prints by Saunders were re-published by Shropshire in 1774. As suggested by Chaloner Smith, it seems that in 1774–5 Saunders put aside engraving and concentrated on a career as a miniature painter. From 1778 to 1800 he exhibited a number of miniatures at the Royal Academy together with several theatrical subjects.

The plate of the '*Register Office*' was purchased between 1775 and 1777 by Sayer & Bennett, passing eventually to Sayer's successors Laurie & Whittle, who listed it in their 1795 catalogue.

The play was first performed at Drury Lane on 25 April 1761

3. **Finished proof with the engraved inscription, before the day of the month:** *"B. Vand.ᵗ Gutcht pinx.ᵗ *** J: Saunders fecit | Publish'd as the Act Directs Dece.ᵗ 1773 by J: Saunders, at N.º 17 Glanville Street Rathbone Place.".*
Impressions: CLB; H.

4. **[With the day of the month added: 'Dece.ᵗ 29: 1773'. (CS)].**

5. **With the added engraved inscription, the image reduced at the base to allow for the new full inscription:** *"M.ᴿ MOODY and M.ᴿ PACKER, in the FARCE of the REGISTER OFFICE, | Done from the Original Picture, in the Posefsion of the R.ᵗ Hon.ᵇˡᵉ Earl Besborough.".*
Impressions: BM; TM; H.

6. **With the publication line altered:**
"Publish'd as the Act Directs, Dece.ᵗ 29: 1773 by H. Bryer N.º 12, Stephen Street, Rathbone Place.".
Impressions: CLB P27,343 (impression exhibited); BM.

7. **[Re-published by Sayer & Bennett, June 1777 (R)].**

☜ *The Register Office* by Joseph Reed was a satire on Fielding's scheme to provide a form of employment agency for London in the 1750s; those seeking a job paid a small fee to a central bureau which then recommended them to potential employers. In the play, Gulwell (Packer) advertises non-existent jobs in Ireland, Wales and America, collecting fees from unsuspecting 'gulls', and also provides character references at prices from five shillings to five guineas. The basis of the farce lay in the characters of the applicants and the manner in which they were treated by Gulwell. Moody, who excelled in this type of part, played an Irishman.

but enjoyed only moderate success until 1767, after which time it was performed almost every year until 1781. The re-birth of the play was undoubtedly brought about by the fact that it was suitable for topical adaptation. In 1773–4, the season in which this print was published, Moody made several appearances in this part at the Haymarket, playing a further six performances at Drury Lane in the winter, including one for his benefit on 6 April. The revival of his reputation was apparently closely connected with his success in this part; one critic considered that Moody had been 'very near sliding into his original obscurity, till the appearance of the Register Office'.[1]

A reviewer in *The Public Advertiser* commented that the play had, 'great Merit … though our fine gentlemen may call it low', commenting that in the print, 'Mr Moody's Figure is a great likeness and gives a good representation of the manner of that excellent Actor'.[2]

John Hayman Packer was born in the Strand in 1730 and was a saddler until about the age of twenty-four, when he made his first performance in Newcastle under the name of Hayman. No doubt appearing at other provincial theatres beforehand, he played in London for the first time in January 1758 at Drury Lane. He was by all accounts a pleasant character, and played a vast number of minor roles for over fifty years on the stage. He was a very useful performer, if lacking in 'animation and fire',[3] but some critics sneered at his efforts:

I pry'thee, dear sister, bid PACKER retire
To a wide easy chair, and warm social fire;
Let him spend his last days unembitter'd by pain,
Smoke his pipe, and reflect on the Kings he has slain.[4]

He died, poor and disregarded, in 1806.

[1] *Theatrical Biography*, I, p. 132.
[2] *The Public Advertiser*, 3 May 1773.
[3] TDB.
[4] *ibid.*

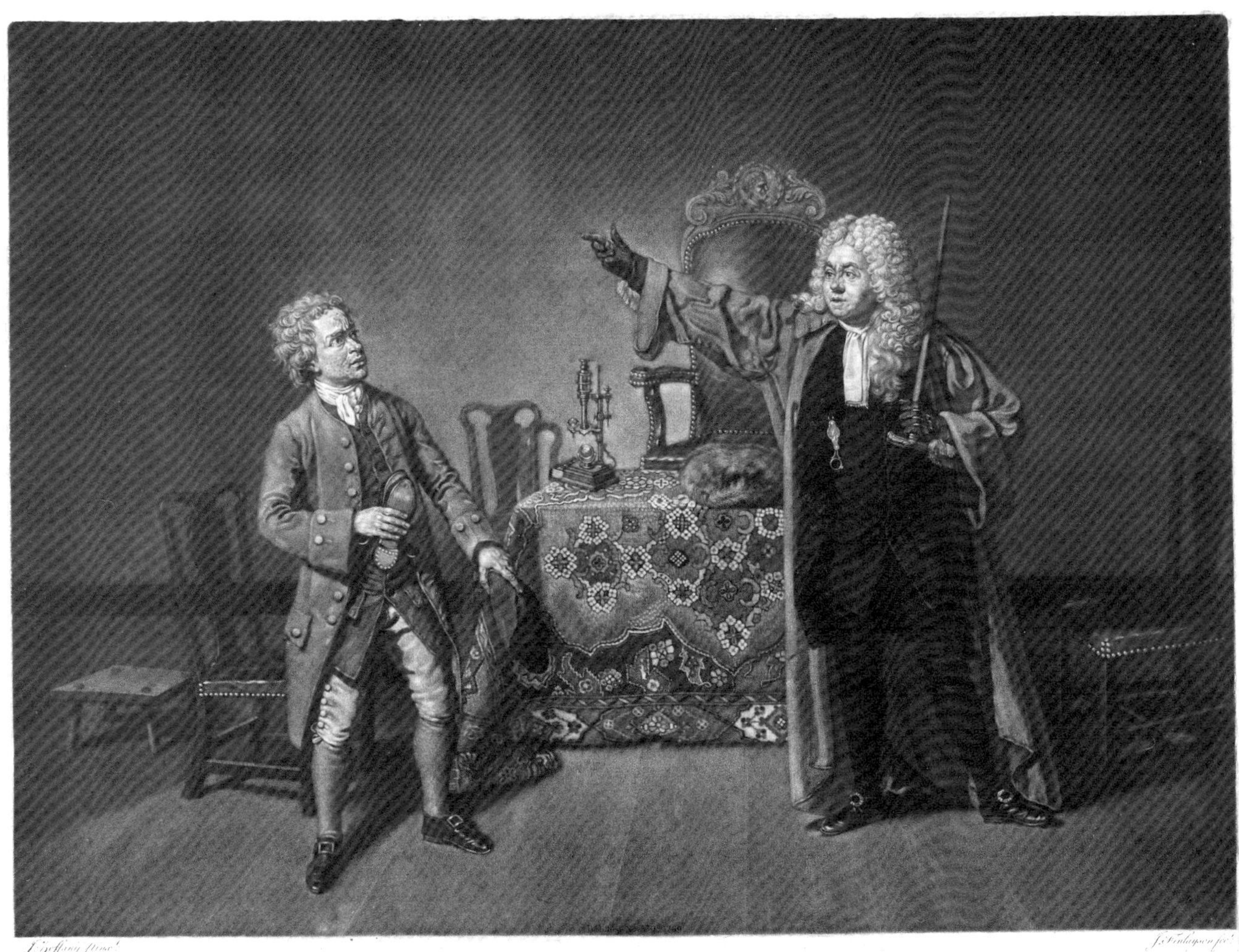

27 Mr. Foote & Mr. Weston, in the Characters of The President & Dr. Last

Engraved by John Finlayson
after Johann Zoffany

Published 30 November 1769

[Re-published by] sold by Johann Zoffany,
John Finlayson and Henry Parker

423 x 557; 457 x 559 Pl.

References: CS 6; O'D (Foote) 16

1. With the engraved inscription: In c, at the
base of the image: "Publifhed Nov.r 30.th 1769.".
In inscription space below: "*J: Zoffanij Pinx.t* ***
J,, Finlayson fec.t".
Impressions: CLB P37,988 ex. coll. W. F. Tiffin, *Lugt*
1051 (impression exhibited); BM.

2. With the added engraved inscription: "*Mr.*
FOOTE & Mr. WESTON, in the Characters of

Johann Zoffany's painting, now in a private collection, was exhibited at the Society of Artists in 1769. It was painted for Samuel
Foote and bequeathed to his executor, but soon afterwards was
acquired by George Colman.[1] John Finlayson exhibited the mezzotint at the Society of Artists the following year. The print, initially published by Zoffany and Finlayson, was acquired by Robert
Sayer and subsequently by John Boydell, together with two other
plates after Zoffany; this is discussed under the first of these three
prints, '*Love in a Village*' (see page 35). A number of copper-plates
from the stock of Benjamin Beale Evans were sold on 26 May
1824; he did not seem to own the plate at this time but since five
prints and a proof were being sold, he may previously have had an
interest in it.

'The President' caricatures Sir William Browne, who was
elected President of the Royal College of Physicians in 1766. At
this time there was a violent dispute over membership of the
College between the Fellows and the Licentiates. Browne was a
defender of the privileges of the Universities and published a
pamphlet that had caused offence to the Licentiates. The College
had for many years insisted that to become a fellow (a member of
the governing body), an individual had to be a graduate of an

THE PRESIDENT & D.ʳ LAST. / "Now D.ʳ Laft___ "I am come for my Shoes. *** *Devil on two Sticks, Act 3.ᵈ Scene 2.ᵈ | Sold by M.,ʳ Zoffanij, in Lincoln's Inn Fields, M.,ʳ Finlayson, *** & M.,ʳ Parker, at N.,º 82 in Cornhill.".*
Impressions: CLB; BM; TM; H.

☛ In Samuel Foote's play *The Devil upon Two Sticks*, the plot centres on two lovers, Harriet Maxwell, daughter of the British Consul in Madrid, and her father's clerk, Invoice. While they are in Spain, their romance is discovered by the angry father and in haste they escape to an adjoining apothecary's shop. Here they find the Devil imprisoned in a bottle. In return for his freedom, he agrees to take them on his coat tails to London. Having been brought up abroad, Harriet and Invoice are bewildered by their circumstances and ask the Devil to explain English manners and customs. In order to do so the Devil shows them, amongst other things, the Royal College of Physicians.

English University (i.e. either Oxford or Cambridge) and consequently could not be nonconformist. All others who wished to practise medicine – graduates of other universities and those who had served an apprenticeship in surgery or physic – had to be content with a 'licence' and joining the Licentiates. The main injustice of this lay in the fact that Edinburgh was one of the leading medical schools of the time and many of the nonconformist graduates were often most able individuals. After the first performance of the play, Browne sent a card to Foote complimenting him on the accuracy of his portrayal, even enclosing his own muff to complete the likeness.

The humour of the scene depicted in this print lies in the fact that the President, whilst turning away genuine applicants who were prevented from becoming fellows, elevates Last the cobbler to the ranks of the Licentiates, although he is the epitome of a quack doctor; Last had served an apprenticeship and therefore fulfilled all the requirements. Now licensed and able officially to practise as a doctor, the shoemaker returns to the President worried only about his shoes, still a shoemaker at heart.

Foote's play *The Devil upon Two Sticks* was first performed on 30 May 1768. Genest suggests that: 'There was little or no plot, but this is amply compensated by the excellence of the dialogue'. In 1769 a reviewer for *The London Chronicle* remarked: 'The critical reader will doubtless perceive that the plot of the above piece is taken from *L'Malade Imaginaire* of Moliere'. Like many of Foote's productions, the play relied upon his own performance on the stage. The play centred upon personal satire and the ridicule of certain fashions, including a vicious attack on Garrick's Shakespeare Jubilee as well as a snipe at the managers of the two patent theatres. Although successful, the play depended heavily on capturing the audience's attention with the subject that it satirised; when the subject was no longer contentious and the personalities that it targeted were forgotten, the play was bound to be overlooked. Yet with Foote's death Davies believed that, '… the publick lost a great check on notorious vice and fashionable irregularity …'.[2]

The plot of *The Devil upon Two Sticks* was used for a Harlequin Book or 'turn-up', which was published by Robert Sayer in 1771, and priced at 6d plain or 1s coloured. There is no mention of any items of this type in Sayer's 1766 catalogue, but Sayer & Bennett's catalogue for 1775 lists fifteen examples. The same group are listed again in Laurie & Whittle's catalogue for 1795, 'for the entertainment and instruction of youth, usually called turn-ups; neatly fitted-up with blue glazed paper; coloured, eight shillings a dozen; plain, four shillings'.

---

[1] In Colman's sale at Christie's, 3–4 Aug. 1795.
[2] Davies, II, p. 263.

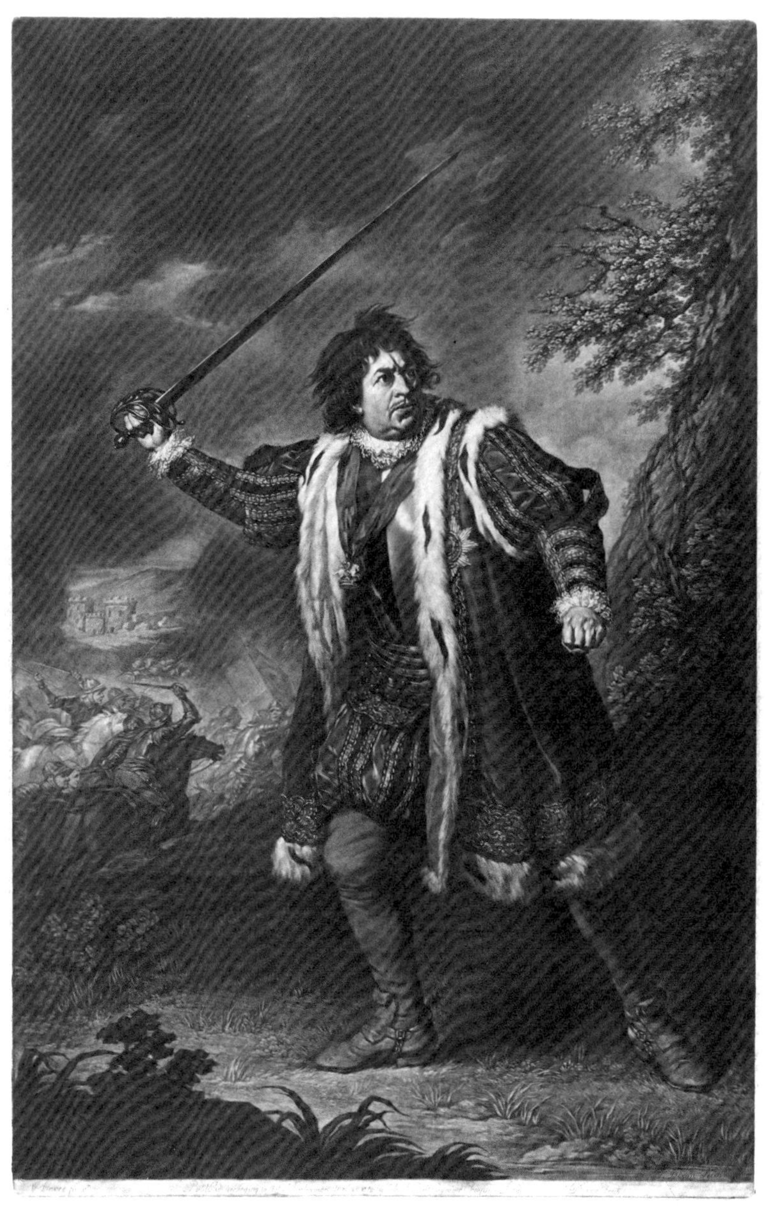

28 Mʳ Garrick in Richard the Third

Engraved by John Dixon after Nathaniel Dance

Published by John Boydell 28 April 1772

625 x 395 I; 635 x 396 Pl.

References: CS 15; O'D 81; Hall 250

1. Finished proof with the scratched inscription: *"N Dance pinxᵗ *** Publishd according to Act of Parliament April 28 1772 by John Boydell Engraver Cheapside London *** J Dixon Fecit"*. Scraped to l. at base of image *"Dance pinx"* and to r. in scratched letters *"J Dixon Fecit"*.
Impressions: CLB P4,552 (impression exhibited); BM; TM.

Nathaniel Dance's painting, now owned by Stratford-upon-Avon Town Council, was exhibited at the Royal Academy in 1771. It was acquired by Sir Watkin Williams Wynne who had bought it for one hundred and fifty guineas, reputedly even outbidding Garrick himself, who had promised to buy it for his wife. In 1772 Dixon exhibited his preparatory drawing from Dance's painting, with his mezzotint next to it, at the Society of Artists. Dance, born in 1735, was a successful portrait and history painter. In 1790 he married a very rich widow, gave up his profession and entered Parliament. He died, Sir Nathaniel Dance-Holland Bt., in 1811.

The print was published by Boydell and listed in his catalogue for 1773 at 10s 6d. A 'fine proof' sold by Robert Grave in 1809 cost £1 11s 6d; the plate was finally sold in 1818 after Josiah Boydell's death in a lot with three other theatrical plates for £18 7s 6d. Murphy states that Garrick admired this 'excellent mezzotinto print' and 'sent it to his select friends' with complimentary lines printed and pasted on the back. The print was also used as a

2. With the engraved inscription: *"N,, Dance Pinxt. *** J,, Dixon Fecit* / M.ʳ GARRICK in RICHARD the THIRD. / Publiſh'd April 28ᵗʰ 1772, by John Boydell Engraver Cheapſide London.".*
Impressions: CLB; BM; H.

The Morning Post, 28 May 1773.

Mr. Garrick appeared in Richard the Third last night, for the first time these four years, and performed it throughout to the astonishment and admiration of a most numerous, and fashionable audience. As it is the character requiring the nicest judgement, with the full force of all natural, as well as theatrical powers to do it justice, we do not wonder to find him stand single and alone in it, leaving behind the train of imitating monotonists at a prodigious distance … The varying and delicate touches throughout the play, from which he produced so fine a relief of light and shade, form the most striking transitions of acting, and oratory, that ever were displayed, or heard, on any stage … His hypocritical scene with Lady Anne was so exquisitely performed, that we forgot the poet's impropriety, and thought not her yielding to the deceitful tyrant, by any means unnatural … The powers of his voice in the last act were wonderful; and his bodily capacity kept equal pace with them; for in the heat of the action he flew through the narrow pass of trees with such uncommon martial agility, that we thought the house would never have ceased the applause they bellowed upon it.

model for two Derby porcelain statuettes.[1] The fame of Dixon's mezzotint was such that, when Zoffany painted Peter Friell and a fellow connoisseur looking over a portfolio of prints, it was Dixon's mezzotint that was uppermost on the table.

By the time that this print was published, the part of Richard III, in which Garrick had made his formal debut on 19 October 1741, was particularly associated with him. His first appearance at Drury Lane the following year was commemorated in a painting by Thomas Bardwell.[2] The most important picture of Garrick as Richard III was that painted by Hogarth, which depicts the king starting from his couch. When Dance came to paint this subject, the image was well known through Grignion's[3] engraving, which was still available despite having been published twenty-five years earlier.

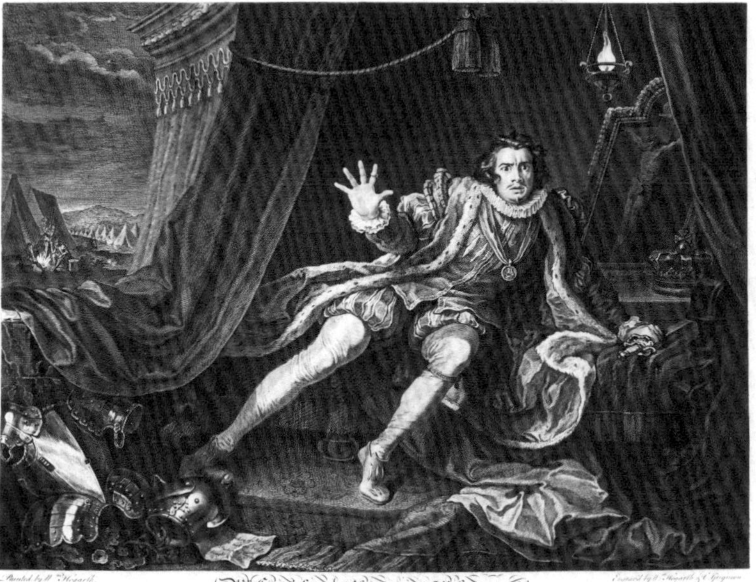

Like Bardwell, Francis Hayman chose to show Richard on the battlefield in his painting of 1760. This painting, which was shown at the Society of Artists, was the first picture of Garrick to be exhibited in public. Dance too, set the actor on the battlefield but the figure of Richard III is more monumental and imbued with greater heroism. Gentleman praised Garrick's performance:

The Public have set up Mr Garrick as a standard of perfection in this laborious, difficult part; and if we consider the essentials, his claim to such distinction will immediately appear indisputable … variations of voice, and climax of expression, in both which he stands without an equal; graceful attitudes, nervous action, with a well-regulated spirit, to animate within natural bounds every passage, even from the coldest up to the most inflamed. Mr Garrick also preserves a happy medium, and dwindles neither into the buffoon or brute.[4]

---

[1] Bradshaw *Derby*, pp. 185–6.
[2] Russell-Cotes Art Gallery, Bournemouth, no. 310. Bought at Christie's 7/7/1916 for 8 guineas by Alderman Russell-Cotes. The painting is signed and dated 1741.
[3] Charles Grignion I (1717–1810), engraver.
[4] Gentleman, I, p. 11.

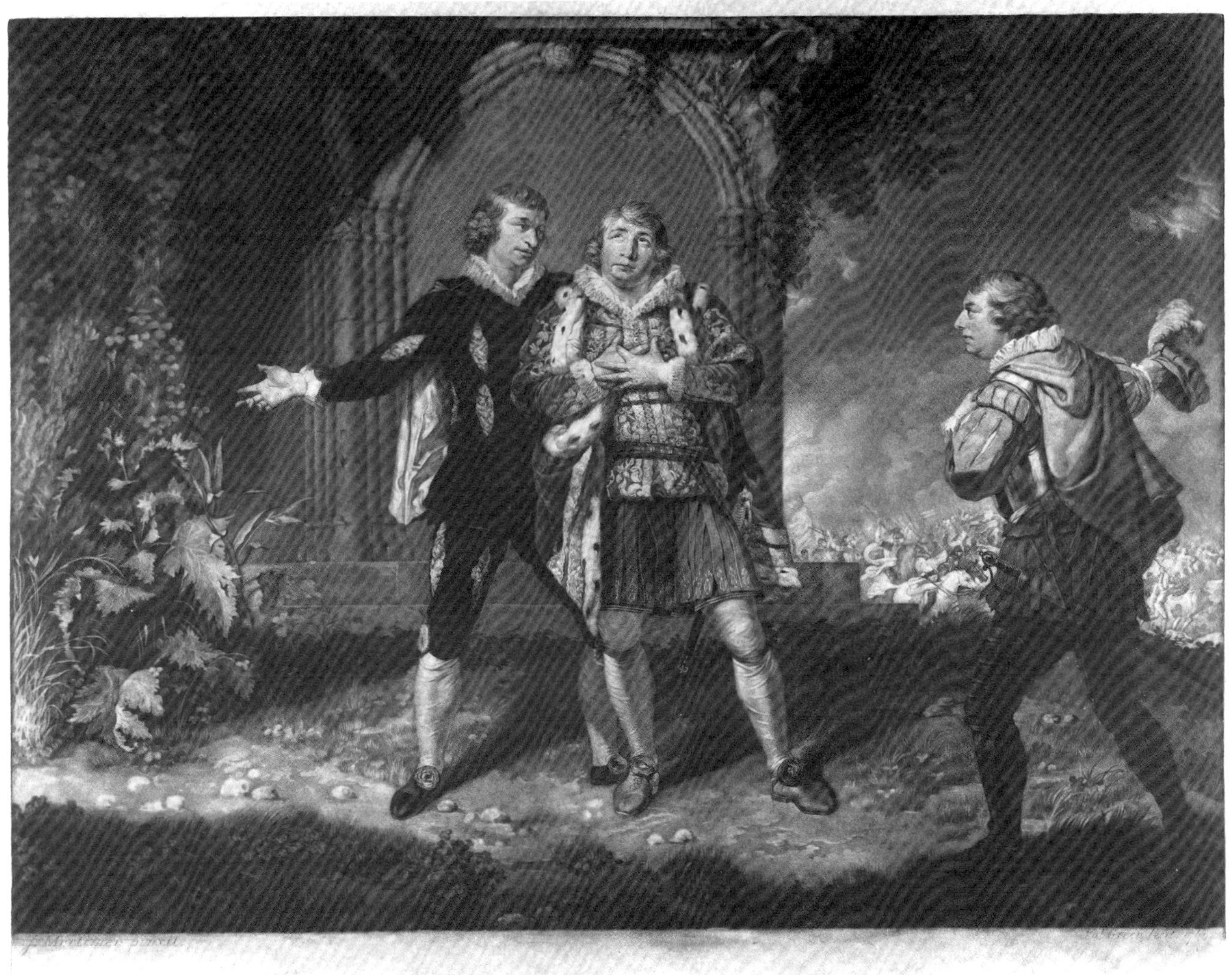

29 M.r Powell and M.r Bensley, in the Characters of King John and Hubert

Engraved by Valentine Green
after John Hamilton Mortimer

Engraved 1769; [re]published by William Wynne Ryland 9 January 1771

420 x 550 I; 455 x 550 Pl.

References: CS 104; W 9; O'D (Bensley) 8

1. Finished proof with the scratched inscription: "*J. Mortimer pinxit. *** Val. Green fecit 1769.*".
Impressions: CLB P11,424 (impression exhibited); BM.

2. With the added scratched inscription: "*Published as the Act directs Jany 9: 1771 by the Proprietor W. Wynne Ryland in Cornhill.*".
Impressions: CLB; BM; TM.

John Hamilton Mortimer's painting, once in the collection of Charles Matthews and now in the Garrick Club, was exhibited at the Society of Artists in May 1768 and again in September at a special exhibition for the King of Denmark. The engraving was not exhibited. The plate was finished by Valentine Green in 1769 who may then have issued the prints himself. William Wynne Ryland seems to have owned the plate by March 1771 at the latest; he had been in partnership with Henry Bryer from 1766 until their bankruptcy in December 1771 and it is interesting to note that the plate seems to have remained Ryland's property, not that of the partnership, the assets of which were advertised for sale on 6 March 1772. In 1771 an impression (presumably very fine) was listed in Walter Shropshire's catalogue at 16s and in 1773 he listed two proofs at 12s each. In 1780 the print was included in Green's four page catalogue of his own works, priced at 10s 6d.

On 26 July 1783 Ryland was arrested on a charge of forgery. He was accused of counterfeiting an acceptance to two bills of exchange for payment of £7,114, thus attempting to defraud the East India Company. He was found guilty and was executed on 29 of August.[1] The whole account of Ryland's crime, flight, attempted suicide (by cutting his throat), capture and execution is

3. With the engraved inscription: "*Painted by J. Mortimer. *** Engrav'd by Val. Green. | MR POWELL and MR BENSLEY, in the Characters of KING JOHN and HUBERT. | King John – Act 5th Scene 5th | Publish'd as the Act directs March the 26. 1771. by Wm Wynne Ryland in Cornhill*".
Impressions: CLB; BM; H.

4. The plate re-worked and the publication line altered: "*Published as the Act directs March the 1st 1785 by* [John Walker] *N_o 148 n^r Somerset House Strand*".
Impressions: H.

☞ King John is threatened with war by King Philip of France and the Duke of Austria, who support the strong claim to the throne of Arthur, John's nephew. John and Philip, the bastard son of Richard I, invade France, but peace is secured by the marriage of John's niece to the Dauphin. However, Philip reneges on the alliance. The English are victorious, the Bastard kills the Duke of Austria, and Arthur is captured and sent to England to be executed by Hubert de Burgh. King John's sister-in-law, Constance (Arthur's mother) goes mad with grief and dies. This print represents Act V, Scene III, in which a messenger informs John of this, and the King replies: 'Thou hast made me giddy with these ill tidings'. Hubert cannot bring himself to injure Arthur who, however, kills himself in trying to escape, but much of the English nobility suspect John of Arthur's murder and join the Dauphin who is invading England. King John is poisoned by a monk and dies at Swinstead Abbey. Meanwhile the rebellious lords discover the Dauphin's treachery and the play ends with the retreat of the French before an England united under the new king, Henry III.

remarkable, particularly since by his own claim he was financially secure at this time.[2] The forgery was remarkably fine and James Whatman, the paper-maker, was called in to examine the evidence. The forgery was dated 5 October 1780 but Whatman recognised that the paper, of his own manufacture, had not been available until May 1782; this, it was claimed, convinced the jury of Ryland's guilt.[3] Ryland might have been reprieved, had he not already used his position as engraver to the King to secure the reprieve of one of his brothers, who had been convicted of highway robbery. In the following April, what seems to be the last of Ryland's stock was sold; this included the copper-plate to '*Powell and Bensley in King John*' which was then purchased by 'Palmer' for £1 11s 6d. It is highly likely that this would have been William Palmer, a printseller at 159, the Strand, who in 1784 took in subscriptions for the relief of Ryland's widow Mary. He probably bought it on behalf of, or sold it on to, John Walker[4] who clumsily re-worked it in the shadows and dark areas and re-issued it in March 1785.

Powell first played King John on 20 March 1766, alongside William Havard (see page 27) as Hubert. Robert Bensley was Hubert to Powell's King John on only three occasions, twice in 1767, the performances celebrated in this print, and on one further night on 3 May 1769. Genest identifies the messenger in this print as William Smith and suggested that 'as the likeness of Smith and Bensley is good, it is probable that of Powell may be so likewise'.[5] This was to be Powell's final appearance on the stage; he died just two months later. It seems that King John was a play that was rarely performed, but it may have been familiar through the printed text to a great many people. It was this, combined with the reputations of Mortimer and Green, that kept the print popular in the 1780s.

Powell's performance as King John had its faults; Francis Gentleman felt that Powell had been characteristically under-prepared for a part to which he was ill-suited anyway: 'too boyish, he wanted weight and depth of expression to excel'.[6] Despite this opinion, when Powell played the part on 7 February 1767, Garrick was sufficiently concerned by his success to write to his brother the following day, sick with jealousy:

Sick– Sick– King John beshit– bouncing, strutting, Striding, Straddling, thumping, grinning, Swaggering, Staggering all be shit . . .[7]

Robert Bensley had been an army officer serving in North America. Having performed in private plays at the end of the war, he got himself recommended to Garrick and appeared at Drury Lane for the first time in 1765 as Pierre in *Venice Preserv'd*, the audience being chiefly made up of his fellow officers. From 1755 until his retirement in 1796, he played at the Haymarket in the summer and Drury Lane in the winter. He was generally considered to be a good, sensible man and competent actor, in marked contrast to Gentleman's view that, 'his person is slight, his features contracted and peevish, his deportment falsely consequential, his action mostly extravagant, and his voice rather harsh'.[8] His last performance was in a production of the *Grecian Daughter* for his benefit in May 1796 opposite Mrs Siddons. On leaving the stage he became Barrack-Master at Knightsbridge barracks.

---

[1] Christie and Ansell, 7 April 1784, lot 70.

[2] Ryland claimed an income of £2,000 net from his business, a Royal Pension of £200 and 22 shares in the Liverpool Water Works worth at least £7,000.

[3] For a full account of Ryland's downfall see *The Authentic Memoir of William Wynne Ryland . . . to which is added . . . his Trial*, John Ryall, London 1784.

[4] John Walker (fl. 1770–90), printseller and publisher in Parliament Square and later in the Strand.

[5] Genest, V, p. 185.

[6] Gentleman, II, p. 168.

[7] *Letters*, no. 445, [8 Feb. 1767].

[8] Gentleman, II, p. 491.

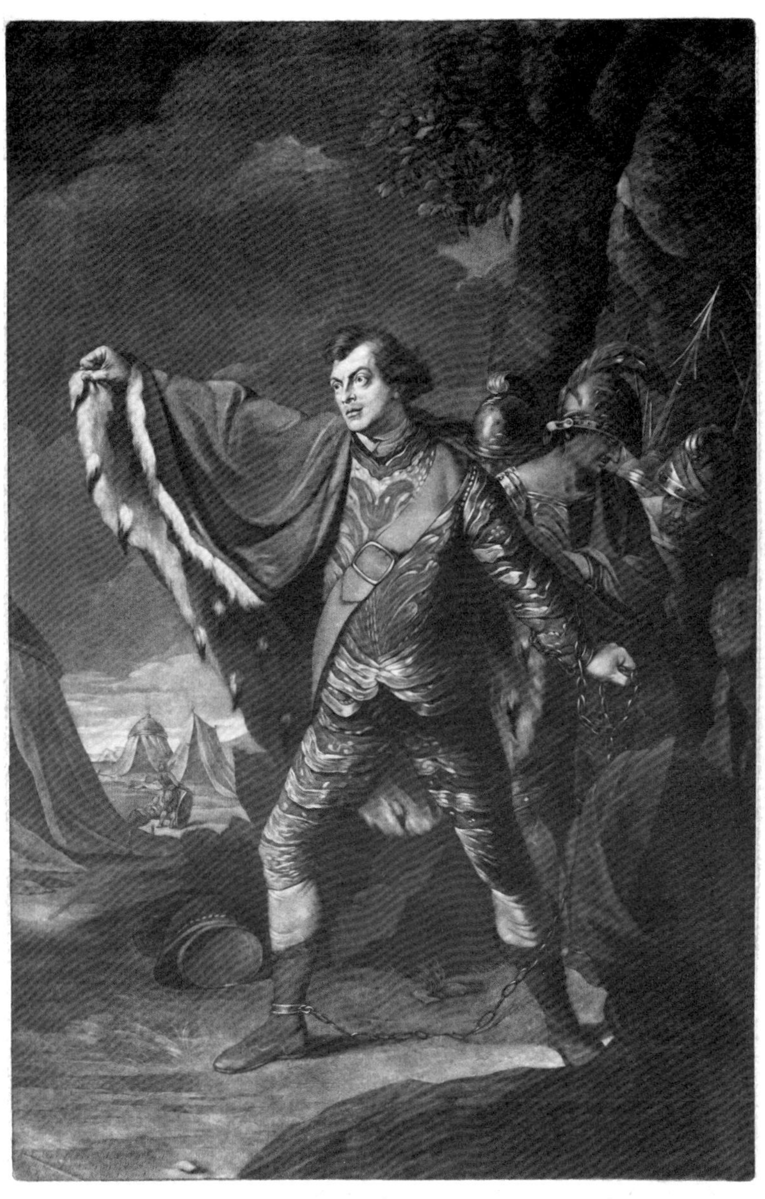

30 Mr. Reddish, in the Character of Posthumus

Engraved by Valentine Green
after a painting by Robert Edge Pine

Published by Valentine Green
19 November 1771

615 x 391 I; 617 x 392 Pl.

References: CS 108; G 31; O'D 4; Hall 7

1. Finished proof with the scratched inscription: "R.E. Pine pinxit ∗∗∗ Val. Green fecit. Publish'd Novr 19th 1771 by V. Green Salisbury Street London".
Impressions: CLB P5,520; BM.

2. Re-published by John Boydell with the

The painting by Robert Edge Pine was exhibited at the Society of Artists in 1768 and had supposedly been commissioned by Reddish with this exhibition in mind. It was said that Posthumus was:

> ... a part which, from the kindness of an indulgent audience
> on the first appearance, he flattered himself he was original in;
> and for the sake of handing down to posterity such uncom-
> mon merit, he was at the expence[sic] of 65 guineas in having
> a whole length of himself painted in that character for the
> then exhibition at Spring Gardens, where he regularly
> attended above 4 hours every day, for the space of 6 weeks,
> like a second Narcissus.[1]

The print, published three years later, was not exhibited. Initially, the plate seems to have been issued by Valentine Green alone, although John Boydell may have been involved in its publication from the outset. The addition of 'John Boydell Excudit

added engraved inscription: "M! REDDISH, in the Character of POSTHUMUS – Act the fifth, Scene the last. / John Boydell Excudit 1771".
Impressions: CLB; BM; TM.

3. The plate reduced to 238 x 181 I; 244+ x 181 Pl: "R.E. Pine Del. *** SAMUEL REDDISH as POSTHUMUS. / OBIT 1787.".
Impressions: H.

☞ In Shakespeare's *Cymbeline*, the plot centres on Imogen, daughter of Cymbeline the King of Britain, who has secretly married Leonatus Posthumus. The Queen, Imogen's step-mother, who had intended her son Cloten to marry Imogen, reveals this secret marriage to the King who banishes Posthumus. The latter, now in Rome, boasts of Imogen's virtue and makes a bet with Iachimo that if he can win Imogen's favour he shall have the diamond ring that Imogen gave to Posthumus. Iachimo gains false evidence against her fidelity and so wins the ring. Posthumus writes to Pisanio, his servant at the court, directing him to kill Imogen but Pisanio instead disguises her as a boy and leaves her in a forest. A Roman army invades Britain and Imogen is captured and made the page of a Roman general, who is in turn taken prisoner, together with Iachimo. Posthumus, who has returned to fight for Cymbeline, now surrenders himself for execution as he has broken the terms of his banishment. The Roman general asks Cymbeline to spare Imogen which he does, also granting her a request. She asks that Iachimo be forced to tell how he came by his ring; he discloses his treachery and Posthumus, learning that his wife is innocent but believing her dead, laments as pictured here, before she reveals herself.

'1771' in the second state is significant and implies that Boydell had complete control over the plate by this stage. Boydell included the print in his catalogue for 1773 priced at 10s 6d and it was listed at the same price in Green's catalogue for 1780, but noted as being the property of another publisher. By 1791 impressions were available from William Richardson at the reduced price of 7s 6d. The plate was eventually sold in 1818 after Josiah Boydell's death, in a lot which included six proofs and thirty-eight impressions, as well as three other theatrical plates; the lot was sold to Colnaghi for £18 7s 6d.[2] At some stage between 1818 and 1830 the plate was drastically cut down.

Reddish seems to have been criticised by almost every commentator who cared to mention his name, but the indications are that he had a considerable number of loyal followers. Posthumus seems to have been a part with which he was particularly associated, and it is unlikely that Boydell would have invested in the plate had he been such a poor actor. The rather cruel opinion of the critic in *The Theatrical Review* may obscure the purpose of Reddish's lengthy visits to the Society of Artists; perhaps it was here that he persuaded both Valentine Green and Boydell to become involved in the scheme to publish the mezzotint. The composition of this picture may have been influenced by the portrait of Garrick in the part of Richard III painted by Francis Hayman, which was exhibited in 1746. Reddish or Pine may have known this painting in 1771 and it would undoubtedly have appealed to Reddish to be ranked alongside Garrick by being depicted in a fine history painting. It is remarkable that so few actors in this period followed Reddish's example in commissioning artists to paint their portraits; Reddish merely emulated Garrick by publicising his own merit. It is particularly interesting to compare this portrait with Dance's picture of Garrick as Richard III (see page 67), which it predates by three years.

This print depicts Posthumus as he realises Imogen's innocence in Act 5, Scene V:

O, give me cord, or knife, or poison
Some upright justicer! Thou, king, send out
For torturers ingenious: it is I
That all th' abhorred things o' th' earth amend
By being worse than they. I am Posthumus,
That kill'd thy daughter: villain-like, I lie;
That caus'd a lesser villain than myself,
A sacrilegious thief, to do't. The temple
Of Virtue was she; yea, and she herself.

Samuel Reddish was born in 1735 in Frome, the son of a tradesman. Initially he was apprenticed to a surgeon at Plymouth where he tried unsuccessfully to join the theatre. He managed to join the Norwich company, appearing there and at Richmond for two years in minor parts. Failing to gain employment at Drury Lane or Covent Garden, he went to Smock Alley in Dublin, where he gained both a good reputation and heavy debts. He first appeared at Drury Lane in September 1767 in *The Provoked Husband*, a performance that according to Hopkins was well received. Cross[3] considered him to be an indifferent figure, but suggested that he would be a useful player in the company. Reddish remained at Drury Lane for the following ten seasons until he played Hamlet at Covent Garden in 1778. 'By particular desire' he was seen as Posthumus for his benefit in May 1779, his last appearance on the stage. By this time his memory was failing; it is said that whilst in the Green Room prior to taking the stage as Posthumus, he continually lapsed into the part of Romeo, but to everyone's relief once on the stage he actually played rather better than usual, being 'more natural and less assuming.'. He died at York asylum in December 1785, having gone completely mad.

He tended to be very violent in his acting and was a troublesome character, as Garrick wrote to Hopkins:

> Mr Reddish wants more Indulgence from ye Managers, they wish that he would indulge himself with less Swearing before ye Performers, & dressers in his room, that damn him if he would walk again ... let Mr Reddish know ... his treatment of his Brother Comedians ... is ungenerous, & unjust ...'.[4]

Lichtenberg was particularly uncomplimentary about him and declared: 'I still think that Reddish, who played the devilish Iago, an odious creature. Alas for all lips and noses which resemble his, if ever I write a treatise on physiognomy!'[5]

Reddish was never considered a first-rate performer; after columns praising a memorable portrayal by Garrick of Richard III, one reviewer could only add that: 'The rest of the drama was not in general so well filled as we could wish. – Mr. Reddish ranted poor King Henry into Ribbons. &c.'. His form was 'stiff and heavy', his face 'rigid' and his voice 'monotonous'. When playing the character of Vainlove for the first time, Reddish was hissed off stage by the audience; he made a grovelling apology and explained that he had only had very short notice, with just two rehearsals: 'So great a Lye was never delivered to an audience by any Actor or Actress before', snorted Hopkins, saying that Reddish had been given the part six weeks beforehand and had only attended three of the six rehearsals.

[1] *Theatrical Biography*, I, p. 107.

[2] Sold with '*Garrick as Richard III*', '*Yates as the Tragic Muse*', and a print of Garrick in an oval, possibly the one by Robert Stewart.

[3] Richard Cross (d. 1760), Drury Lane prompter (1740–60)

[4] *Letters*, no. 659, [11 Nov. 1771].

[5] Lichtenberg, p. 32.

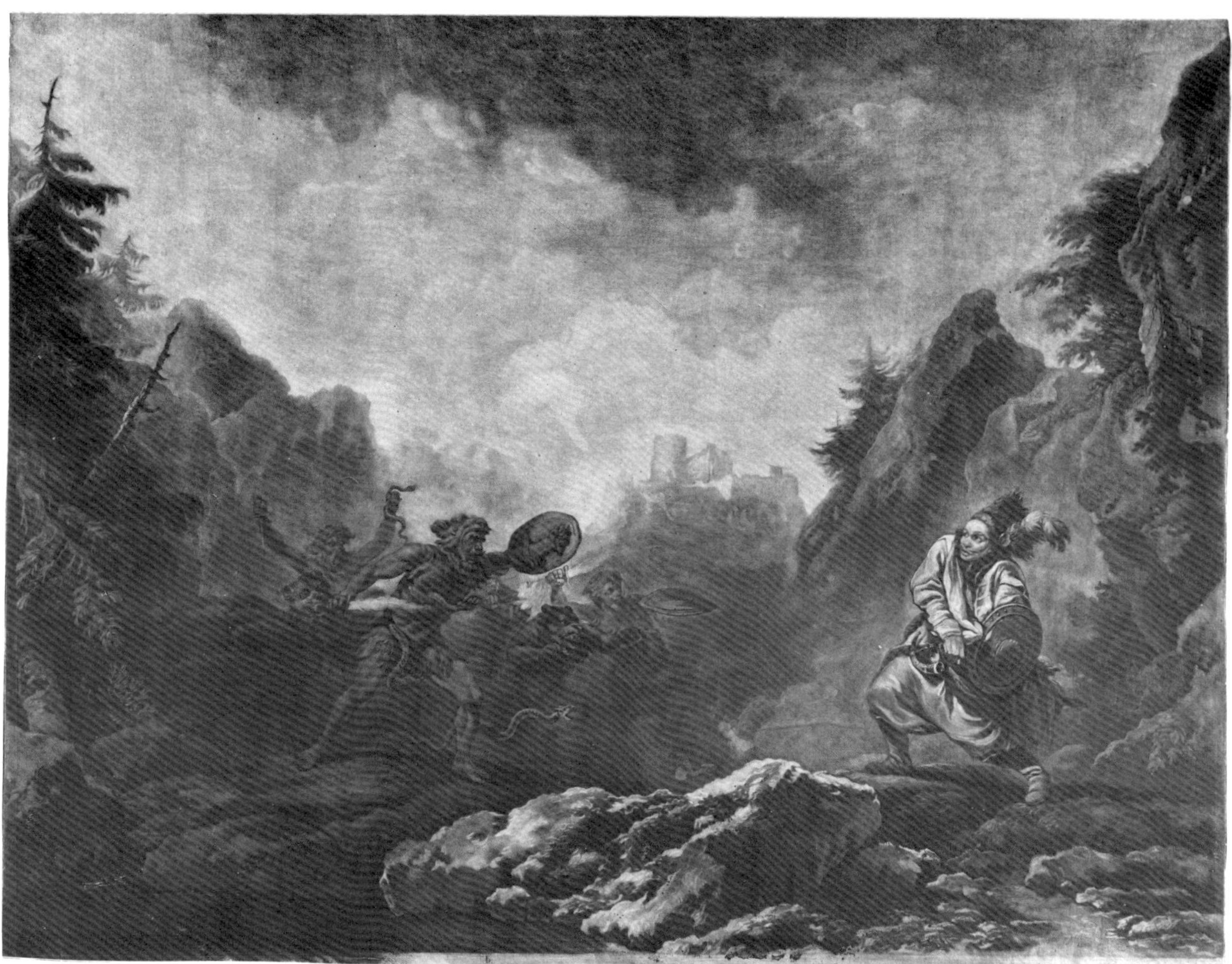

31 M.r Weston in the Character of Tycho, Encountring the Evil Spirits

Engraved by Charles Phillips
after Philippe Jacques de Loutherbourg

Published by Victor-Marie Picot 29 May 1776

Image cut to 465 x 585

References: CS 4

1. Unfinished proof before all letters.
Impressions: CLB P36,002 (impression exhibited).

2. Finished proof with the engraved inscription: "P. I. de Loutherbourg Painter to the King of France, pinx.! *** Charles Phillips fecit. / [in three columns] M.r WESTON in the CHARAC-TER of TYCHO, Encountring [sic] the Evil SPIRITS. // The 3.d Scene of the 4 Part of the CHRISTMAS TALE. – / Pub May, 29, 1776. by M.r Picot N.o 16 in y.e Strand // This PLATE is ADDRESS'D to DAVID GARRICK, Esq.r, as a Lover & Friend of the ARTS, by his Friend & Servant P,, I,, De,, Loutherbourg.".
Impressions: BM (cut); H.

De Loutherbourg exhibited the painting at the Royal Academy in 1774 and it has not been seen since.[1] The mezzotint, which was dedicated to Garrick, was exhibited at the Society of Artists in 1778 and in 1779. Little is known about Charles Phillips, whose work can be extremely fine. It seems that he was active from about 1766–80 and engraved a number of plates for Boydell, particularly in his early years. This print may have been intended as a tribute, either to Garrick upon his retirement from the stage, or to Weston, who died at the end of December 1775.

The print was published by the engraver and printseller Victor Marie Picot, who engraved at least five other plates after de Loutherbourg. Picot was born in Monthières and is said to have been brought over to England by William Wynne Ryland in 1766. Once in England, he lived with François Simon Ravenet, possibly working as his assistant, and later married his daughter Angelique. In 1771 he was in partnership with Jean Marie Delattre, who appears to have worked for John Boydell. The plate seems to have remained in Picot's possession and was never re-published. Only three impressions of this print are known and no references to the plate or to any impressions have been found amongst the many printsellers' catalogues that have been consulted.

De Loutherbourg was born in 1740 at Strasbourg, the son of a miniature painter to the Court of Darmstadt. He became the pupil of Carle van Loo and learnt engraving from Jean-Georges Wille.[2]

In *The Christmas Tale* Camilla is advised by her father, who lies on his deathbed, to marry only the man who can give proof of 'what the enchanted wood unfolds'. Written in gold on a laurel there appear the words Valour, Constancy and Honour. Her lover Floridor is the son of the good magician Bonoro, who warns him never to set eyes on the bad magician, Nigromant, unless it is to destroy him. Camilla needs protection from Nigromant and so Bonoro prepares a sword and shield for Floridor, asking him to meanwhile guard a prison, in which he has gathered the evil spirits. Floridor delegates responsibility to his squire Tycho, who falls asleep; the spirits escape amidst thunder and lightning to plague the isle where they 'revel, dance & sing'. The evil spirits are of an eighteenth-century fashion – a Jesuit, an attorney, an actress, a gamester and so forth. Bonoro forgives Floridor, who acquits himself with valour, constancy and honour. Floridor follows Nigromant first to a lake of fire and then to his castle from which he rescues Camilla; the castle then burns down in the finale.

His success was considerable and he was nominated as 'peintre de roi' in 1766. He came to London in 1771 with a letter of introduction to Garrick, who soon employed him as a scenery painter. De Loutherbourg first had an opportunity to display his talents with the pantomime *The Pigmy Revels*. De Loutherbourg abandoned stage design for illustration and genre painting at the end of 1781, for no one was prepared to pay him the high salary that he had demanded of Garrick. He was recognised as a history painter and elected to the Royal Academy. He died in 1812.

Performed for the first time on 27 December 1773, *The Christmas Tale* was said to have been written in haste by Garrick, in order to display 'some fine Scenes which were design'd by Mons De Loutherberg particularly a Burning Palace &c. which was extremely fine & Novel'.[3] Genest remarked '– if it had been brought out as an afterpiece and a spectacle, it might have passed without censure, but such things when produced as first pieces must excite the indignation of all but barren spectators ...'.[4]

De Loutherbourg's revolutionary effects were overwhelming and Garrick's faith in him justified; a reviewer wrote after the first performance:

... The scenes are all new, excellent in their kind, have beautiful effects, and do g[r]eat humour to the Painters. The first is a river, with a castle at a distance; the second a Gentleman's seat, seen through an avenue arched with trees; the third is a cave, with separate dungeons enclosed with grates; the fourth a wood, in which the trees change colour alternately from green to red, resembling fire; the fifth a piece of ruins, with a sarcophagus; the sixth distant rocks, with a river of (very unnatural) fire, which at the blowing of Tycho's horn, disappears, and discovers a beautiful bay, with a castle on a promontory; the front of a castle next appears; seventh, (and the fourth act) are closed with a triumphal entry of the spirits in chains, followed by Tycho riding on a rhinoceros the eighth is a triumphal Turkish throne, as we mentioned before, succeeded by a horrid scene of fire, with the ebullition of blood, and the stage darkened. This is followed by a blue scene (the ninth) and the rising of the moon; a cloud then descends, and opening discovers the Hermit within them; soon after it rises again and exhibits to view a castle by the sea side.[5]

As can be seen from this description, De Loutherbourg's stage innovations were ambitious and hugely imaginative. These were all intended to further illusion and to encourage the audience to suspend disbelief. He utilised spectacular new devices, such as the introduction of mechanical scene drops, which prevented interruptions from stage hands, and subtle lighting which could be changed by the use of silk screens and transparencies. De Loutherbourg used additional stage tricks such as setting moons and rising suns to control the exits and entrances of players. Stage sets were redesigned by breaking up the wing flats and borders into a number of smaller pieces, creating a convincing effect of depth and distance; realistic landscape scenery was added, with rocks, caves, rolling hills, forests and lakes, adding diversity and a natural irregularity.

Thomas Weston was born in 1737. He went to sea as a midshipman, but soon left and joined a theatrical company playing around London. In the summer of 1761, he was at Drury Lane under

NEVER PERFORMED.

By His MAJESTY's COMPANY,

At the Theatre Royal in DRURY-LANE,

This present Monday, Dec. 27, 1773,

Will be presented a New Dramatic Entertainment, call'd

A Christmas Tale.

The PRINCIPAL CHARACTERS by

Mr. VERNON, Mr. BANNISTER,
Mr. WESTON, Mr. PARSONS,
Mr. CHAMPNES, Mr. HURST,
Mr. DIMOND, Mr. W. PALMER,
Mr. ACKMAN, Mr. WRIGHT, Mr BURTON,
Mr. Griffith, Mr. Wrighten, Master Blanchard,
Mr. Fawcett, Mr. Kear, Mr Blanchard, Mr. Courtney,
Mrs. WRIGHTEN, Mrs. SCOTT,
Mrs HUNT, Mrs. JOHNSTON, Miss PLATT,
And Mrs. SMITH.

The DANCES by

Sig. COMO, Sig. GRIMALDI, Mr. ATKINS, Sig. GIORGI,
Signora CRESPI, Mrs. SUTTON, Signora GIORGI, &c.

With a PROLOGUE,

After which a New OVERTURE.

New Scenes, Dresses, Music, Machinery
and Decorations.

To which will be added,

MISS in her TEENS.

The Doors will be opened at FIVE o'Clock.

To begin exactly at SIX o'Clock.   Vivant Rex & Regina.

Foote and Murphy who rented the theatre for twenty three performances. He was again with Foote at Drury Lane in the summer of 1763 where his performance as Jerry Sneak in Foote's *The Mayor of Garrat*, a part written for him, was highly acclaimed. Weston was very much the mainstay of Foote's theatre in the Haymarket, a tribute to the quality of his acting.

His personal life continually let him down; he was a heavy drinker and his extravagance was legendary. On one occasion his debts at Drury Lane forced the management to take stern measures:

> Last night, between the play and farce at Drury-lane theatre, a disturbance arose, which continued a full hour. Mr Weston, it appeared was in debt to the Managers a sum of money, on which account they had impounded all the cash received on his benefit night; this the Comedian did not like, and therefore yesterday sent word that he could not play, as he was arrested, and detained in a Spunging-house.[6]

It was announced that Weston would be unable to play due to 'suddenly being taken ill'; at this moment, Weston, released on bail for the evening, popped up from his position in the upper gallery and attempted to explain the situation from his point of view. He was eventually persuaded to come down and play the part of Sneak.

Weston was a master of timing, the perfect 'straight man' in comedy; Lichtenberg felt that he was more 'droll' than Garrick:

> Weston is a strange creature, whom nature seems to have designed to move others to laughter without having given him the faculty of laughing himself. I have never seen him laugh on stage, nor have I observed the least sign that he had any difficulty suppressing it; and I am told that he laughs very seldom off the stage: nevertheless, his form and his whole nature are quite unsuited to grave things and he would absolutely ruin a serious part.[7]

Characteristically, Weston once chose to play the part of Richard III for a benefit performance; Lichtenberg suggests that this was probably the only time that Shakespeare was deliberately 'profaned' in the theatre. At the end of the play when the moment came for Richard to die, the audience was so delighted by his antics that they clamoured for him to rise up and die once again.

Weston died in January 1776 of 'habitual drunkenness', and was summed up by Garrick as having been, 'a good Actor, & a very bad Man – ...'.[8]

[1] There is a drawing of *Floridor fighting Negromant and the Demons* at the Musée des Beaux-arts, Strasburg and another of *Bonoro's cell* in the collection of Sir Brinsley Ford. There is also an anonymous etching of the latter in the British Museum.
[2] Jean-Georges Wille (1715–1808), engraver.
[3] William Hopkins' Diary quoted in *The London Stage*, IV, p. 1774.
[4] Genest, V, p. 401.
[5] *The London Chronicle*, 28 Dec. 1773.
[6] *ibid.*, 25 April 1772. His debts stood at nearly £12,000.
[7] Lichtenberg, pp. 2–3.
[8] *Letters*, no. 954, 7 Nov. [1775].

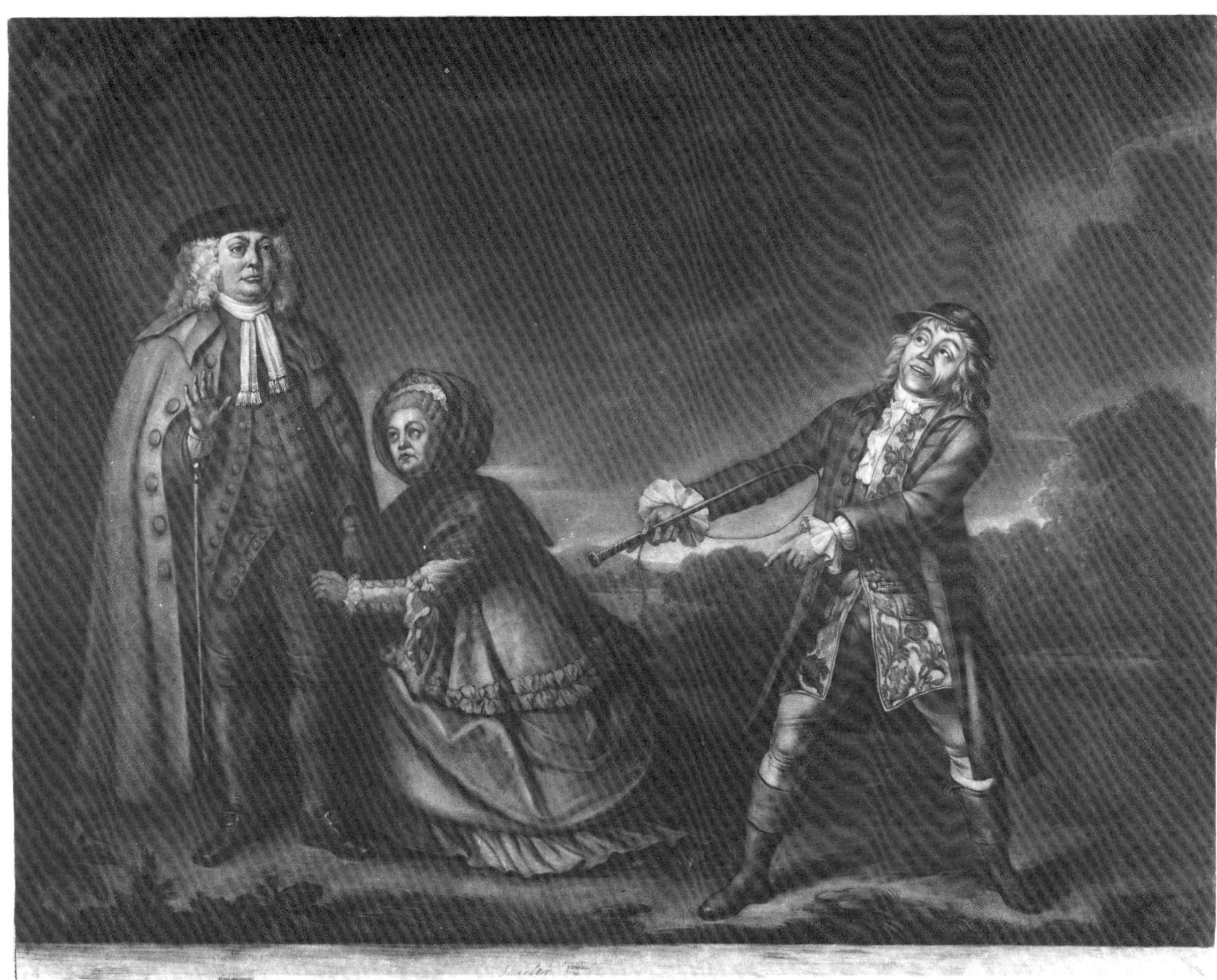

32 M.ʳ Shuter, M.ʳ Quick and M.ʳˢ Green in the Characters of Hardcastle, Tony Lumpkin & M.ʳˢ Hardcastle

Engraved by Robert Laurie
after Thomas Parkinson

Published by Robert Sayer and John Bennett
4 July 1776

432 x 550 I; 454 x 550 Pl.

References: CS 35; O'D groups p. 29

1. Finished proof with the scratched inscription: "[…] Digna Societas […]diem […] perficiet […]".
Impressions: CLB P14,141 (impression exhibited).

2. [Finished proof with the scratched inscription: "Tho.ˢ Parkinson pinx.ᵗ ∗∗∗ R. Laurie fecit.". (CS)].

Thomas Parkinson exhibited his painting at the Royal Academy in 1774. It now hangs in a private collection in Toronto. It is possible that the mezzotint was published to commemorate Shuter's last performance at Drury Lane, which was his own benefit in May 1776. This print, which was not exhibited, was engraved by Robert Laurie whilst he was still Robert Sayer's apprentice; Laurie was not released from his apprenticeship until May 1777, when he attempted to set up as an independent engraver. By 1788 at the latest, Laurie had returned to help in Sayer's business in some capacity. An entry in the rate assessments for the parish of St Dunstan's in the West records that Sayer's successors, Laurie & Whittle, were printers in Sayer's premises in Bolt Court; this was at a time when Sayer was still trading in Fleet Street. Described as his 'assistants in trade', Laurie & Whittle may well have also acted as in-house printers. The fact that Laurie won a premium from the Society of Arts 'for disclosing his method of printing Mezzotinto in colours' reinforces this suggestion.

Laurie's engraving style is usually harsh and brassy and he lacks finesse in his draughtsmanship. Some of these defects are evident in this plate, although they are less offensive than in other plates by him; this is probably because Laurie's abilities rather suit

3. Finished proof with the engraved inscription: "*Tho,' Parkinson pinx,', *** R. Laurie fecit. /* London, Printed for R. Sayer & J. Bennett, No 53 in Fleet Street, as the Act directs 4 July 1776.".

Impressions: CLB; BM; H.

4. [With the engraved title added: "Mr Shuter, Mr Quick and Mrs Green in the Characters of Hardcastle, Tony Lumpkin & Mrs Hardcastle She Stoops to Conquer, Act V. Scene I.". (CS)].

☞ In Goldsmith's comedy *She Stoops to Conquer, or The Mistakes of a Night*, Sir Charles Marlow has proposed a match between his son and a certain Miss Hardcastle. In order to meet her, young Marlow sets out with his friend Hastings. Losing their way, they arrive at an inn where the mischievous Tony Lumpkin, Mrs Hardcastle's son by a previous marriage, directs them to another nearby. This 'inn' is actually the Hardcastles' house. Young Marlow, apt in general to be overly shy and retiring, is somewhat more bullish in the company of barmaids and serving girls; he treats his prospective father-in-law as a landlord and makes fierce advances on his prospective wife, under his misapprehension. Fortunately, all is explained when Sir Charles arrives.

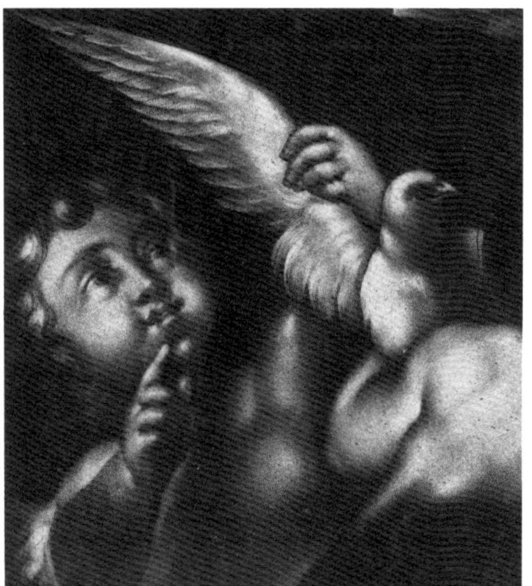

Venus and Cupid (detail).   R. Laurie

Parkinson's wooden style. His faults are perfectly illustrated in the dreadful print that he engraved of Venus and Cupid after Carlo Cignani (see detail below). His harsh reworking of McArdell's '*Venice Preserved*' is unmistakable. In addition to Carington Bowles's version of this plate, Sayer & Bennett's similar sized mezzotint anticipated the publication of Laurie's print.

Jane Green was born in 1719, daughter of the comedian John Hippisley. She was first referred to, as 'Hippisley's Daughter', in the bills for March 1735. In 1740–1 she became a member of the Goodman's Fields troupe, playing a variety of different parts. She probably met Henry Green in Bristol in the summer of 1743. In 1747–8 she was part of the company put together by Garrick in this, his first season as manager of Drury Lane.

Jane Green kept her connection with the Bristol theatre, performing there every summer from 1756–72. She was at Covent Garden until the end of the 1779–80 season and sang in the first performance of Sheridan's *The Duenna*. She was the first Mrs Hardcastle in *She Stoops to Conquer* and gave her last performance in this role in May 1780. When presented for the first time on 15 March 1773 at Drury Lane, the play was extremely well received and it is said that four thousand copies of the text sold within three days. Garrick took great time and care over her, leading to rumours that they had an affair, and even that this resulted in a child, Samuel Cautherley the actor.

She began her career as sweet-voiced characters in ballad-operas, but 'early corpulence' meant that Mrs Green was better suited to playing country girls and domestics. While she did attempt to create a style of her own, her acting derived much from that of Mrs Clive:

> Mrs Green, of all the female players, in comic humour came the nearest to this admirable comedian. It was Mrs Green's misfortune to live at the same time with Clive. I shall as soon expect to see another Butler, Rabelais, or Swift, as a Clive.[1]

Tate Wilkinson asserted that at Covent Garden Mrs Green was held in 'universal and deserved admiration', although it was difficult for her to make her mark in a theatre dominated by such formidable leading ladies as Clive:

> … Her person is well suited to the dignity of the part[2] but an endeavour too much to please, in some degree destroyed the design; a fixed smile almost constantly remained on her countenance, that marred the effect of tragic expression, which her eyes seem well calculated to make … Neither had she acquired that easy deportment, that graceful action which prejudice so much in favour of a Yates or Barry … however … she may be an ornament to the stage in such a dearth of tragic actresses.[3]

She died in August 1791 at her house in Bristol and was buried in Clifton Church.

Her supporting actors, John Quick and Edward Shuter both had distinguished careers: Quick was engraved in '*The Duenna*' (see page 102) and together with Shuter in '*Love in a Village*' (see page 115). Unlike the other actors portrayed in this print, Shuter's fame was sufficiently great for his portrait to be engraved (see page 91).

[1] *Dramatic Miscellanies*, III, p. 324.
[2] Queen Elizabeth in the *Earl of Essex*.
[3] *Town and Country Magazine*, Nov. 1773.

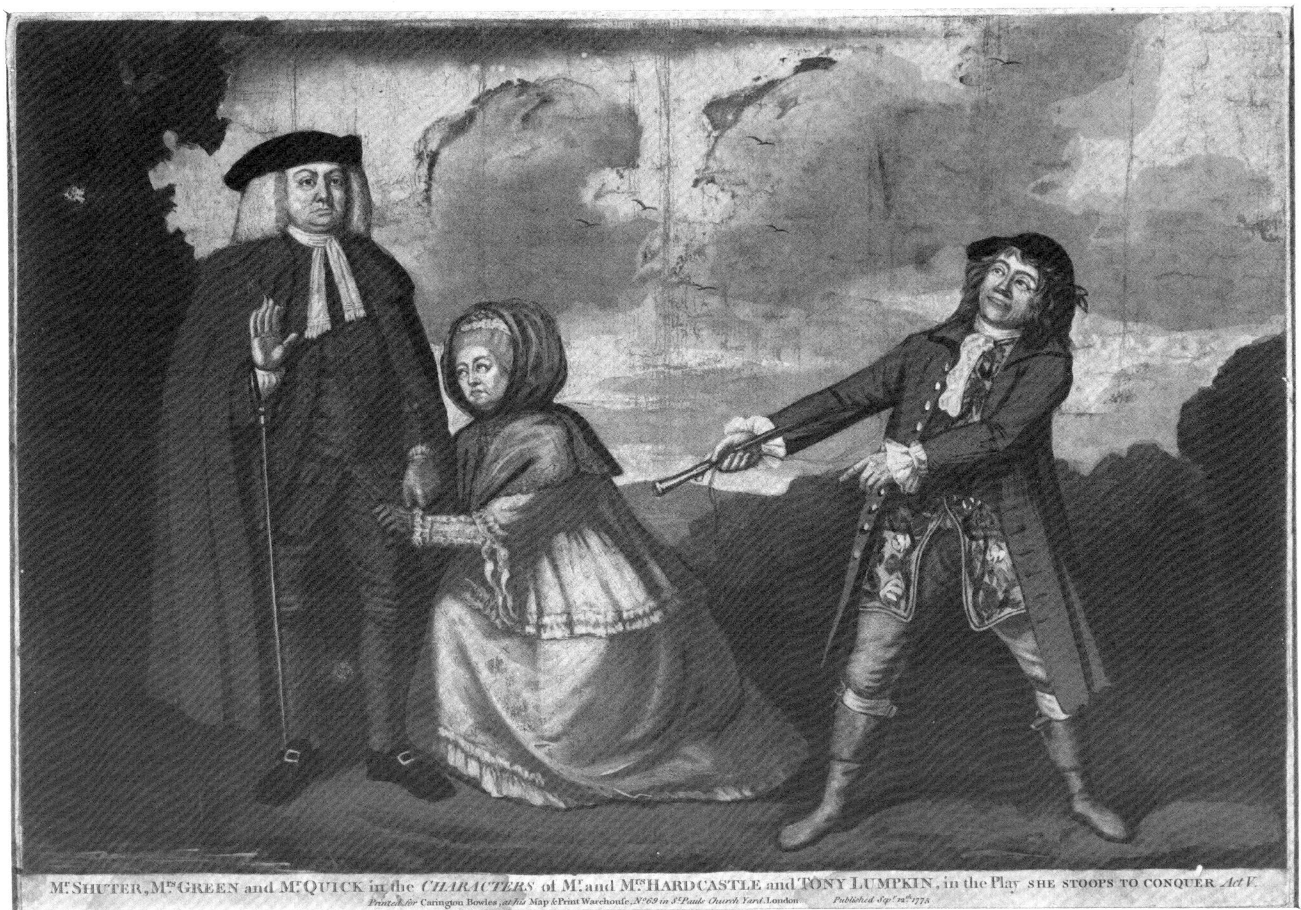

33 M.ʳ Shuter, M.ʳˢ Green and M.ʳ Quick in the Characters of M.ʳ and M.ʳˢ Hardcastle and Tony Lumpkin, in the Play She Stoops to Conquer

Anonymous mezzotint after Thomas Parkinson

Published by Carington Bowles
12 September 1775

240 x 352 I; 251 x 353 Pl.

References: CS p. 808

1. Finished proof before all letters.
Impressions: CLB.

2. Finished proof with the engraved inscription: "M.ʳ SHUTER, M.ʳˢ GREEN and M.ʳ QUICK in the CHARACTERS of M.ʳ and M.ʳˢ HARDCASTLE and TONY LUMPKIN, in the Play SHE STOOPS TO CONQUER Act V. / *Printed for* Carington Bowles, *at his* Map & Print Warehoufe, *N.º 69 in S.ᵗ Pauls Church Yard*, London. *Published Sep.ᵗ 12.ᵗʰ 1775.*".
Impressions: CLB P32,737 (impression exhibited); TM.

Engravings of this size could be produced quickly by journeyman engravers or apprentices and were sold as popular prints which would have cost 1s uncoloured or 2s for a hand coloured impression. Usually, since they could be engraved and printed in days rather than weeks, this format was used for piracies. Robert Sayer was the most flagrant in his use of copyists and it is from this practice that he is said to have made his fortune. His main rivals were John Bowles and his son Carington, who ran separate businesses in the City. The Bowles family and Sayer pirated each other's prints, but also produced copies of prints by major engravers and other publishers (see page 27).

Carington Bowles's anonymous 'half-sheet' mezzotint was the first print after Thomas Parkinson's painting to be published; in February 1776 Sayer & Bennett published another mezzotint of the same size. It is possible that Sayer was aware of the successful sales of Bowles's print and so decided to make a copy. Both publishers, no doubt, were aware of the popular appeal of the play. Sayer & Bennett then published another plate in July, engraved by Robert Laurie, which was nearly twice the size of the earlier prints (see page 77). This was probably prompted by news of Shuter's impending retirement.

Normally it would be safe to assume that Carington Bowles's mezzotint was a piracy; this is unlikely in this case, since there is no indication that Sayer & Bennett's large plate was authorised by Parkinson and there was no need for Bowles to pre-empt Sayer &

NEVER PERFORMED.

THEATRE-ROYAL
In COVENT-GARDEN,

This present MONDAY, MARCH 15. 1773,
Will be presented a NEW COMEDY, call'd

She Stoops to Conquer;

Or, The MISTAKES of a NIGHT.

The PRINCIPAL PARTS by

Mr. SHUTER,
Mr. QUICK,
Mr. LEWES,
Mr. DU-BELLAMY,
Mr. GARDNER,
Mr. SAUNDERS, Mr. THOMPSON, Mr. DAVIS,
Mr. HOLTOM, Mr. STOPPELAER, Mr. BATES,
Mrs. GREEN,
Mrs. KNIVETON,
Mrs. BULKLEY,

To which will be added

THOMAS and SALLY.

The Squire by Mr. MATTOCKS,
Sailor by Mr. DU-BELLAMY,
Dorcas by Mrs. GREEN,
Sally by Mrs. MATTOCKS.
With a Hornpipe by Miss BESFORD.

The Doors to be opened at FIVE o'Clock.
To begin at SIX o'Clock. Vivant Rex & Regina.

Bennett's large print, which was not published for ten months.

Carington Bowles's output included maps, humorous mezzotints, good quality topography, some portraits and a staple of general engravings like drawing books. He died in 1793 aged sixty-nine. His son, Henry Carington Bowles, married well and continued the business in partnership with Samuel Carver, his father's manager; they ceased trading in about 1830 but the Bowles family prospered, receiving a baronetcy in 1926. Carington Bowles produced a few theatrical engravings, which, with the exception of two versions of '*Dibdin as Mungo*' (see page 85) and another of '*Mattocks and Quick in the Duenna*' (see page 102), were all piracies of large mezzotints. Although nowadays his business is considered to be have been on a par with Sayer's, it was less extensive since he issued far fewer large plates.

It is not known who coloured this type of print. They could have been coloured by apprentices, although printsellers may have contracted the work out to professional colourists. Certainly, colouring was a service offered by the printsellers and most 'posture' mezzotints were advertised 'plain' or 'coloured'. The colouring tends to be in body colour, watercolour with chalk added, which sits above the surface of the mezzotint. Some think this method of colouring is crude but it is highly prized by collectors and it is now rare to find examples of this sort.

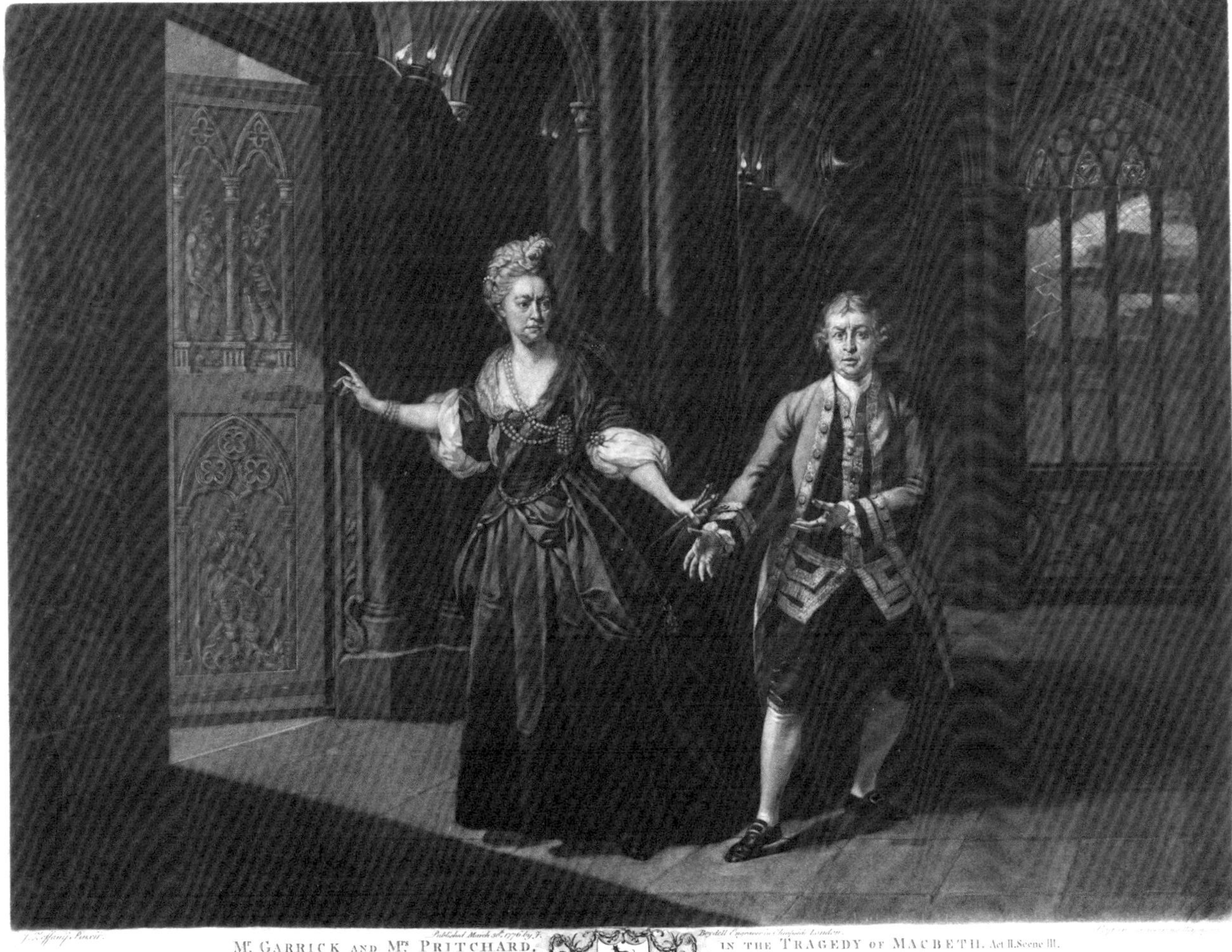

34 Mʳ Garrick and Mʳˢ Pritchard in the Tragedy of Macbeth

Engraved by Valentine Green
after Johann Zoffany

Published by John Boydell 30 March 1776

423 x 554 I; 455 x 555 Pl.

References: CS 47; R 47; W 6; Hall
(Garrick) 236

**1. [Finished proof with the scratched
inscription:** "J. Zoffanij Pinxit. Published
March 30ᵗʰ 1776, by J. Boydell Engraver in
Cheapſide, London. V. Green, Engraver to his
Majesty fecit" (R)].
Impressions: said to be at Harvard.

**2. Finished proof with the scratched inscrip-
tion (arms etched in c.):** "*Published March 30ᵗʰ
1776, by J. Boydell, Engraver, *** in Cheapſide,*

The original painting, which was not exhibited, is now in the
Baroda Museum, India. At the time that the print was published,
the painting was in the possession of George Keate, to whom
Boydell applied for permission to have it engraved. The painting
was probably intended to commemorate Hannah Pritchard's retirement; after a partnership of twenty years, she and Garrick played
these parts for the last time at her farewell benefit on 25 April
1768. On this occasion tickets for the pit and boxes cost 10s 6d, the
price charged for this print by Boydell. Garrick wrote the farewell
address and Mrs Pritchard entreated people to send their servants
by three o'clock and to arrive early themselves. The plate,
together with thirty-one proofs, was eventually sold in 1818 after
Josiah Boydell's death. It was purchased by 'Walker' for sixteen
guineas, together with the plates to '*Garrick and Miss Bellamy in
Romeo and Juliet*' and '*The Mayor of Garrat*' (see page 33). In 1780
the print was included in Green's four page catalogue of his own
works, priced at 10s 6d.

The print illustrates the scene in which Macbeth returns to his
wife with two daggers in his blood-soaked hands, having just murdered Duncan. A particularly taxing part, it was not one which
Garrick played frequently; he appeared in 'the Scottish play' thir-

London. | J. Zoffanij, Pinxit. *** V. Green, Engraver to his Majesty, fecit. | MR GARRICK AND M^{RS} PRITCHARD IN THE *TRAGEDY OF MACBETH*, ACT *II*, SCENE *III*.".
Impressions: CLB P34,779 (impression exhibited); BM; TM; H.

3. With the engraved inscription: "I. Zoffanij Pinxit. *** V. Green Engraver to his Majesty fecit. | *Published March 30.th 1776 by J. *** Boydell Engraver in Cheapfide London.* | Mr GARRICK AND Mrs PRITCHARD, IN THE TRAGEDY OF MACBETH. Act II. Scene III. | *From the Original Picture painted by J. Zoffanij, *** in the poffeffion of George Keate Esqr, | To whom this PLATE *** is Inscribed, by his Most Humble Servant. | *** *** JOHN BOYDELL.*".
Impressions: CLB; BM; TM; H.

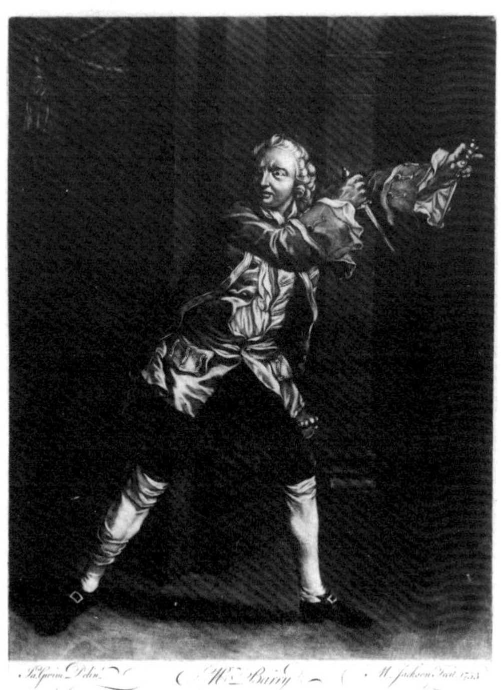

teen times in 1744 but then only another twenty-four times in his entire career. Garrick had adapted the play himself in 1744, replacing Davenant's version which had been used for the previous seventy-five years. His revised version 'broke through the fetters of foolish custom and arbitrary imposition' and gave him more scope to express the emotions of horror and grief.

Garrick added a new dying speech for Macbeth since he 'excelled in the expression of convulsive throes and dying agonies, and would not lose any opportunity to show his skill in that part of his profession'.[1] The dagger scene was one of Garrick's particular specialities:

> when he was in Italy, and requested by the Duke of Parma to give a proof of his skill in action, to the admiration of that prince, he at once threw himself into the attitude of Macbeth's seeing the air-drawn dagger. The duke desired no further proof of his excellence, being perfectly convinced by this specimen, that he was absolute master of it.[2]

Thomas Davies, who played Ross in this production, describes Garrick and Mrs Pritchard in their roles:

> The beginning of the scene ... was conducted in terrifying stage whispers. Their looks and agitation of the mind supplied the place of words. You heard what they spoke, but you learned more from the agitation of the minds played in their action and deportment ... The dark colouring given by the actor to these abrupt speeches, makes the scene awful and tremendous to the auditors. The wonderful expression of heartful terror, which Garrick felt when he shewed his bloody hands, can only be conceived and described by those who saw him!... The representation of this terrible part of the play, by Garrick and Mrs Pritchard, can no more be described than I believe it can be equalled ... the merits of both were transcendent.[3]

Mrs Pritchard was held to be the greatest Lady Macbeth of her day, despite Garrick's opinion that she was 'apt to blubber her sorrows'. She was engraved by McArdell after Hayman (see page 18) and by Aliamet as Hermione in *The Winter's Tale*, as well as in *Miss in her Teens* and *The Roman Father*. Garrick's main rival, Spranger Barry, appears in the same scene in a mezzotint by Michael Jackson after James Gwynn (see left).

[1] *Dramatic Miscellanies*, II, p. 118.
[2] *ibid.*, II, p. 141.
[3] *ibid.*, II, p. 148.

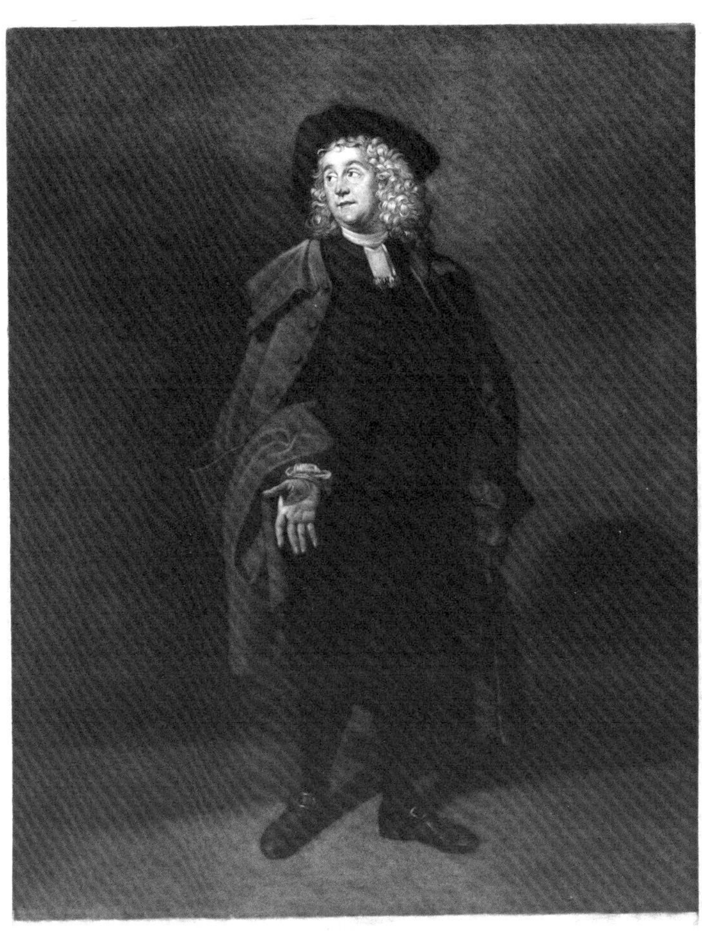

35 M.ʳ Moody, in the Character of Foiguard

Engraved by Giuseppe Marchi
after Johann Zoffany

[Published by] sold by John Wesson [1769–71]

462 x 354 I; 505 x 354 Pl.

References: CS 11; R 11; O'D 9; Hall 5

1. Progress proof before white highlights and before the face and hands were finished and etching was added.
Impressions: CLB.

2. Progress proof before all letters, almost finished.
Impressions: BM.

3. Finished proof before all letters.
Impressions: CLB P34,777 (impression exhibited); BM.

4. With the engraved inscription: "Sold by I. Wefson, in Litchfield Street Soho. / *Zaffanij pinx! *** Marchie fecit* / M.ʳ, *Moody, in the* Character *of Foiguard.* ".
Impressions: CLB; BM; H.

The painting was exhibited at the Society of Artists in 1764. The print was never exhibited and it may have been engraved some years after the picture was painted. Giuseppe Marchi, an Italian from Rome, was brought to London by Reynolds in 1752 as an assistant. When he attempted to set up on his own account, he was unsuccessful and returned to Reynolds's studio. He engraved about a dozen portraits, half of them after Reynolds, using a silvery technique like other engravers associated with the latter's studio.

The dating of this print has been suggested from the fragmentary publishing history of the printseller John Wesson. He was briefly in partnership with Ryland & Bryer in 1768 and appears to have been in business on his own from 1769, his last known publication being issued on 17 December 1771. The print does appear frequently in printsellers' catalogues of stock in the early 1770s, but the plate never seems to have passed into the stock of another publisher.

John Moody was born in 1727, the son of a Cork hairdresser, and he initially followed his father's trade. He went to Jamaica, apparently to escape conscription during the 1745 uprising, and acted with a company in Kingston. On his return in 1758 he became a principal actor at Norwich, and in September of the following year Cross recorded that Garrick had engaged Moody 'a stroler'.[1]

During the Half-Price riots in January 1763, he incensed the public by removing a burning torch from a maniac in the audience

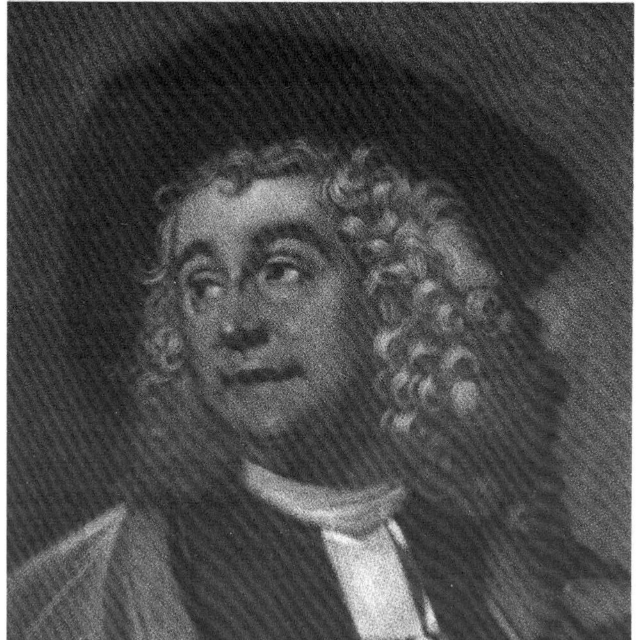 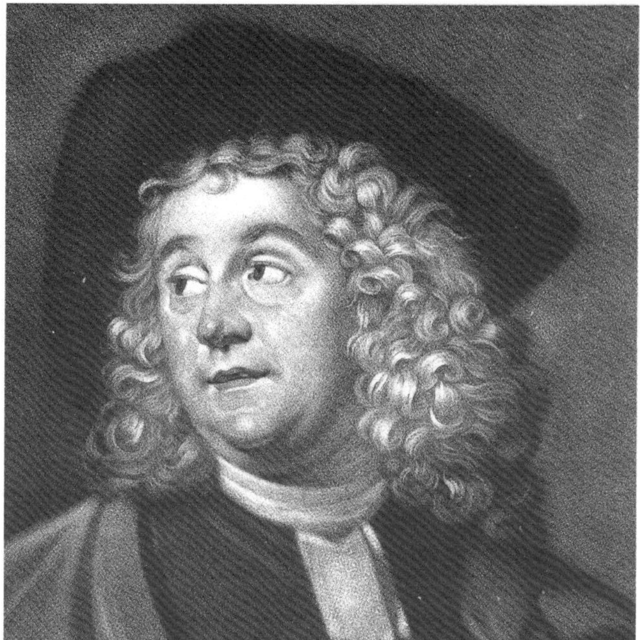

The details above show Marchi's method of engraving. In the progress proof (left) *he has finished most of the print but still has to work on the face and the hands, and to add the final highlights.*

☞ In *The Beaux' Stratagem* by George Farquhar, Aimwell and Archer, two friends who have spent their inheritance, arrive at an inn in Lichfield in search of adventure and heiresses. Archer pretends to be Aimwell's servant. There is much speculation as to who they are, and Boniface the landlord concludes that they are highwaymen. This curiosity is shared by Dorinda, daughter of the wealthy Lady Bountiful, who falls in love with Aimwell at first sight, and Mrs Sullen, wife of Lady Bountiful's son, who falls for Archer. Aimwell, thinking Dorinda a suitable prey, tricks his way into Lady Bountiful's house with Archer. An attack by rogues upon the house enables Aimwell and Archer to come to the rescue of the ladies, and both press the advantage just gained. But Aimwell, who has passed himself off as his elder brother, Lord Aimwell, is smitten with remorse and confesses the fraud to Dorinda. At this moment news arrives of the death of the real Lord Aimwell and of the accession of Aimwell to title and fortune. Sullen at the same time willingly agrees to a dissolution of his marriage, so that his wife is free to marry Archer. Amongst other people at the inn is Macshane, an Irishman, posing as Father Foiguard, a priest from Brussels who the young beaux threaten to expose.

who was about to set fire to the house. As Moody refused to apologise to an irate audience, Garrick was compelled to promise that he would not appear on the stage whilst the audience were displeased with him; Moody however confronted the ring-leader Fitzpatrick and forced a reconciliation, consequently reappearing on stage the following month.

He established a reputation as a comic Irishman, in roles that were especially written for him, such as Major O'Flaherty in *The West Indian* (see page 46). Although he was not a trained vocalist, he was often required to sing and was apparently intended for the role of Mungo in *The Padlock* (see page 85).

In 1774–5 Moody expressed dissatisfaction to Garrick about his salary, particularly as Yates, who was paid more, was taking some of his roles. By 1788 his performance had deteriorated and during his last years, he was criticised for being lazy and lethargic: 'he jogs the same trot he did ten years before ... As he knows he can charm us whenever he'll please, 'Tis a shame he gets fat and enjoys so much ease'.[2] Some critics thoroughly disliked him:

Moody devoid of spirit, humour, grace!
No strong expression of his face we find;
No passion marks the features of his mind.
Dull, sluggish, cold insensible and tame,
He gives no pleasure, and deserves no fame.[3]

Some went so far as to say that throughout thirty-seven years on the stage, 'he seldom exhibited any ambition to extend his line or exert any creative effort'.[4] He was forced to retire in 1796 but emerged again in 1804 in *The Devil to Pay*.

He died on 26 December 1812 in Shepherds Bush.

[1] Cross quoted in the TDB.
[2] Pasquin.
[3] *The Modern Stage Exemplified*, 1788.
[4] TDB.

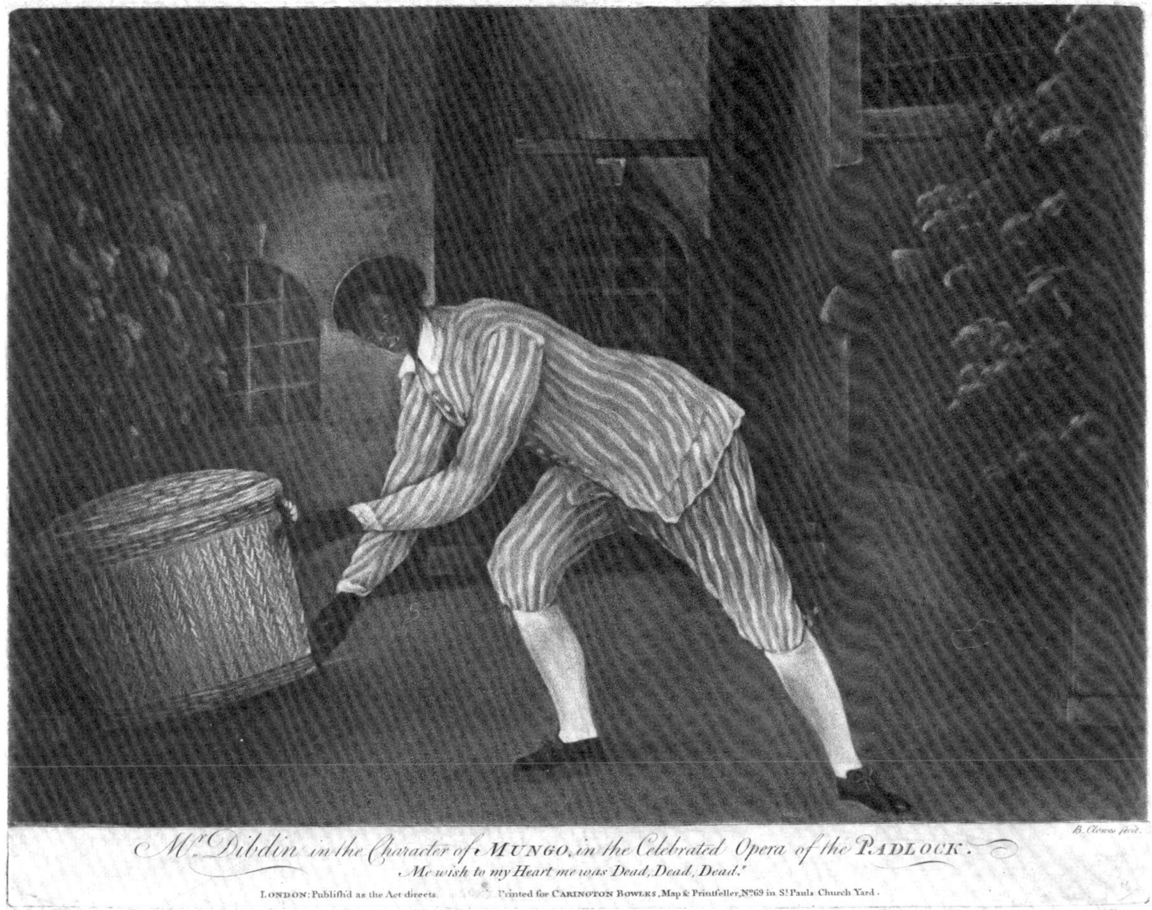

36 Mr. Dibdin in the Character of Mungo, in the Celebrated Opera of the Padlock

[Designed?] and engraved by Butler Clowes

Published by Butler Clowes 1 January 1769

Re-published by Carington Bowles

246 x 313 I; 277 x 316 Pl.

References: CS 7; O'D 11; Hall 15

1. With the engraved inscription: *"Publiſhed accordᵍ to Act of Parliamᵗ Janʸ 1. 1769. *** B. Clowes fecit.".*
Impressions: BM.

2. With the added inscription: "Mr. DIBDIN / *In the Character of Mungo, in the Celebrated OPERA of the Padlock. | "Me wish to my heart me was Dead, Dead, Dead.".*
Impressions: CLB.

3. With the plate reduced in size to 233 x 312 I; 251 x 316 Pl, with the re-engraved inscription: *"*** B. Clowes fecit. | Mr. Dibdin in the Character of MUNGO, in the Celebrated Opera of the PADLOCK. | Me wish to my Heart me was Dead,*

This rather strange print was probably engraved by Butler Clowes after his own design. Initially it seems to have been published by Clowes too, but the plate was then obtained by Carington Bowles. Bowles listed it in his catalogues for 1782 and 1784 at 1s, together with a smaller version, also by Clowes. Little is known about Clowes, who seems to have been engraving and publishing from about 1763 until at least 1775. Between 1773–5, whenever James Watson published one of his own prints he did so jointly with Clowes, although the reasons for and terms of this association remain unclear. Bromley felt that Butler Clowes was an eccentric amateur who '... amused himself with scraping the heads of his family and acquaintances from the life, without previous drawings. Few of them have any resemblance ...'.[1]

As Chaloner Smith points out, this is too severe a criticism, for despite the fact that these small portraits are crude, some of Clowes's mezzotints are excellent. His earliest plates date from 1769, and include a series of large humorous mezzotints after Dawes and Collett, which he engraved for Robert Sayer and John Smith[2] of Cheapside. Clowes also worked as an 'engraver in general', designing and engraving a number of book-plates, heraldic plates and trade-cards.

The Padlock, first produced at Drury Lane in October 1768, was an immediate success; according to Hopkins it was, '... a very compleat, pretty piece, – the music very striking ... much applauded'. It had fifty-two performances in its first season and

Dead, Dead." / LONDON: Publiſh'd as the Act directs, Jany. 1ſt. 1769. Printed for CARING-TON BOWLES, Map & Printſeller, N.º 69 in S.ᵗ Paul's Church Yard.".
Impressions: CLB P26,667 (impression exhibited); BM; TM.

☞ Isaac Bickerstaffe's comic opera *The Padlock* follows the plot of a novel by Cervantes, in which the ageing Don Diego is the temporary guardian of the young Leonora and intends to marry her. However during his absence, Leander, a young lover, arrives and, cajoling the duenna and Mungo, the negro servant, gains admission to the lady despite a large padlock on her door. Diego returns unexpectedly, but sensibly accepts the situation and handsomely endows Leonora.

nearly two hundred performances over the next decade, earning Bickerstaffe around £1,700 although Dibdin the composer earned a mere £45. The part of Mungo was originally intended for Moody, but Dibdin made the music too difficult for him since he wanted the part for himself.

Charles Dibdin was born in Southampton in 1745. His father, a parish clerk, intended him for the church. He was a chorister at Winchester Cathedral where he later became a principal singer at the Subscription Concerts. In London, he began to visit theatres whilst earning a living by playing the organ at various churches. He met John Beard, who produced a pastoral operetta for him in 1764.

The following year he played in Bickerstaffe's *The Maid of the Mill*, which ran for more than fifty nights, but was eventually driven away from acting by the envy and opposition of fellow actors and returned to his love, operatic music.

Garrick, with whom Dibdin was said to argue frequently, felt particularly strongly about Dibdin's desertion of his mistress, Harriet Pitt. He discharged Dibdin over the affair, also rejecting his *Waterman*, which later met with great and lasting success when accepted by Foote at the Haymarket.

In order to avoid angry creditors, Dibdin went to France, and on his return was engaged at Covent Garden. Again pursued by creditors, he attempted to go to India, but failed and took lodgings near the Old Bailey, hoping to make a fresh start. This was his most successful time, as he concentrated on his sea songs, considered to be his greatest achievement. He retired from the theatre in 1805, selling his stock and copyright to Anne Bland and E. Weller of Oxford Street. He lived in Camden Town and died in 1814.

[1] 'Bromley, Henry *pseud.*'[i.e. Andrew Wilson] *A Catalogue of Engraved British Portraits from Egbert the Great to the Present Time*, 1793, p. 400.
[2] John Smith (1654–1720), engraver.

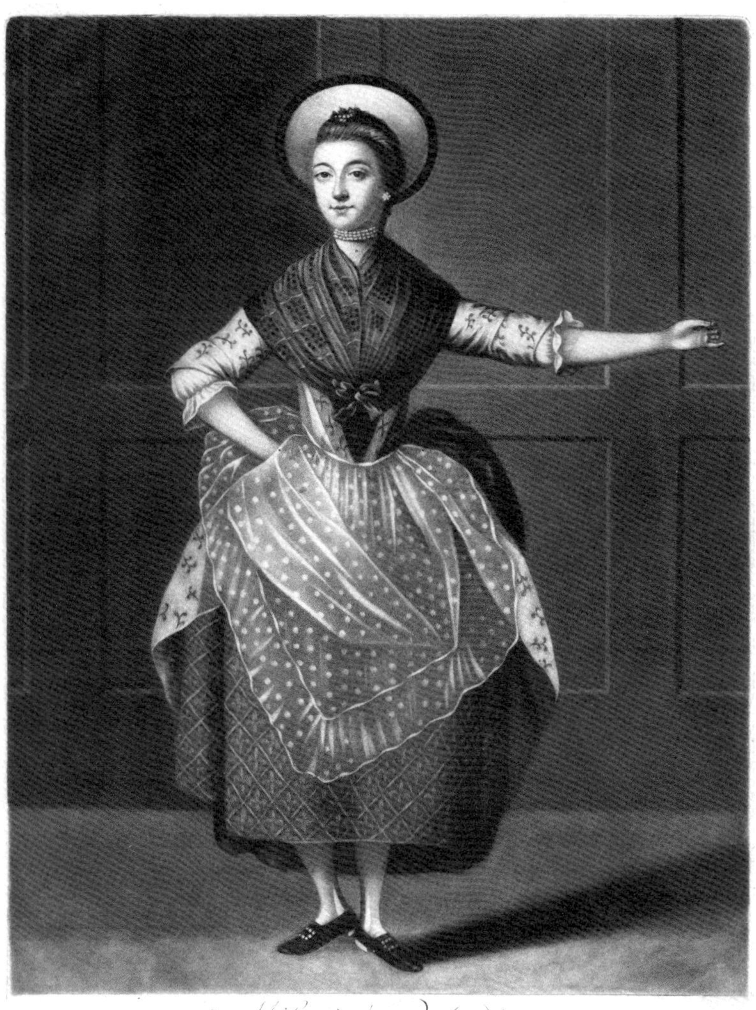

37 Miss Nancy Dawson

[Engraved and] published by
Michael Jackson [c. 1760]

Re-published for Robert Sayer [before 1768]

331 x 249 I; 353 x 251 Pl.

References: CS 2; R 2; O'D 3; Hall 2

1. With the engraved inscription: *"Miſs Nancy Dawson / Printed for M,, Jackson, at Rembrandt's Head, Fleet Street, Pr: 2,ˢ".*
Impressions: BM.

2. Re-touched, the address and price erased and replaced with: *"London Printed for Rob! Sayer Map and Printseller at the Golden Buck near Serjeants Inn Fleet Street.".*
Impressions: CLB P22,353 (impression exhibited).

3. With a door introduced in the wall to l.
Impressions: CLB.

4. Coarsely re-touched and numbered '153' bottom right.
Impressions: CLB; BM; H (and a masked proof).

Chaloner Smith firmly attributes this print to Michael Jackson. The plate was evidently a success, since it was printed extensively throughout almost half a century. Miss Dawson was at her most notorious between 1759–61 and it would be logical to suppose that the prints are from this period. In later states, as the plate wore down, a door was inserted into the background. Several examples have been encountered which were printed in sanguine; this was probably in an attempt to allow the now extremely worn plate to remain saleable, but as a novelty print. This print was listed in Sayer and Bennett's 1775 catalogue at 1s. Numerous copies exist: Robert Sayer, who acquired the original plate from Jackson, issued a 6 x 4¹/₂ inch mezzotint copy, which also appears in Sayer and Bennett's 1775 catalogue at 1s. A more elaborate copy was engraved for George Pulley, who seems to have acquired Jackson's premises in Fleet Street, although not his plates. The long inscription explains her charms as she danced the hornpipe:

Come all ye Bucks and Bloods so grim, / Who love the rousing Hornpipe trim, / Behold how Nancy moves each limb, / The Charming Nancy Dawson. // How easily she trips the stage, / Her heaving breasts all eyes engage, ... She's only for N-d S-rs arms, / The Charming Nancy Dawson ...

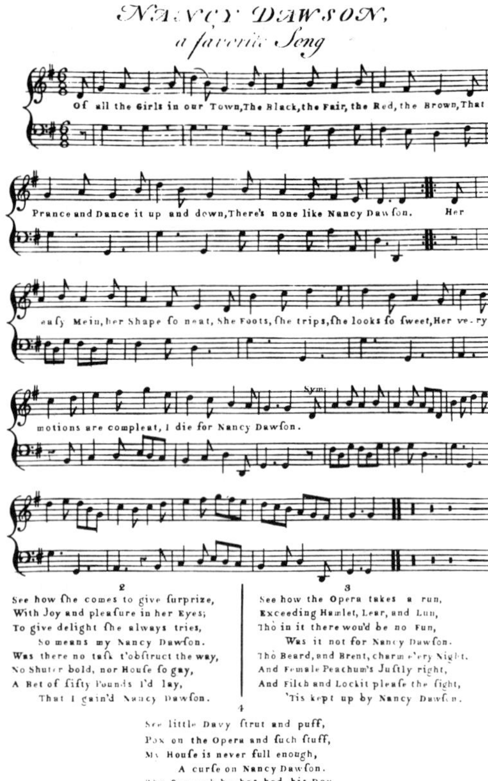

Two other small engraved copies were made: one for her *Authentic Memoirs ...* , the other, in the Burney Collection, probably for the *Genuine Memoirs ...* , no copy of which survives. This was advertised and reviewed in 1760 as being 'adorned with a neat copper plate'. A reviewer in *The Critical Review* considered that the book was, 'an Impudent, obscene and dull performance, the author of which merits not only critical reprehension but bodily correction'.[1] She was also drawn by Charles Spooner and engraved by both him and James Watson.

Nancy Dawson was born in about 1730, the daughter of a 'pimp and porter'. She lost her mother early and was deserted by her father soon after. She then joined the company of Griffin, a puppet-showman who taught her to dance, and a dancer from Sadler's Wells, taken by her performance, arranged for her to be engaged at his own theatre. The following season she appeared at Covent Garden, under the aegis of Edward Shuter.

In October 1759, due to the illness of the man who danced the hornpipe in *The Beggar's Opera*, she took his place, and from then on her reputation was made. The hornpipe was danced to the tune of *Here we go round the Mulberry Bush* which became known as *The Ballad of Nancy Dawson*. For a long time this was the popular air of the day, even to the point of being introduced into *Love in a Village* and mentioned in the epilogue of *She Stoops to Conquer*. The dance also contributed to the success of *The Beggar's Opera* at Covent Garden which enjoyed an unusually long run, much to Garrick's chagrin.

Offered a salary rise and enticed by Shuter, her lover, she moved to Drury Lane, where her first performance was in a production of *The Beggar's Opera* in September 1760. She continued to appear there over the following three years in a variety of entertainments including 'Jiggs', 'specially scripted ballads for two or more actors singing a cross dialogue of a lewd nature with lascivious gestures and dancing'.[2]

Although beautiful and graceful in her dancing, Alsager Vian[3] states that she 'possessed no claim to recognition'; similarly, Robert Lowe considered her to be a 'lady with no character worth mentioning'.[4] She was saucy, precocious and regarded as a heartless mercenary. She lived with Polly Kennedy, a popular young courtesan, in fashionable Manchester Square and between 1763–5, when they lived in Bedford Street, they welcomed visitors such as Henry Frederick Duke of Cumberland. Although Pulley's print implies that Nancy was faithful to Shuter, she seems to have been more widely available at a price.

She died in May 1767 on Haverstock Hill and was buried in Bloomsbury. After her death, her memory was maintained by the publication of *Nancy Dawson's Choyce Ditties*, a selection of her famous smutty songs.

[1] *The Critical Review*, 1760, p. 327.
[2] Burford, E. *Wits, Wenchers and Wantons*, p. 124.
[3] DNB.
[4] Lowe, Robert *A Bibliographical Account of English Theatrical Literature*, 1888, p. 83.

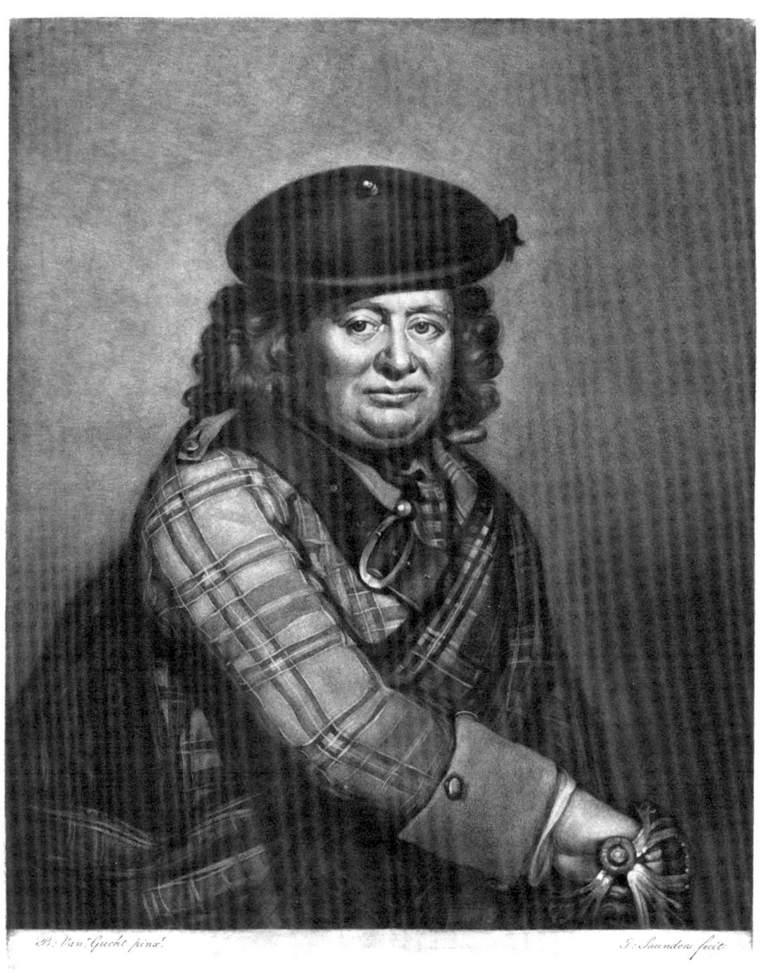

38 Mr Johnston in the Character of Gibby in the Wonder

Engraved by Joseph Saunders
after Benjamin Vandergucht

Published by Joseph Saunders
14 December 1773

Re-published by Henry Bryer 16 May 1774

336 x 274 I; 376 x 274 Pl.

References: CS 7; R 7; O'D (Alexander Johnston) 1; Hall (Alexander Jonston) 1

1. Finished proof with the engraved inscription: *"B: Van.r Gucht pinx.t *** J: Saunders fecit / Publish'd as the Act Directs Decem;r* [in ms *"14.th"*] *1773 by J: Saunders N.o 17 Glanville Street Rathbone Place."*.
Impressions: CLB P28,442 (impression exhibited); BL.

2. With the day of the month engraved and with the added engraved inscription:

The painting, a kitcat,[1] was exhibited by Benjamin Vandergucht at the Royal Academy in 1773 together with his painting of Mr Moody and Mr Packer, in the Farce of the Register Office. Although it has previously been assumed to represent the Drury Lane Housekeeper and Box book-keeper Alexander Jonston, it is now presumed to be of the actor John Johnston (fl.1742–81). This print shows him in the part which he had selected for his benefit on 27 May 1773, and raises doubts about the validity of the contemporary claim that his performance in this role was 'so contemptible, as to raise critical indignation'.[2]

Saunders exhibited both this print and an impression of '*Moody and Packer in the Register Office*' (see page 63) at the Society of Artists in 1774 in the hope that they would be taken up and distributed by a printseller. He seems to have been successful since Henry Bryer acquired both plates. Before the exhibition had ended, it was re-published by Bryer, who seemingly cut the plate down to the more usual size of 14 x 10 inches. In 1774 Shropshire listed an impression in his stock catalogue at 5s. The plate eventually passed to Robert Wilkinson[3] and was sold in his sale of stock in 1826 together with seventeen impressions.

Johnston's first named part on 6 November 1756 was Gibby in a revival of *The Wonder! or a Woman Keeps a Secret* by Susannah Centlivre, in which Garrick played Don Felix, also for the first time.

"M:^R JONSTON in the Character of GIBBY in the WONDER".

Impressions: CLB; BM.

3. With the plate reduced to 323 x 254 I; 362 x 254 mm Pl. and the publication line altered: "Publish'd as the Act Directs May 16.th 1774 by H. Bryer at N.º 12 Stephen Street Tottenham Court Road.".

Impressions: BM.

☞ In the play, Don Felix is the headstrong and proud son of a Portuguese Grandee, Don Lopez. Escaping from a forced marriage, has seriously wounded a fellow Portuguese, Antonio, and fears for his life should the latter die. He returns from flight because of his love for Violante, Don Pedro's daughter. Felix's sister, Isabella, under similar pressure from Don Lopez to marry for convenience, escapes her room, is rescued by a Scot, Colonel Briton and taken to her friend Violante's house. Felix catches sight of Briton, visiting there the next day (no man is supposed to visit Violante) and flies into a rage, thinking that Violante has taken a lover. Isabella begs Violante not to disclose her hiding place; this secret Violante keeps at her own near peril as events unfold. A game of dodging and disguise follow, complicated by Felix's jealousy until all is happily resolved. Gibby, a stage Scotsman, is Colonel Briton's retainer.

John Johnston was a regular performer in the Drury Lane company by 1751–2. He played in *Harlequin Ranger* in January 1752, performing this role again in the following season, in addition to various other parts including one of the witches in *Macbeth*, and several female characters in pantomime. He played characters both in plays and in pantomime for the following twenty-five seasons, although he never rose to prominence.

In 1766 he became the secretary of the Drury Lane Theatrical Fund, of which Garrick was chairman. The date of his death is not known, but he was playing at Drury Lane until at least 1780–81. Johnston's wife Helen also performed at Drury Lane at this time, and in the 1770s they lived nearby at 97, Craven Buildings. A Master Johnston, who sang at Drury Lane and Ranelagh Gardens in 1762 may have been their son.

---

[1] A traditional size of painting, measuring 36 x 28 inches.

[2] *The Theatrical Review*, 1772.

[3] Robert Wilkinson (1779–c. 1825), map and printseller at 58, Cornhill 1779–1816.

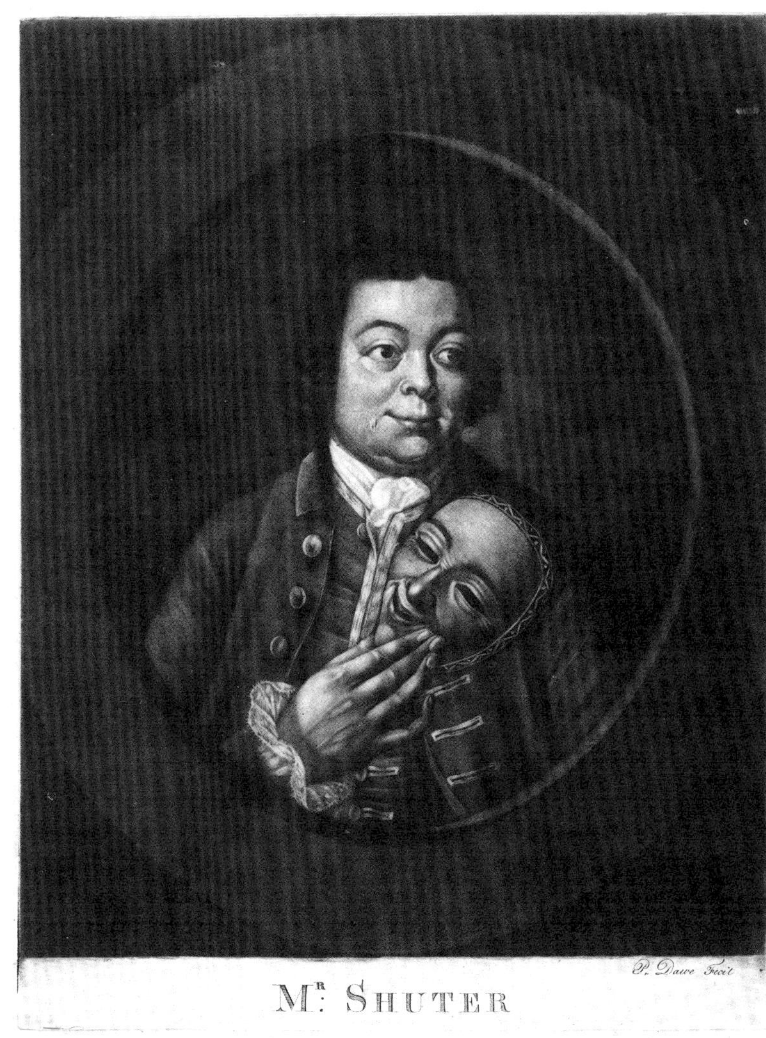

39 M.r Shuter

[Designed?] and engraved by Philip Dawe

Published by Philip Dawe and William Darling 12 June 1773

Re-published by Baldwyn

Re-published William Richardson [after 1784]

316 x 248 I; 350 x 248 Pl.

References: CS 10; O'D 5; Hall 1

1. Progress proof with the hands dark, the waistcoat without buttons, buttonholes or lace, the mask without the trim and the inscription space uncleaned.
Impressions: BM.

2. With the engraved inscription: "*** *** *P,, *Dawe Fecit* | M.R SHUTER | *Publish'd June 12, 1773 by P; Dawe, N.º 4 Goodge Street, Tottenham Court Road, & W.m Darling in Great Newport Street,*".
Impressions: CLB; NPG.

This print of Edward Shuter, probably designed by Philip Dawe as well as being engraved by him, was not exhibited. Dawe executed a number of decorative plates for Carington Bowles after Henry Morland, said to have been his master and a relation, which are extremely fine examples of their type. Among the genre plates that he engraved, the pair '*Morning at Work*' and '*Evening at Rest*' are excellent examples of the type of decorative print then in demand.

Dawe's earliest plates date from 1769 and he appears to have been active as an engraver until at least 1780; it is thought that he died the following year. He seems to have been an independent engraver who worked for a number of different publishers, including Robert Sayer, and the Bowles family; these two firms made use of journeyman engravers to provide them with cheap decorative prints. This practice proved to be extremely profitable and helped Sayer to accrue a considerable fortune: a complete valuation of Sayer's stock was called for in 1774 when John Bennett was made a partner in the business, at which point the stock was valued at £13,500. The inventory generated by this valuation was used as the basis for Sayer & Bennett's 1775 catalogue.

This plate was published by Dawe in conjunction with William Darling,[1] a well known 'engraver in general', who engraved a great

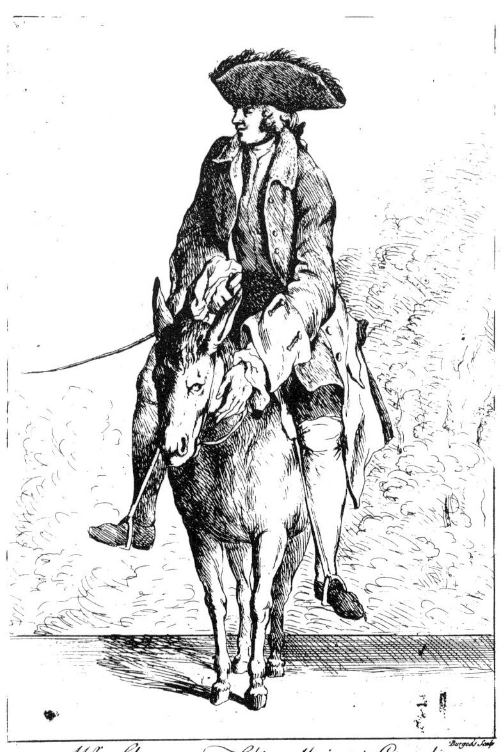

3. With the publication line altered:
"Publifhed by Baldwyn Catherine St Strand London.".
Impressions: BM.

4. With the publication line altered:
["Publifhed by W Richardson Antient and Modern Print Warehouse 164 Strand."(CS)].

5. Re-published with the plate reduced at the bottom to 340 x 251 mm and the publication line consequently cut off.
Impressions: CLB P 8,206 (impression exhibited); BM; TM; H.

---

¹ William Darling (fl. 1771–99), engraver, publisher and printseller in Great Newport Street.
² Unidentified press cutting mounted with a print of Shuter at Harvard (Hall V).
³ *Theatrical Biography*, II, p. 43.
⁴ Lichtenberg, p. 54.
⁵ Gentleman, I, p. 212.

many trade-cards and book-plates in partnership with John Peter Thompson. Nothing is known of Baldwyn, who probably re-published the plate in the 1780s. Towards the end of the century the plate was acquired by William Richardson.

Edward Shuter was born in about 1728 in St. Giles. He is thought to have worked as a vintner near Covent Garden. He was then taken on as an apprentice by Chapman, an actor at Drury Lane, and soon became known as 'Comical Ned'. He played with country companies, first appearing in 1744 at Chapman's theatre in Richmond. He performed at Covent Garden in the following year for Chapman's benefit, and at Goodman's Fields in 1746–7 with a company that was described as being 'inferior'. In 1747 he was employed at Drury Lane where he remained until 1753, playing a variety of comic parts. Shuter's reputation was initially made in his portrayal of Master Stephen in *Every Man in his Humour*, a part in which he is portrayed in numerous engravings. He discovered and 'kept' the dancer Nancy Dawson (see page 87).

Shuter left Drury Lane in 1753, and apart from visits to Ireland and occasional performances at the Haymarket, he remained at Covent Garden where he was given more important parts including Richard III and Sir John Brute. He received considerable publicity for his delivery, seated upon an ass, of Joseph Hayne's epilogue to *Unhappy Kindness* (see margin). It is has never been advisable for an actor to perform with children or animals, as Shuter was to discover:

> On Wednesday evening Mr Shuter spoke an epilogue riding on as ass at Covent Garden house, but it being somewhat difficult to get the sluggish animal forward on the stage, the house seemed very much diverted, the excellent humourist, however soon changed the laugh at him to one with him, by declaring the Ass was very disconcerted it being his first appearance on the stage.²

Shuter's last appearance was as Falstaff in May 1776, for his benefit, and he died later that year, in November. Garrick reputedly described him as the greatest comic genius he had ever seen:

> with strong features, a peculiar turn of countenance and natural passion for humour, he has the happiness of disposing and altering the muscles of his face into a variety of laughable shapes which, though they border on grimace, are, however, on the whole irresistible.³

Shuter was described as being decadent, quick-witted and amusing, although Lichtenberg accused him of 'constant exaggeration', despite the fact that 'every word he uttered was applauded'.⁴ A similar criticism was levelled at his performance in *The Provoked Husband*: 'forgetting every trace of character, [he] burlesques it with ten thousand unmeaning transitions of countenance, and as many ill-applied breaks of voice'.⁵

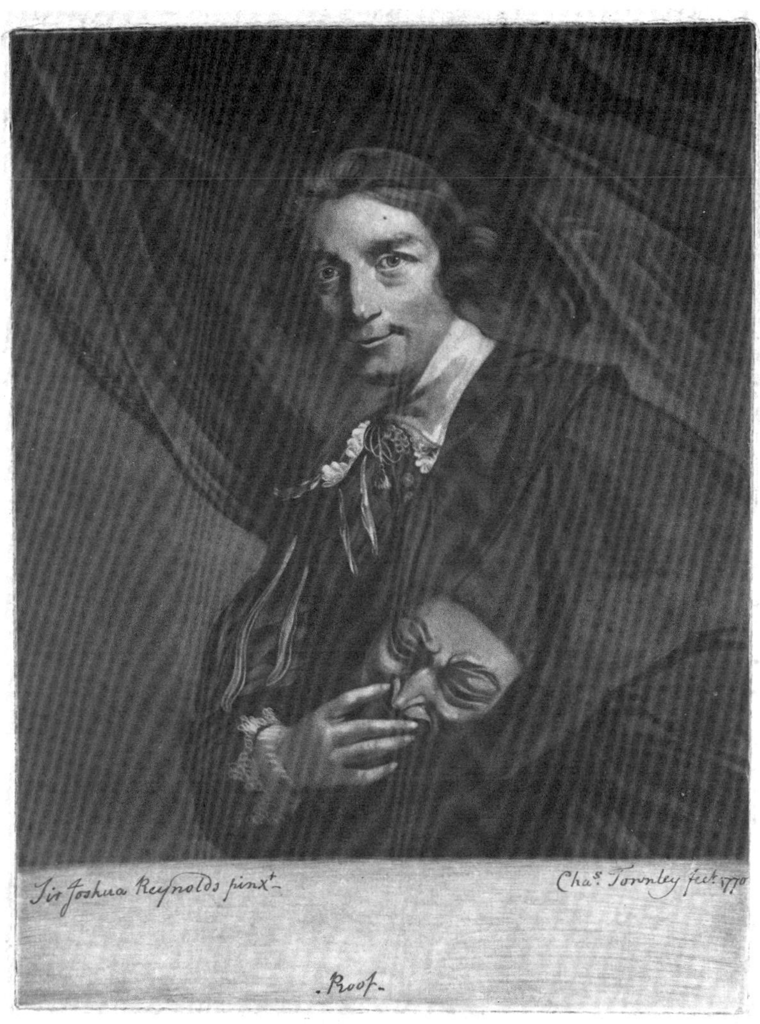

40 Henry Woodward

Engraved by Charles Townley
after Sir Joshua Reynolds

Presumably abandoned before publication

262 x 226 I; 306 x 227 Pl.

References: CS (Watson) 157 & noted
(Townley) p.1393; H p.73–4; G (W) 7

**1. Unfinished proof before all letters, before
the inscription space was cleaned.**
Impressions: CLB P2,871 ex. coll. Duke of
Buccleuch, *Lugt* 402 (impression exhibited); BM.

The two proof prints of Henry Woodward by Charles Townley
and James Watson (see page 100) are excellent examples of the
different ways in which a mezzotint engraver could 'translate' a
coloured painting into a black and white print. James Watson, the
finer of the two engravers, has managed to reproduce faithfully the
facial features in the painting, whereas Townley has attempted to
copy the painting almost brush stroke for brush stroke with a most
unsatisfactory result, since the eyes stare and the face leers.

Technically, this working proof displays Townley's vices. His
work is soft and his use of the burnisher to reproduce brushwork is
especially noticeable in his early work. His mezzotint ground is
broadly laid and rather crude when compared with that of Watson,
whose technique has a sharper, more silvery appearance.
Townley's portrait of Dr Joseph Allen after George Romney has
the same over-stated features, a fault that is not to be found in
Romney's paintings. The clumsy highlighting on the face of this
proof can also be seen in finished proofs of his portrait of Dr
Johnson after John Opie.

Charles Townley, the son of Garrick's friend James Townley,
author of *High Life Below Stairs* and the headmaster of Merchant
Taylor's School, practised as a miniature painter. Having studied
in Rome and Florence in the 1770s, he worked as an engraver in
London up to 1786, when he left for Berlin; several mezzotint por-

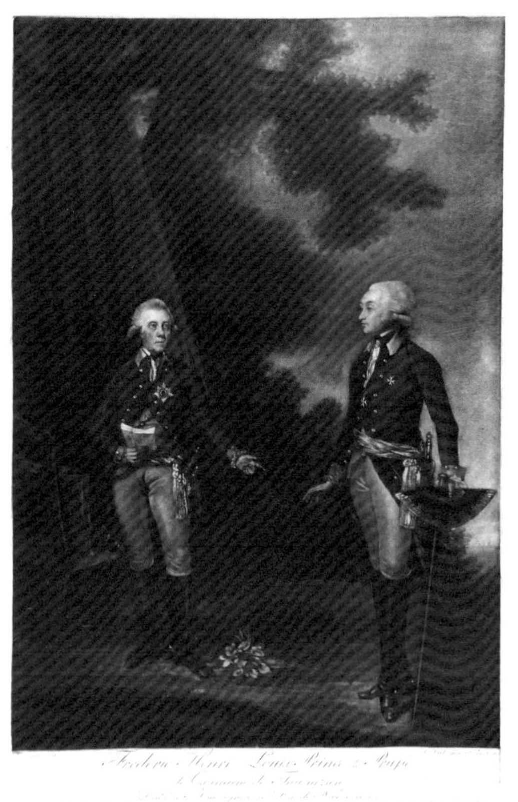

Frederic Henri Louis Prince de Prusse
E.F. Cunningham   C. Townley 1787

traits date from this period. The majority of these are after Edward Francis Cunningham and, whilst some faults may lie with the painter, particularly the wooden figures in his whole-length portraits, Townley's style hardens and becomes stiffer and flatter. This hard-edged style may have been caused by the use of copperplate, which was made using harder copper. After his return to England in 1790, the soft over-statement in his work occasionally returns and can be seen in his portrait of General Forbes after Romney.

Chaloner Smith suggests that this print of Woodward was probably abandoned as a failure and indeed, since it would have been almost impossible to re-engrave the face satisfactorily, this is plausible. Other examples of unpublished or unfinished plates that were abandoned are recorded in the eighteenth-century,[1] but it is unusual for a progress proof such as Townley's portrait of Woodward to have survived; no other such proofs by him are recorded. It is possible that since prints after Reynolds were in demand, even in the 1770s, this impression would have instantly been considered a rarity.

The impression exhibited is from the Buccleuch Collection and is the one described by Edward Hamilton.[2] It may be the one seen by Chaloner Smith who suggests that Townley's plate is by James Watson, although he had seen an impression inscribed '*Chas Townley fecit 1770*'. Townley's involvement in this plate is supported by evidence of family friendship. Woodward was at Merchant Taylor's with the elder Townley and chose his *False Concord* for his benefit in March 1764, its only performance.

[1] Lot 179 on the third day of the sale of James Bretherton's stock 31/1–5/2/1799, included the unpublished copper-plate of a mezzotint portrait of Stubbs by James Watson. Numerous unfinished plates were sold by William Dickinson after his bankruptcy in 18 February 1794.

[2] Edward Hamilton M.D., physician to the London Homeopathic Hospital

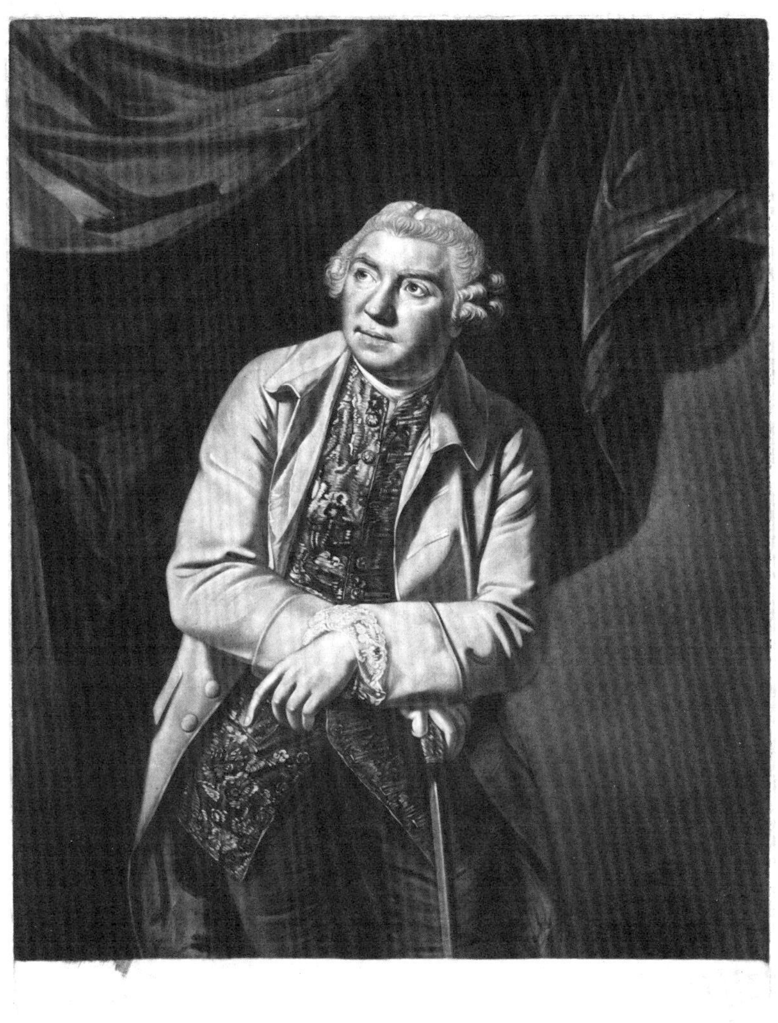

41 Samuel Foote

Engraved by Thomas Blackmore
after Sir Joshua Reynolds

Published by William Wynne Ryland
4 June 1771

415 x 329 I; 458 x 330 Pl.

References: CS 2; H p. 27; Hall 9

1. Finished proof before all letters.
Impressions: CLB P26,384 (impression exhibited).

2. Finished proof with the engraved inscription: *"Painted by Sir Joshua Reynolds. *** Engrav'd by T. Blackmore. | Publish'd June ye 4.ᵗʰ 1771. accorᵍ to Act of Parliament by W.W. Ryland in Cornhill."*.
Impressions: CLB; BM; H.

3. With the added inscription: *"Samuel Foote Esq,.".*
Impressions: CLB; BM.

Joshua Reynolds's painting, which survives, was not exhibited. Very little is known about Thomas Blackmore, an extremely competent engraver who appears to have worked between 1769 and 1771 only. Details of the publishing career of William Wynne Ryland, the publisher of this print are discussed under *'Powell and Bensley in King John'* (see page 69). Boydell did not list the print in his 1773 catalogue, but impressions were certainly available from his stock in 1777 and 1779 at 5s, and in 1803 at 7s 6d. It is impossible to say when Boydell actually obtained the plate, but it was sold after the death of Josiah Boydell to Robert Grave and subsequently remained in the stock of this firm until at least 1836.

Samuel Foote was born in Cornwall in 1721. His father was a commissioner of the Prize Office and at one time Mayor of Truro. His mother was the sister of Sir John Goodere, Bt., who left Foote and his brothers his vast fortune. Foote inherited at twenty-one, when his other uncle, Captain Samuel Goodere, kidnapped Sir John and murdered him on his ship. Foote was educated at Worcester, where his extravagant habits were first apparent. He initially tried the Bar, but abandoned it soon afterwards. He made his debut at the Haymarket Theatre in February 1744 and his early appearances were apparently unsuccessful.

In 1746 Foote played in entertainments at the Haymarket which displayed his innate talent for mimicry. These were initially called 'Diversions of the Morning', but after complaints that he was flouting the Licensing Act of 1737, he was forced to change the manner in which they were presented. In 1747 he began advertising the 'Dish of Tea': 'Mr Foote's compliments to his friends and the public, desiring them to drink Tea at the Little Theatre at the Hay-Market, every morning at the Play-house Prices'.[1] His bold claim that he was not presenting plays appealed to the public and meant that the house was filled for the next few years. The majority of these shows consisted of impersonations of actors, particularly Garrick.

Foote became manager of the Haymarket Theatre in 1747 and ran it successfully for the next thirty years. Although many people were slandered in his productions, complaints served only to increase public interest in them.

In 1757 he visited Dublin with Tate Wilkinson, who at one performance gave a wickedly amusing impersonation of Foote which raised cries of, 'Foote undone!', to Foote's obvious chagrin. Foote returned to Dublin for the following season when he tried out his new comedy *The Minor*, in which he attempted to retaliate against Wilkinson's mimicry, and satirised the fanaticism of George Whitefield and the Methodists, who took great offence. This play is considered to be Foote's best piece and is characteristic of his work in that the plot is non-existent but the characters and wit are superb.

In 1766 Foote had an accident which changed his life and career. While visiting Lord Mexborough, he met a group of people, including the Duke of York, who teased him about his claim to be a fine horseman. Persuaded to ride a high-spirited horse, he was thrown, breaking his leg so badly that it eventually had to be amputated. Feeling responsible, the Duke of York obtained a patent for Foote to erect a theatre in London. It was stipulated that he could show 'dramatic pieces there from 14 May to 14 September during his life.'. Foote purchased his old premises in the Haymarket and put up a new building on the site, which opened in May 1767.

Around 1776 his popularity appeared to wane and even when he appeared at the Haymarket in *The Devil upon Two Sticks*, there was little enthusiasm. In addition, he became involved in a quarrel with the notorious Duchess of Kingston over the libellous play, *Trip to Calais* and was forced to stand trial. Remarkably, many of those whom he had lampooned in the past – including Garrick – came to support him. Although he was acquitted, the experience shocked Foote considerably.

The Haymarket Theatre was leased by Colman in 1776–7, the year in which Foote appeared for the last time in *The Devil upon Two Sticks*. The change in him was apparent – he looked tired, ill and old. He arrived at Dover en route for France on 20 October, but died next morning, another performer to die as a result of his excesses. He was buried in the west cloister of Westminster Abbey.

Foote's personal direction of his numerous satirical plays attracted criticism as well as applause. It is surprising that Reynolds was prepared to paint Foote at all, since he thought that, 'by Foote's buffoonery and broad-faced merriment, private friendship, public decency, and every thing estimable among men were cast under foot'.[2] Dr Johnson found Foote's humour irresistible and Sylas Neville noted that at a performance of *The Orators* even one of the actresses, 'could scarce do her part for laughing at Foote'.

Seemingly consumed by jealousy, Foote plagued Garrick throughout his life. In spite of this Garrick always tried to remain on good terms with him, being friendly, even affectionate, calling Foote in one letter 'my dear Devil'.[3] Garrick asserted that Foote's scathing tongue did not cause him undue anguish:

'In publick wound, in private love me;
The polish'd Lancet cannot move me …'.[4]

Yet it did not go unnoticed that Garrick was extremely quiet when in Foote's company.

Reynolds believed that this was because, 'he disdained to compete with one whose style of talk and wit was vulgar merriment, indecency and impiety'.[5] Egotistical and obstreperous, Foote ignored any hurt he caused, yet he was a lively wit, vivacious, entertaining and sharp-tongued, both admired and feared.

[1] TDB.
[2] Russell, William Clark *Representative Actors*, 1872, p. 137.
[3] *Letters*, no. 506, 2 June 1768.
[4] *ibid.*, no. 581, 25 April 1770.
[5] Fitzgerald, P. *A Biography of Samuel Foote*, London, 1910, p. 88.

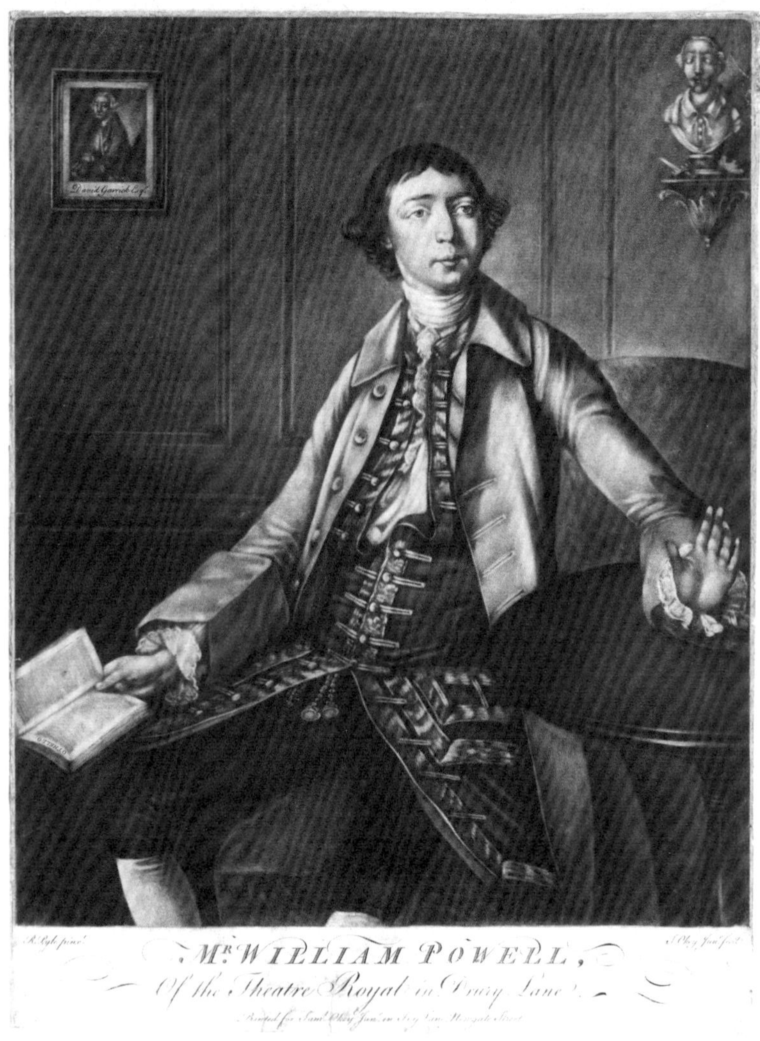

42 Mr William Powell, of the Theatre Royal in Drury Lane

Engraved by Samuel Okey jun.
after Robert Pyle

Published by Samuel Okey jun. [c. 1763–67]

312 x 254 I; 354 x 256 Pl.

References: CS 8; O'D 3

1. With the engraved inscription: "R,, Pyle pinx:, *** S,, Okey Jun:, fecit. / *Mʀ WILLIAM POWELL, / Of the Theatre Royal in Drury Lane.*". In border of portrait in image: "*David Garrick Esq:*".
Impressions: BM.

2. With the engraved publication line and the price in scratched letters added: "*Printed for Sam:, Okey Jun:, in Ivy Lane, Newgate Street. *** Pr. 1ˢ 6*".
Impressions: CLB P36,003(impression exhibited); TM.

Robert Pyle's painting does not seem to have been exhibited. Waterhouse notes that Pyle's figures seem very stiff and wooden, a fault that is emphasised by this rather crude mezzotint. This undated print was almost certainly published whilst Powell was at Drury Lane; he made his first appearance there in 1763 and left for Covent Garden in 1767, having bought a share of Rich's patent. He is shown in this picture with a text of *Othello*, a bust of Shakespeare and a framed print of Garrick, probably Watson's mezzotint after Hudson. The allusion to the text of *Othello* helps a little in dating this print. Powell first appeared in *Othello*, as Iago, in March 1764 for his own benefit and then acted in the play on only three further occasions, in 1765 and 1766 at Drury Lane.

The night of his debut performance in this play was clearly one to remember:

This Night there was the greatest over flow ever known. The Crowd so great it prevented Ladies from coming into the Boxes till near Seven o clock at half past Six begun the play. As the Ladies were not come into the Boxes, being prevented by passage being Stopt up by the Crowd the Gentlemen Cry'd out off off &c. Mr King & Mr Havard remained on the Stage some time but the Noise increasing. Mr King address'd the Audience & told them it would be equally agreeable to the performers to stay half an hour longer, Upon which there was a great Clap and the Curtain was drop'd & a quarter before Seven begun the Play again.[1]

The print was engraved and published by Samuel Okey junior, who won a premium at the Society of Artists in 1765 and is also recorded as having exhibited his work there in 1767–8. In 1773 he seems to have left England for Newport, Rhode Island where he remained until at least 1780. His father was also an engraver and as Chaloner Smith warns, the two may be confused. In 1766 the eminent printseller Thomas Bowles left an annuity to a cousin called Samuel Okey who may have been one of the two.

William Powell was born in 1735, in Hereford like his patron Garrick. He was introduced by Charles Holland to Garrick, who was looking for an actor with the ability to fill his place during his planned visit to the Continent. Coached by Garrick, Powell made his first ever appearance on stage at Drury Lane in October 1763; Hopkins recorded that 'a greater reception was never shown to anybody'. Describing how the audience, 'not content with clapping, stood up and shouted', Horace Walpole considered that Garrick's absence was not going to be noticed. It has been said that Powell burst upon the stage with every perfection but experience; his acting had 'a thousand beauties and a thousand faults'. Gossip even suggested that Powell was Garrick's 'natural' son.

Powell's move to Covent Garden to share the management with Colman broke his contract with Garrick, who was furious. His last appearance was in May 1769 as Jaffeir and he died in Bristol two months later. His death, at the age of just thirty-three, appears to have provided John Goldar with the motive for publishing a mezzotint portrait. This was engraved by John Dixon after William Lawranson and is now the most commonly surviving portrait of Powell. Powell's funeral was memorable, not least due to the late appearance of a drunken Ned Shuter who, 'banged on the doors and cried out the lines spoken by Romeo upon breaking open the tomb of the Capulets'.[2]

Powell tended to take parts that were beyond him, for example in *Macbeth*,

> ... the requisite forces of expression and a proper disposition of features were wanting; as after the murder, his feelings dwindled into a kind of boyish whimpering ... in the third act he seemed unequal to the arduous task of describing extreme horror, and in the fifth, Macbeth's weight of desperation bore him down ...[3]

Although Powell never became a serious rival, his success in certain parts, notably King John, was great enough to make Garrick jealous. Genest, aware of his remarkable talent, believed that 'had he restrained his impetuosity, he might have been twice the actor he was'.[4]

Davies summed up his career thus:

> William Powell had, from nature, many requisites to exhibit, with propriety and skill, lovers and heroes: his person and voice were well adapted to them; his ear was good, nor did he want any thing but time to bring his judgement to maturity ...[5]

[1] William Hopkins' Diary quoted in *The London Stage*, IV, p. 1049.
[2] TDB.
[3] Gentleman, I, p. 110.
[4] Genest, V, p. 37.
[5] *Dramatic Miscellanies*, III, p. 277.

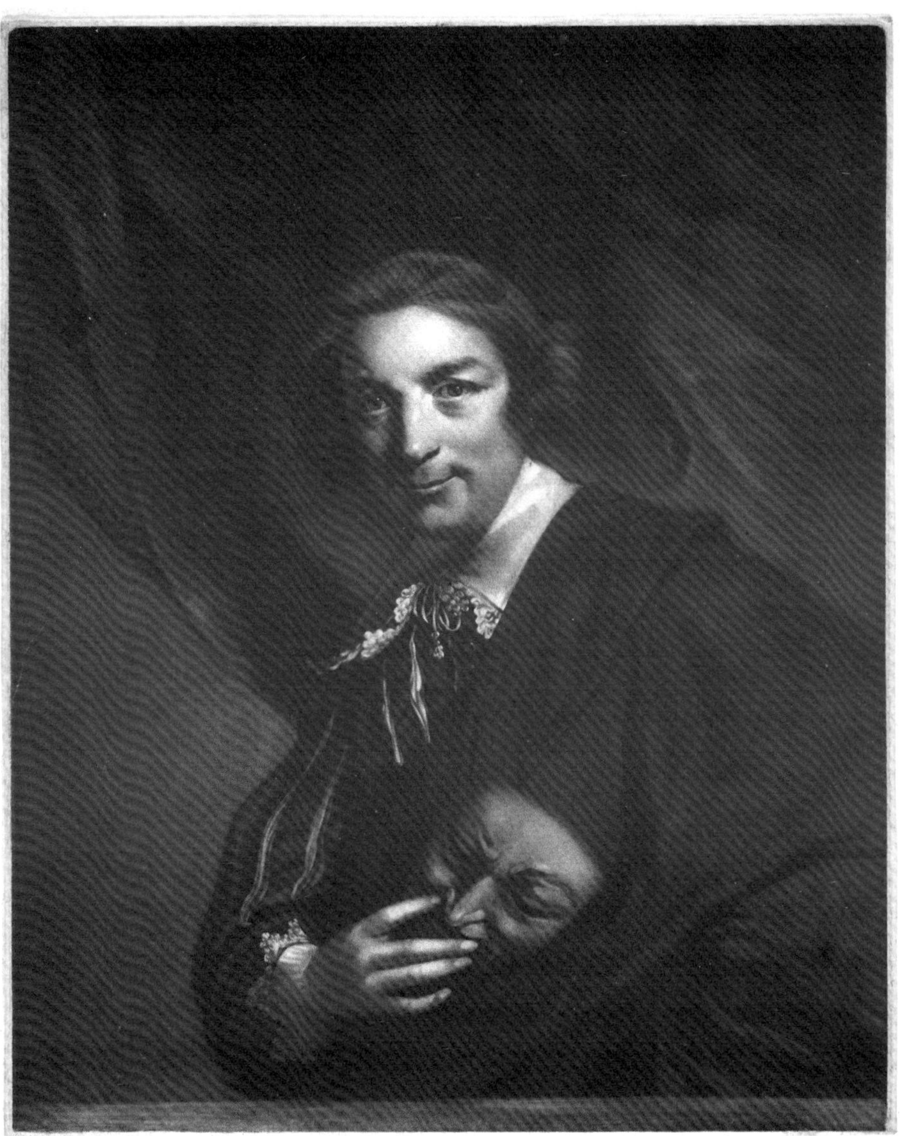

43 Henry Woodward, Comœdus Anglicanus Celeberrimus

Engraved by James Watson
after Sir Joshua Reynolds

Published by Ryland & Bryer [1764]

281 x 227 I; 327 x 227 Pl.

References: CS 156; H p. 73-4; G 67; O'D 3; Hall 1

1. Finished proof before all letters and before the inscription space was cleaned.
Impressions: CLB P33,001 ex. coll. Alfred Morrison *Lugt* 151 (impression exhibited).

2. Finished proof with the inscription space cleaned.
Impressions: CLB.

The painting is now in the collection of Lord Egremont.[1] Penny suggests that the Vandyke costume is similar to that issued for performances of Shakespeare and Ben Jonson, and speculates that Woodward is dressed as Mercutio, perhaps his most famous part. The print may be the one that was exhibited at the Society of Artists in 1764 ('a mezzotinto from Mr. Reynolds'), identified by Grave as portrait of Woodward.[2]

James Watson, the last of the great Irish engravers, was born in about 1740, just before the first wave of engravers arrived in London. He seems to have been trained in London, since no prints by him are known to have been published in Dublin and it is unlikely at this date that there was anyone in Dublin who was capable of teaching him. His early work was for printsellers who employed him to produce prints after Reynolds. By the mid-1760s he was capable of engraving extremely fine full-length mezzotints after Reynolds, occasionally publishing them himself or in conjunction with Butler Clowes (see page 85). After 1775 he ceased to publish, possibly because his fame was such that he could charge what he wished for engraving a plate. He and his publishers rarely

100

3. With the engraved inscription: "*J. Reynolds pinx! *** Ja.* Watson fecit. | Harry Woodward, Comœdus Anglicanus Celeberrimus. | Sold by Ryland & Bryer, at the Kings Arms, in Cornhill.*".
Impressions: CLB; BM; H; TM.

dated his prints. James's daughter Caroline was a fine stipple engraver (see page 123).

Watson's drawing and modelling are exquisite and his technique extremely well suited to reproducing French portraits. He engraved with such superb delicacy and subtlety that some of his portraits of young men are given an air of effeminacy. This portrait of Woodward was among Watson's first ten plates and is not only extremely well drawn and engraved, but has a restraint and sophistication rarely found in the work of young engravers. Chaloner Smith stated that he was fastidious and had destroyed plates which were unsatisfactory. This may be so, since a number of proofs of his plates are to be found which differ in size from the published prints,[3] but the two examples that Chaloner Smith cites are not variants.[4] A small part of Watson's output consisted in small copies of his larger plates; whether Watson engraved them himself or employed pupils to produce them is not known, but they may have been produced to cut out the piracies by Sayer and other printseller. The poorer quality of these small plates has dimmed his reputation considerably.

Henry Woodward was born in 1714, the eldest son of a tallow chandler in Southwark. Educated at Merchant Taylors' school, he was meant to join his father's business, but when the business failed he joined Rich's Lilliputian troupe at Goodman's Fields, where he remained until 1735–6. From 1741–2 until 1746–7 Woodward performed at Covent Garden. He made surprisingly few appearances at Drury Lane during his career.

He wrote pantomimes and was Garrick's Mercutio during the famous Barry-Garrick competition in *Romeo and Juliet*. In 1758 he left Drury Lane and went to Dublin to help Barry to set up the theatre in Crow Street. Unfortunately they quarrelled and Woodward lost half his savings. He returned to England to play at Covent Garden in 1762. In 1770 he appeared in Edinburgh under Foote and also acted under Tate Wilkinson in York but in 1772 finally settled at Covent Garden, where he played until shortly before his death. His last appearance was as Stephano in the *Tempest* in January 1777, but he was too ill to act at his benefit in March and he died on 17 April. He had lived for the last ten years of his life with George Anne Bellamy and left her the bulk of his property, although she never received it.

His appearance was suited to tragedy but it was said that he was 'unable to speak a serious line with effect'. He had few equals in comedy and even at the height of his popularity he had sufficient modesty to play minor parts. His vivacity was astonishing and although Genest thought that he sometimes overacted, he felt that the 'very tones of his voice inspired comic ideas'.[5]

[1] Penny, pp. 212–3.
[2] Graves, Algernon *Society of Artists and the Free Society*, 1907. Graves does not state his source.
[3] For example, '*Ann, Lady Fortescue*' (CS 55).
[4] '*Miss Hale as Allegra*' (CS 69 and 70) is in fact one plate, and the second plate of Woodward is by Townley.
[5] Genest, V, p. 573.

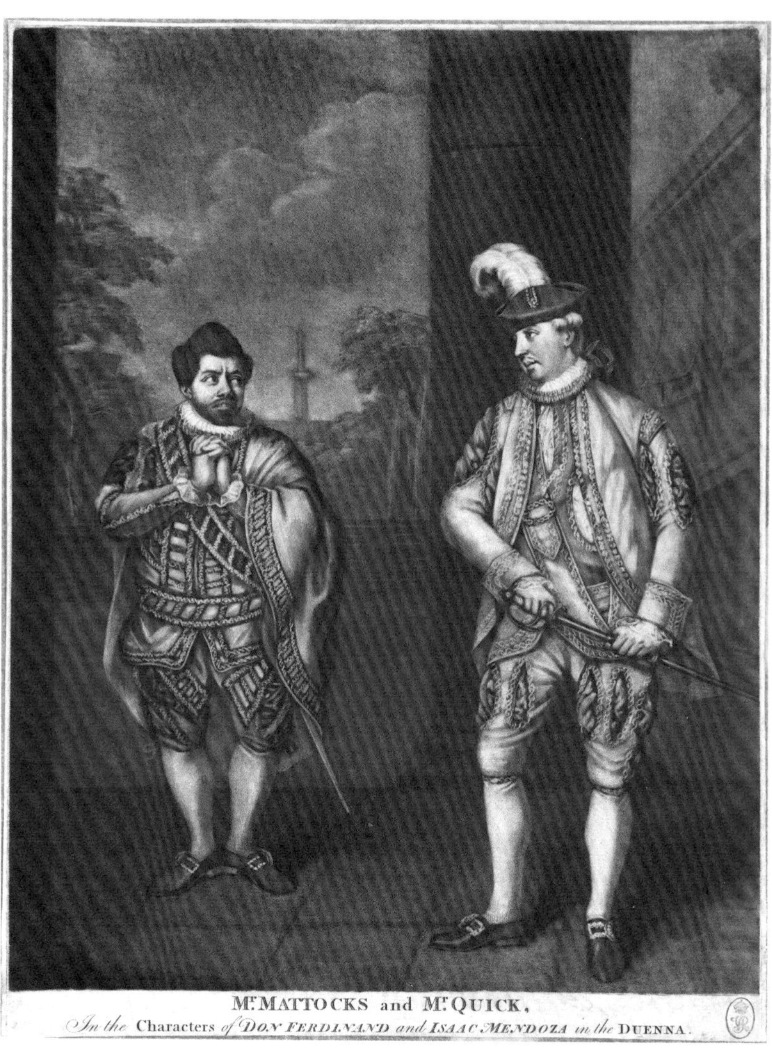

44 M.r Mattocks and M.r Quick, in the Characters of Don Ferdinand and Isaac Mendoza in the Duenna

Anonymous mezzotint

Published by Carington Bowles
10 November 1777

330 x 205 I; 352 x 250 Pl.

References: CS ENA III, 107; O'D (Mattocks) 9; Hall (Mattocks) 5

1. With the engraved inscription: "M.r MATTOCKS and M.r QUICK, *In the* Characters *of* DON FERDINAND *and* ISAAC MENDOZA *in the* DUENNA. / *Printed for & Sold by* Carington Bowles, *at his* Map & Print Warehouſe, *N.o 69 in S.t Paul's Church Yard,* London. Published as the Act directs, 10.th Nov.r 1777.".
Impressions: CLB P3,921 ex. coll. H.M. Queen Victoria, Lugt 2532 (impression exhibited); TM; H.

The painting was sold at the Revelstoke sale at Christie's on 26 July 1929, implausibly attributed to Johann Zoffany. A second painting which is clearly by the same hand, catalogued as a scene from *Every Man in his Humour*, was sold at Christie's in 1925. It is not known where these paintings are today, the only record of them being the Christie's catalogue entries; in these entries the measurements of the two pictures are quite different and, rather confusingly, one of them seems to have been mis-measured. A re-attribution of the pictures to Thomas Parkinson can be suggested, but in the absence of the paintings this is speculative. In 1775, the year that this play was first performed, Parkinson exhibited 'A Scene in Cymon, Act III, scene I, small whole lengths' at the Royal Academy and in the following year, 'A Scene in the Duenna, Act III'; these may have been the two pictures sold by Christie's. The figures are wooden, as Ellis Waterhouse observes of Parkinson's work in general; nevertheless it can be seen from the handful of drawings for Lowndes's *New English Theatre* that he was a competent draughtsman on a smaller scale.

The print was published by Carington Bowles and listed in his catalogues for 1782 and 1784 at 1s plain or 2s coloured. The size of the plate and the number '*369*' indicate that it was a print from the extensive series of 10 x 14 inches, 'half-sheet humorous mezzot-

2. With the number '369'.

Impressions: BM (with the date erased from the print).

☛ Sheridan's *The Duenna, or The Double Elopement* centres around Don Jerome, an obstinate and irascible father who is determined that his daughter Louisa shall marry Isaac, an 'odious little Jew', although she loves Antonio. Don Jerome discovers that the duenna, or chaperone, is acting as an go-between for the two lovers and dismisses her. He locks up Louisa, but she escapes from the house disguised as the duenna, leaving the latter in her place. Isaac is thus fooled into marrying the duenna and into bringing Louisa and Antonio together.

NEVER PERFORM'D.

At the Theatre-Royal, Covent-Garden,

This prefent TUESDAY, November 21, 1775,

Will be prefented a New COMIC OPERA call'd

The DUENNA;

OR, THE

DOUBLE ELOPEMENT.

The PRINCIPAL CHARACTERS by

Mr. MATTOCKS,

Mr. QUICK,

Mr. WILSON,

Mr. DU-BELLAMY,

Mr. MAHON,

Mr. WEWITZER, Mr. FOX, Mr. BAKER,

AND

Mr. LEONI.

Mifs BROWN,

Mrs. GREEN,

Mrs. MATTOCKS.

The MUSIC partly NEW and partly felected from the moft EMINENT COMPOSERS. With a NEW. OVERTURE, SCENES, DRESSES and other DECORATIONS. End of Act II. a New SPANISH DANCE, By Signor and Signora ZUCHELLI, Mr. DAGUEVILLE, Signora VIDINI, & c.

To which will be added (not acted here thefe Ten Years)

The LYING VALET.

Sharp (Firft Time) by Mr. LEE LEWES,

Gaylefs by Mr. DAVIS,

Juftice Guttle by Mr. BOOTH, Dick, by Mr. JONES,

Beau Trippet by Mr. WEWITZER,

Meliffa by Mifs AMBROSE,

Mrs. Gadabout, Mrs. POUSSIN, Trippet, Mrs. MASTERS,

Kitty Pry by Mrs. PITT.

BOOKS of the SONGS in the OPERA to be had at the Theatre. The Doors to be opened at Five o'Clock, to begin exactly at Six, *Vivant Rex & Regina!*

---

[1] For this print see Vol. II/X, p. 65.
[2] *Dramatic Miscellanies*, III, p. 136.
[3] *Macaroni, Savoir Faire, and Theatrical Magazine*, 1773.

ints', which were published and re-published by the Bowles family throughout the second half of the eighteenth-century. Bowles's catalogue asserted: 'The following extensive Collection is chiefly new, and of superior Goodness to all others extant. A Quantity always kept ready framed and glazed at the lowest Prices'. These prints are scarce since they were almost always framed for interior decoration, unlike etched caricatures which tended to be bound in folios. Some of the finest examples of the Bowles' output of mezzotint caricatures survive in two magnificent albums[1] in the British Museum; despite some oxidation, the colours are remarkably fresh.

The print depicts an extremely successful comic partnership; Davies described the two actors as '... born to relax the muscles and set mankind a tittering ...'.[2] George Mattocks, who played the original Ferdinand in *The Duenna* was born in 1735. In September 1747 he sang at a booth at Southwark Fair and was singing and dancing at Bartholomew Fair the following year. He appeared at Drury Lane in 1749 and in December 1751 he stood in for David Ross at late notice, with great success. In November 1757 he appeared as Macheath at Covent Garden where he remained for the next twenty-five winter seasons. He sang in supporting choruses or songs between acts, gradually moving into the leads of ballad, pastoral and comic operas; he was never suited to straight comic or tragic roles. He left the company after the 1782–3 season.

Mattocks was described as hard-working and keen, but not hugely talented. Most critics agreed that:

> ... as an Actor, Mr Mattocks has very little title to public favour, – as a singer he claims very respectful notice: his voice is clear, soft, melodious and expressive. The next is his figure which is well-proportioned; yet he wants that manly grace his sex demands, and animation to inspirit the several characters he performs ... As a vocal performer, I look upon Mr Mattocks to be the best on either theatre in point of voice; and, did he possess more compass in this last-mentioned, he, probably, would be the best on any stage.[3]

John Quick was born in Whitechapel, the son of a brewer. At the age of fourteen he joined a theatrical company in Fulham in which he played various tragic characters. In 1766 he was at Haymarket under Foote, together with Shuter. He performed mainly at Covent Garden throughout his career, although he also appeared at provincial theatres and was the manager of the King Street theatre at Bristol for a time. Initially he played clowns and rustic characters and triumphed in 1773 as the original Tony Lumpkin in *She Stoops to Conquer* (see page 77), a part which Woodward had turned down. The majority of his huge list of original parts were assigned to him following the deaths of Shuter and Woodward in 1776 and 1777.

Quick appeared as Richard III for his benefit in April 1790, in the belief that he was capable of playing tragedy; the performance began well but disintegrated into comedy and laughter. In April 1798 he resigned his long engagement at Covent Garden due to ill health. His last performance seems to have been in *The Wonder* in May 1813 for Mrs Mattocks's benefit. He died on 4 April 1831.

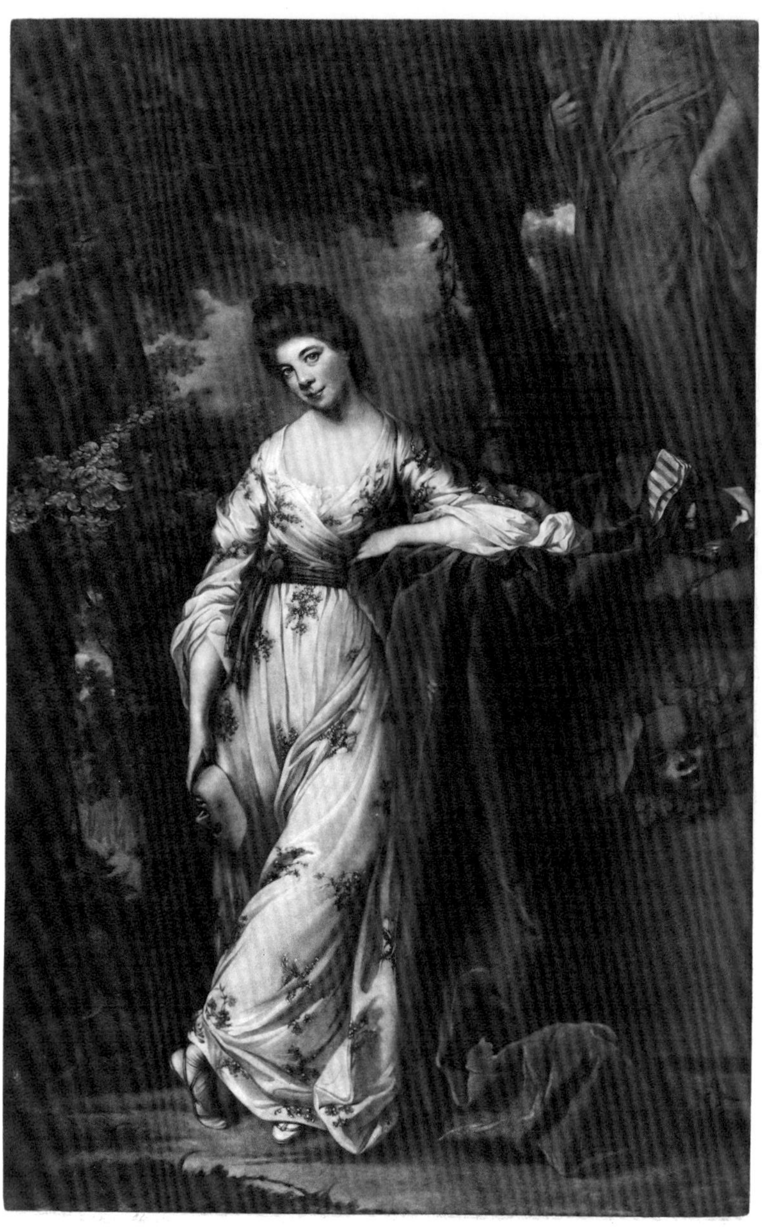

45 Mrs Abington

Engraved by James Watson
after Sir Joshua Reynolds

Published by John Wesson 17 April 1769

615 x 383 I; 616 x 384 Pl.

References: CS 1; G 62; H p. 77; O'D 13

1. Finished proof before all letters.
Impressions: CLB; BM.

2. With the engraved inscription at the base of the image: "*Sr J. Reynolds pinx. *** J^s Watson fecit | Mrs ABINGTON. | Publiſh'd & Sold by I. Wesson, in Litchfield Str^t Soho.*".
Impressions: CLB.

3. With the publication line clumsily altered:

Neither the painting, now at Waddesdon Manor, nor the print was ever exhibited. The painting was altered by Reynolds at a later date.[1] Although the plate was published by John Wesson, it was acquired by William Dickinson and subsequently sold after Dickinson's bankruptcy in 1795 for 11s. It then came into the possession of James Bretherton[2] and was auctioned again after his retirement in 1799.[3] Walter Shropshire, who considered the sitter to be wearing a 'masquerade dress', listed a proof impression[4] in his catalogue for 1773 priced at 15s.

Frances Barton was born in 1737. Her father had served in the Guards and kept a cobbler's stall near Drury Lane Theatre. She sold flowers at first, becoming known as 'Nosegay Fan', and then began singing and reciting at taverns and coffee houses. As the servant of a French milliner in Cockspur Street she is said to have acquired both her taste in dresses and a knowledge of French; she was later a cook maid in a kitchen run by Robert Baddeley, cooking for Samuel Foote.

"Publiſh'd Augᵗ 17. 1769 by I. Wesson,
Litchfield Strᵗ Soho.".
Impressions: CLB; BM.

4. With the publication line altered again:
"Publiſhd as the Act directs, Augᵗ *17. 1769* by I.
Weſson in Litchfield Street Soho".
Impressions: CLB.

5. With the date removed: "Publiſhd and Sold
by I. Wesson, in Litchfield Strᵗ Soho.".
Impressions: CLB P11,691 (impression exhibited);
BM.

She first appeared at the Haymarket Theatre when it opened in the summer of 1755 and was at Drury Lane in 1756, having been engaged on Foote's recommendation. She was first described as Mrs Abington in 1759, the year in which she married her music master, who was one of the king's trumpeters; the marriage was short-lived and eventually she bribed her husband to keep away from her. Her success at Drury Lane was overshadowed by that of Mrs Pritchard and Mrs Clive who were the leading ladies at this time, and so she went to Dublin where she was extremely popular.

Persuaded by Garrick to return, she remained at Drury Lane for some eighteen years. She transferred to Covent Garden in 1782 and was absent from the stage altogether between 1790–7. She was seen on the stage for the last time in April 1799 and died 4 March 1815.

Mrs Abington was praised for her wit, charm and beauty. Lichtenberg thought that 'this bewitching charmer' was 'unique on the English stage'.[5] In comedy he felt that:

> She is as different from Mrs Yates and Mrs Barry as the comic from the tragic muse. She is inferior to them, and especially to the latter, in majesty of demeanour and the expression of tender emotion; but she surpasses them in a talent for convincing the innermost heart of the spectators that she does not feel herself to be acting a part, but presenting reality in all its bitter truth, each trifling characteristic feature bearing witness to her own powers of observation. She is superior to them also in her art … and … in showing off her magnificent form … She certainly surpasses all other English actresses in wit. One perceives that the cardboard world of Drury Lane is too restricted for her … Little as she is suited to tragedy, she is less so to low comedy.[6]

Mrs Abington does not seem to have been aware of such limitations, as one commentator mentioned:

> Like many of her profession, she thought herself capable of characters not within the scope of her powers. I once saw her play Ophelia to Mr Garrick's Hamlet; and to use the simile of my old friend Dr Monsey, she appeared like a mackerel on a gravel walk.[7]

She held a distinguished position in society and had many admirers, including Horace Walpole, Samuel Johnson and General Paoli – even Reynolds was said to be bewitched by her. Both on and off the stage she was a much copied figure of fashion and many women went to the theatre just to see what she would be wearing; the 'Abington Cap' was all the rage. A reviewer in *The London Chronicle* noted that:

> … the public took upon her over-dressing her characters as a harmless piece of vanity, and applaud that elegance of taste which leads her into this error. Mrs Abington, it must be observed however, is rarely absurd, altho' she may sometimes o'erleap the bounds of critical propriety. She would never dress a chamber maid like a woman of fashion, in the dress of a shepherdess at a masquerade.

She was also stubborn and petulant, 'the worst of bad women' according to Garrick, who was often driven to distraction by her, complaining, 'I never saw Mrs Abington theatrically happy for a Week together'.[8] Exasperated, he beseeched her:

> for Heavens' sake let ye poor Manager have some respite from his many labours, & enjoy a few unmurmuring Weeks in the Summer; the Month of September will soon be here, & then it will be as Natural for you to find fault with him, as for Him to find fault with You ...[9]

To others, he was more outspoken:

> – what you mean by the black but fair defect, Except that most Worthless Creature Ab[ington], I dont't[sic] know – she is below the thought of an Honest Man or Woman – she is as Silly, as she is false & treacherous – .[10]

[1] Waterhouse suggests that the appointments in October 1772 and early 1773 were for this purpose.

[2] James Bretherton engraver and printseller 134 New Bond Street 1771–99.

[3] *A Catalogue of the Extensive and Valuable Stock of Ancient and Modern Prints ... Mr. James Bretherton, Drawing Master and Printseller ...*, London, Christie, 31 January, 1799 (3rd day, part lot 164).

[4] He also listed it as a 'painting on Glaſs ... in an elegant green and gold frame' at 2 guineas.

[5] Lichtenberg, pp. 68–9.

[6] Lichtenberg, pp. 33–4.

[7] Taylor, John *Records of my Life*, 1771, II, p. 417.

[8] Boaden, J. ed. *The Private Correspondence of David Garrick*, 1831, II, p. 140.

[9] *Letters*, no. 847, 18 June 1774.

[10] *ibid.*, no. 1038, 31 July 1776.

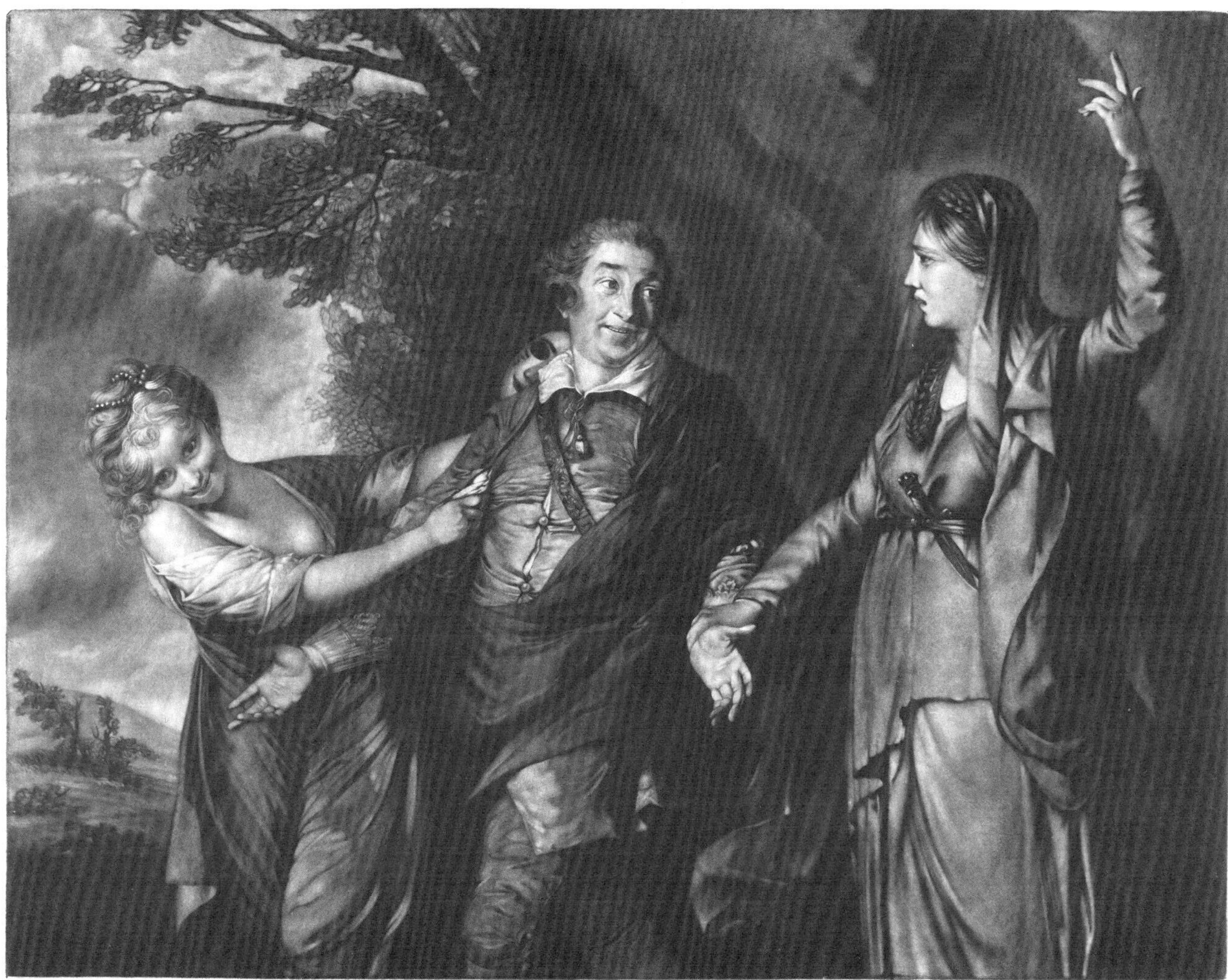

46 [Mr Garrick between Tragedy and Comedy]

Engraved by Edward Fisher
after Sir Joshua Reynolds

Published by Edward Fisher, John Boydell,
Elizabeth Bakewell and Henry Parker
10 November 1762

402 x 502 image plate; 25 x 502 inscription
plate.

References: CS 20; H p. 29; Hall 83

1. Finished proof without inscription space.
Impressions: CLB P20,758 (impression exhibited).

2. With the inscription, on a separate plate:
*"J. Reynolds Pinxit. *** E: Fisher ſculpsit Londini
1762. | Reddere Personæ scit convenientia cuique. |
Sold by Edwᵈ Fisher, at the Golden Head the South
Side of Leicester-Square, John Boydell Engraver, at
the Unicorn, Cheapside, and E: Bakewell, & H:
Parker, PrintSellers in Cornhill, opposite Birchin
Lane, London. *** Price 10/6".*
Impressions: CLB; BM; H; TM.

Reynolds's painting and Fisher's mezzotint were both exhibited at the Society of Artists in 1762 and the former was subsequently purchased by the Earl of Halifax for three hundred guineas. Reynolds's composition and treatment derive from paintings by Guido Reni and Paulo de Mateis.[1]

Control of the plate seems to have eventually passed to the Boydells, since the plate was sold from their stock after Josiah Boydell's death in 1818. It was lotted up with *Garrick as Kitely* and a portrait of Dr James Beattie and sold to Robert Cribb for £27. The other shareholders had all ceased to trade or had died by 1782. A proof from the collection of Nathaniel Hillier made £1 7s at auction in 1784. Shropshire listed an impression, 'very fine & scarce', in his catalogue for 1774 at £1 11s 6d, as did the Magazin des Estampes in 1775.

In 1769 Valentine Green appears to have engraved a version of Reynolds's painting of *Garrick between Tragedy and Comedy*. The print has never been identified, although Green listed it, as 'whole lengths', in his 1780 catalogue amongst plates made for other printsellers. It may have been a second plate made to replace Fisher's mezzotint. There is no evidence that this plate was ever published and it was possibly destroyed.

In 1764 Garrick had written home to his brother:

3. [Later impressions with the separate plate (CS)].

I am so plagu'd here for my Prints or rather Prints of Me–that I must desire You to send me by ye first opportunity six prints from Reynolds's picture, You may apply to ye Engraver he lives in Leicester fields, & his name is Fisher, he will give you good ones, if he knows they are for Me ...[2]

By the following year George Colman reported to Garrick that J.E. Haid's copy was available in Paris:

There hang out here in every street, pirated prints of Reynolds's Picture of you, which are underwritten, 'l'Homme entre le Vice et la Vertu'.[3]

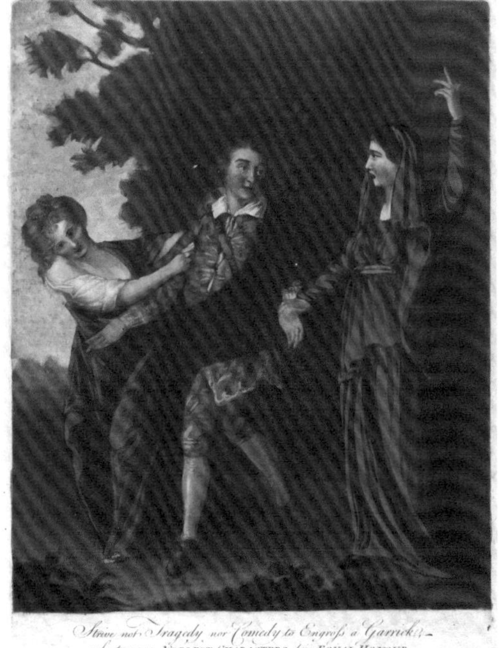

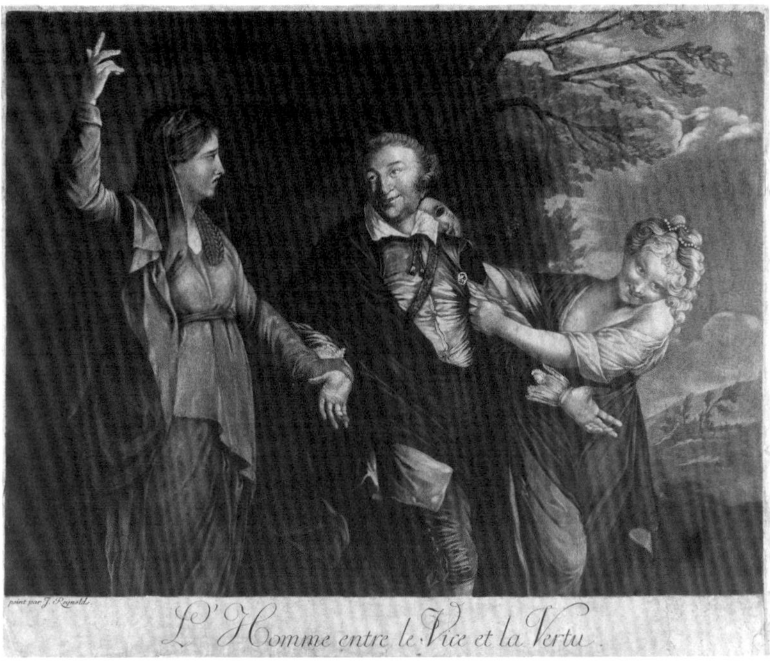

By 1769 when Richard Cumberland composed the epilogue for his play *The Brothers*, the print had already become one of the most famous images of its subject:

Who has but seen the celebrated Strife
Where Reynolds calls the Canvas into Life:
And, twixt the Tragic and the Comic Muse,
Courted of both, and dubious where to chuse,
Th' immortal Actor stands ...

A large number of piracies of this print were engraved in various sizes: a mezzotint (352 x 405 Pl.) was engraved by Purcell and published jointly by Sayer and Bowles; another smaller version (250 x 352 Pl.) was published by Robert Sayer; these were both published in or before 1766, since they are listed in Sayer's 1766 catalogue. An anonymous posture mezzotint (350 x 250 Pl.) was published by Carington Bowles in which the figures were made into whole lengths (see left).

Tuesday November 10. *will be publish'd,*
Price ten Shillings and Sixpence,
A Print done in Mezzotinto by EDWARD FISHER, of Mr. GARRICK, between the Comic and Tragic Muses, from the celebrated Original Picture, designed and painted by Mr. REYNOLDS.
N.B. Gentlemen who are desirous of choice Impressions, are requested to send in their Names and Directions to John Boydell, Engraver, at the Unicorn in Cheapside; E. Bakewell and H. Parker, Printsellers, opposite Birchin-lane, Cornhill; or E. Fisher, at the Golden Head in Leicester Fields.

The Public Advertiser, 2 November 1762.

[1] Penny, pp. 205–7.
[2] *Letters*, no. 343, 20 Nov. 1764.
[3] Boaden, J. *ed. The Private Correspondence of David Garrick*, 1831, I, p. 232.

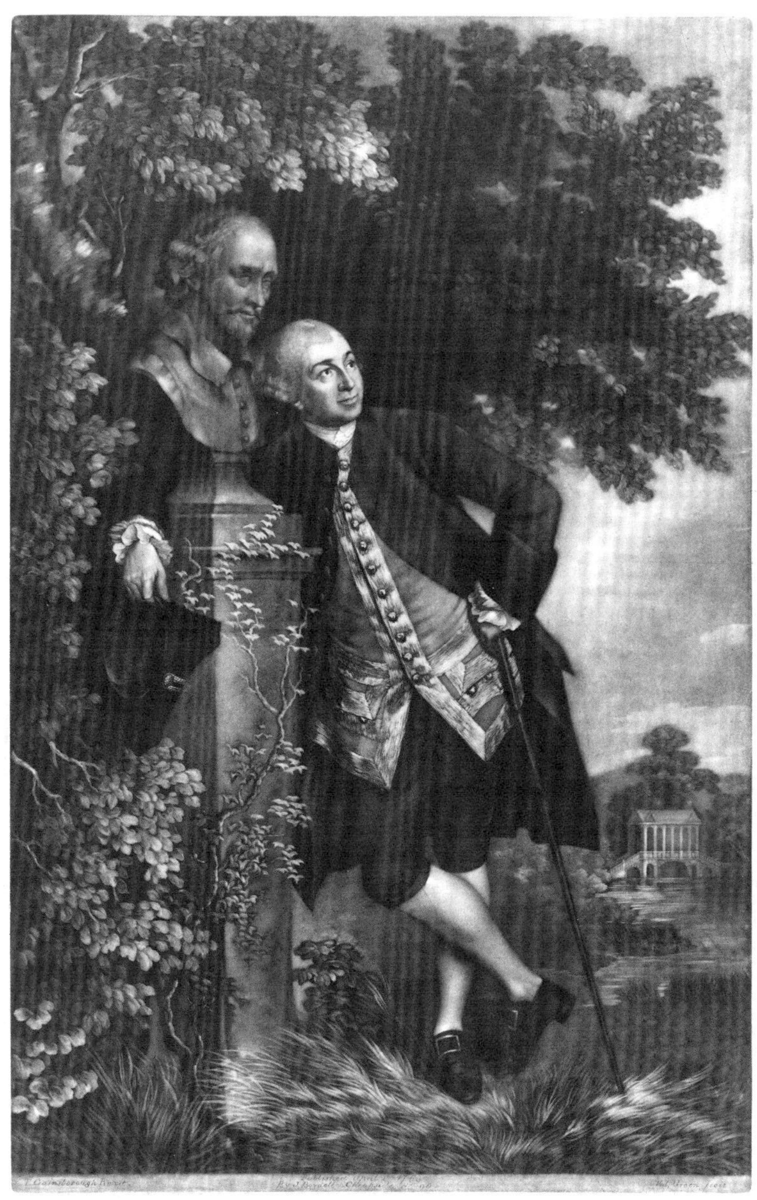

47 David Garrick Esq.ʳ

Engraved by Valentine Green
after Thomas Gainsborough

Published by John Boydell 2 April 1769

605 x 384 I; 616 x 386 Pl.

References: CS 46; R 46; W 7; O'D 8; Hall 9

1. Finished proof before all letters, the inscription space grounded.
Impressions: CLB.

2. Finished proof with the scratched inscription: "*Published April 2ⁿᵈ 1769 | T. Gainsborough Pinxit. *** Val, Green fecit | By J Boydell Cheapside N.º 90.*".
Impressions: CLB P22,295 (impression exhibited); BM.

Garrick commissioned this painting from Gainsborough, who, delighted with Garrick's patronage, wrote:

> I intend with your approbation my dear friend to take the form from [Shakespeare's] pictures and statue[1] just enough to preserve his likeness past the doubt of all blockheads at first sight, and supply a soul from his works; . . .

Exhibited at the Society of Artists in 1766, it was considered by his wife to have been the best portrait of him ever painted. Two years later the Corporation of Stratford invited Garrick to present a picture of himself for the new Town Hall and Garrick requested Gainsborough to re-work this painting. The background of the painting is Prior Park, the home of Garrick's friend Bishop Warburton. The painting was destroyed by fire in 1946.

Valentine Green was born in 1739. He was apprenticed to a lawyer and appears to have been taught engraving by Robert Hancock, who produced transfer prints for the Worcester porcelain

109

3. With the title added, scraped in white letters in c. at the foot of the image: "DAVID GARRICK Efq!".
Impressions: CLB; V&A; H.

T. BECKET, Bookfeller in the Strand, begs leave to acquaint the Nobility, Gentry and the Public in general that he shall publish on Wednesday, the 6th of September, at Stratford upon Avon, [...]
4. A fine Metzotinto Print (done from a Capital Painting of Mr Gainsborough) now in the Great Hall at Stratford, of Mrs [sic] Garrick, with a Bust of Shakefpeare [...].

factory. In 1765, abandoning law, Green came to London where he was successful as an engraver, particularly in the late 1770s. In 1789 he undertook to engrave the paintings in the Electoral Gallery at Dusseldorf, but the war with France that engulfed Europe a few years later ruined him. His mezzotints are excellent and he shines as an interpreter of Reynolds, although in the spring of 1783 they quarrelled and Green never engraved from Reynolds's work again. Green published most of his own works and became one of the most important engraver-publishers. He died in 1813.

Impressions were listed in Boydell's 1773 catalogue at 10s 6d and by 1803 the price he charged had risen to 15s. The plate was eventually sold in 1818 after Josiah Boydell's death for £4. The print was also advertised, as part of a long list of wares, by the established bookseller Thomas Becket in *The London Chronicle* for 1769.

The Jubilee was well advertised by all those who could profit from it: those who published Shakespeare's works, or memoirs and anecdotes of Shakespeare and Garrick; proprietors of 'fine' lodgings in Stratford, and innkeepers on the road to the celebrations. Tickets and 'programmes' were available from London booksellers and every imaginable trinket and souvenir seemed to be on sale. Most magazines had special supplements, often embellished with prints. In today's terms, Garrick's Shakespeare Jubilee was beyond the wildest dreams of even the most imaginative advertising consultant; although 'weak logistic support [was] actually given by the Town for the unexpectedly large crowds [...] Housing was meagre, prices seemed exorbitant, food supplies insufficient, and the heavens opened to a three-day downpour which flooded the race-course, wet down the improvised ball-room floor, and extinguished Domenico Angelo's fireworks'[2], the scale and audacity of the project was remarkable.

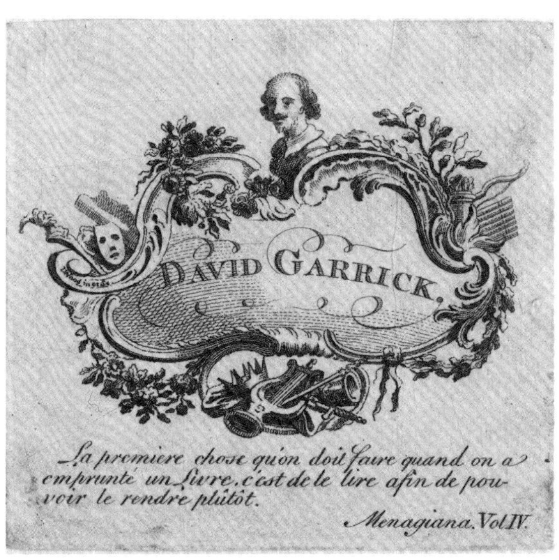

Garrick's book plate.

[1] The latter by Peter Scheemaker after Kent, Stratford Church.
[2] Stone and Kahrl, p. 581.

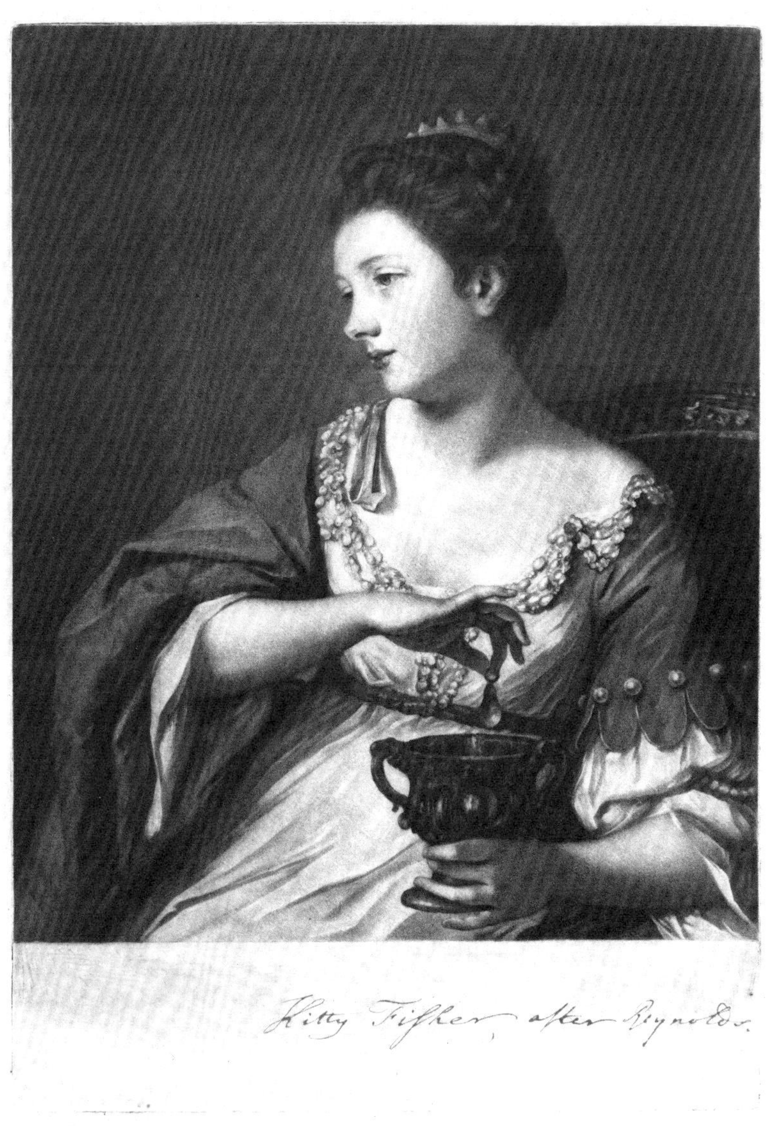

48 Miss Kitty Fischer

Engraved by Richard Houston
after Sir Joshua Reynolds

Published by Richard Houston and
by Robert Sayer [1759]

279 x 225 I; 330 x 226 Pl.

References: CS 36; R 36; H p. 98;
O'D (Norris) 2

1. Before all letters.
Impressions: CLB P8,167 (impression exhibited).

2. With the engraved inscription: "*J. Reynolds
Pinx! *** Rich.ᵈ Houſton Fecit. | Miſs Kitty
Fischer~ | Sold by Rich.ᵈ Houston, at Charing Croſs.
*** P~s 2.ˢ*".
Impressions: CLB; BM.

**3. [Re-published by Robert Sayer with the
engraver's name erased: "at the Golden Buck
near Serjeants Inn Fleet Street." (R)].**

The picture of Kitty Fischer may have been painted by Sir Joshua Reynolds for Sir Charles Bingham [later Lord Lucan] and is now at Kenwood, but an advertisement for the print which was published in *The London Chronicle* for 12–14 July 1759 suggests that the picture was owned by the sitter:

A Curious Metzotinto Print of Miſs KITTY FISCHER, done from an Original Picture in her own Poſſeſſion. lately painted from the Life, by Mr. REYNOLDS.
    Printed for and ſold by Robert Sayer, Printſeller, oppoſite Fetter-Lane, Fleet-Street ; aud T. Ewart, at the Bee-hive, oppoſite Hartſhorn-Lane, in the Strand.

The plate remained in Sayer's stock throughout his life and was passed on to his assistants Laurie & Whittle, when Sayer's executors sold the business to them in May 1794. It is listed in Sayer's catalogue for 1766, Sayer & Bennett's catalogue for 1775 and Laurie & Whittle's 1795 catalogue.

This is not a theatrical portrait, although it could be mistaken for one. Reynolds depicts the famous courtesan Kitty Fischer in the character of Cleopatra who, to impress Mark Antony at a feast, dropped a giant pearl into a glass of wine and drank it, dissolved.

4. With the publication line altered: *"London Printed for Rob.! Sayer, opposite Fetter Lane Fleetstreet."*.
Impressions: CLB; BM.

Fischer is playing a part, but not a part in a play; she never acted on the stage. When Casanova met her in London in 1764, covered in diamonds and about to go to a ball, he was told that she had once clapped a twenty pound note into a bread and butter sandwich and eaten it.[1]

By painting her in this character, using a composition closely adapted from a picture by Trevisani, Reynolds unites portraiture with history painting. Portrait commissions at this date were the mainstay of most artists – Reynolds himself painted over four thousand – but history painting was considered to be a more noble, higher form of painting to which artists should aspire. The portrait of Harriet Powell as Leonora in *The Padlock*, a part she sang fifty-three times in 1768–9, is another example of a portrait in the guise of a history painting.

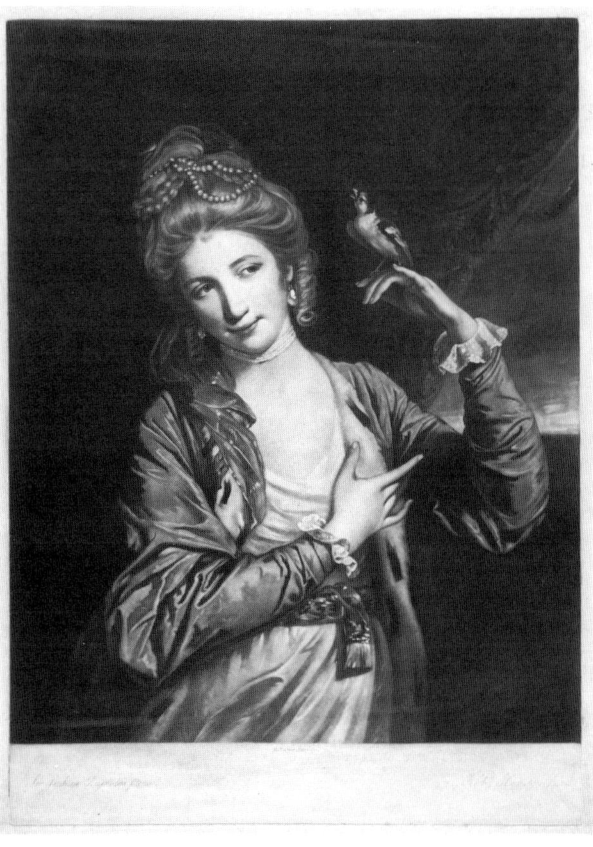

Although Penny suggests that, 'without evidence of the prints which are given the title used here, it may be doubted whether Reynolds's painting would have been recognised as a likeness of Kitty Fisher, or indeed considered as a portrait at all'[2], it seems that the painting was well enough known by September 1759, although admittedly the print had already been issued, causing one critic [possibly William Kenrick] to bring it to the attention of readers of *The London Chronicle*:

In Answer to the two Lines, wrote under Miss Fisher's Picture [print], in the character of Cleopatra.

TO Cleopatra's character what right?
Tho' full as wanton, yet not half so bright;
In manners most unlike you'll find they prove,
The one a W——e for hire, the one for love.

W.K.[3]

[1] Penny, p. 195.
[2] *ibid.*, p. 27.
[3] *The London Chronicle*, 22–24 Sept. 1759.

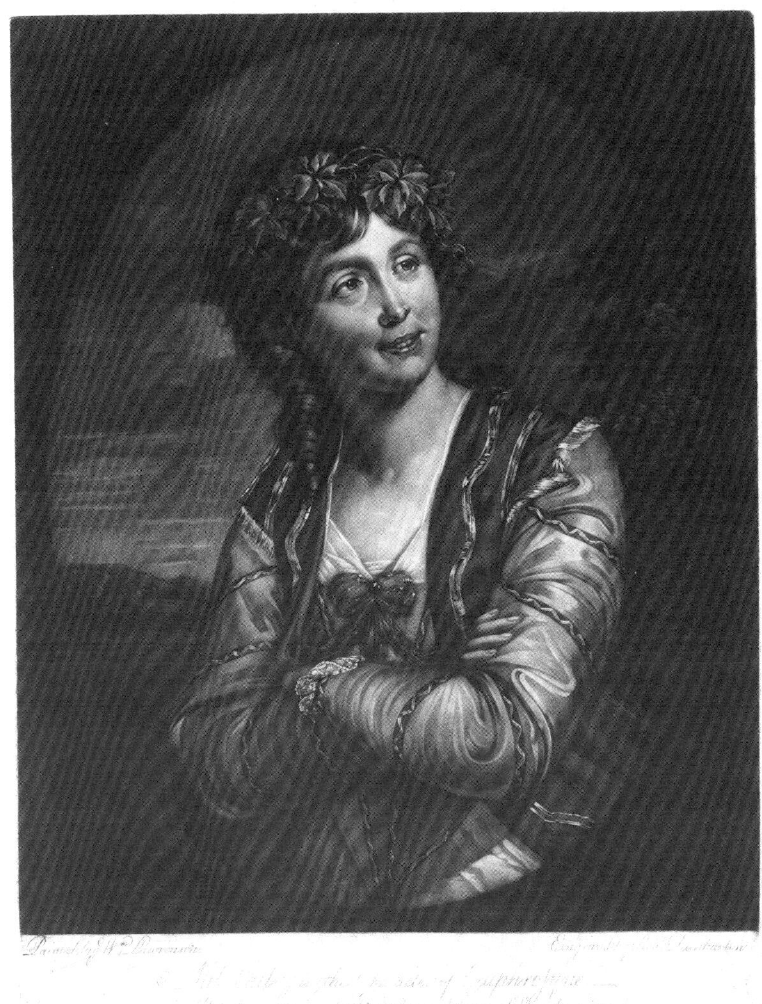

49 Miss Catley, in the Character of Euphrosyne

Engraved by Robert Dunkarton
after William Lawranson

Published by Robert Dunkarton 15 April 1777

348 x 278 I; 383 x 278 Pl.

References: CS 13; O'D 3; Hall 6

1. Finished proof with the scratched inscription: *"Painted by W.m Lawrenson *** Engrav'd by Rob.t Dunkarton | Miſs Catley, in the Character of Euphroſyne. | Publish'd April 15,th 1777 by Rob.t Dunkarton N.o 452, opposite Villers Street Strand.".* Impressions: CLB P28,393 (impression exhibited); BM.

2. With the engraved inscription: *"Painted by W.m Lawrenson *** Engrav'd by Rob.t Dunkarton | MISS CATLEY in the Character of EUPHROSYNE. | "All I ask of Mortal Man, Is but to Love me while he can". Vide Comus Act 2.d Scene 1.st | Publiſhed April*

Both artists involved in this print were minor figures: Lawranson combined the practice of a portrait painter with that of a genre painter, often imitating Reynolds and Wheatley; Robert Dunkarton, a former pupil of the engraver William Pether, began his career as a portrait painter. He exhibited his work at the Society of Artists from 1768 to 1771 and at the Royal Academy between 1770 and 1779. He engraved a large number of mezzotints between 1770 and 1781, and although his work is not of the calibre of engravers such as Valentine Green and John Raphael Smith, a number of his plates show considerable merit; this portrait of Ann Catley displays some of Dunkarton's skills and conveys her beauty and vivacity.

Miss Catley appeared as the pastoral nymph in Milton's 'pastoral comedy' *Comus* at Covent Garden in 1762, but she did not play the part of Euphrosyne until October 1773. She received a benefit performance in this part in March 1777 but did not play it again for three years; her rendition of 'Sweet Echo' made the song famous. *Comus* seems an unlikely play for a wanton to appear in; however on this occasion Miss Catley showed that she was an able actress and could adapt her performance:

... With pleasure we re-mark this Lady seems to have

113

*15th 1777. by Rob! Dunkarton N° 452, oppofite
Villers Street Strand.".*
Impressions: BM; H.

☞ In Milton's masque, Comus, son of Bacchus
and Circe, is a pagan god who waylays travellers
and tempts them to drink a magic potion which
changes them into wild beasts. Lost in a forest
with her two brothers, Euphrosyne is attracted
by Comus's revels and becomes lost. She meets
him, disguised as a shepherd, and he offers to
shelter her in his cottage. The brothers discover
what has happened from the good Attendant
Spirit, who is disguised as the shepherd Thyrsis;
she warns them of the magic powers of Comus
and gives them the root of the plant Haemony
as a protection. Comus, with his rabble, is discovered urging Euphrosyne to drink the magic
potion. The brothers burst in and the mob
retreats, but Euphrosyne cannot be released
from an enchanted chair as Comus still has his
magic wand. Thyrsis invokes Sabrina, a
goddess, who frees Euphrosyne. After an ode of
thanks, she and her brothers return safely to
Ludlow Castle.

profited by the animadversions made on the licentious mode
of her performance last season; for excepting a few liberties
she took with some of the songs, it must be acknowledged she
executed her department in a most bewitching manner; and
by her figure, voice and deportment, in the song beginning
'The Wanton God' exerted the warmest applause from the
audience.[1]

She was born in 1745 near Tower Hill, the daughter of a
hackney coachman. Her singing attracted the attention of William
Bates, a musician who arranged her first engagement.

In 1763 Catley was engaged by Thomas Lowe at Marylebone
Gardens, where she sang at the opening night. Now under the
pupilage of Charles Macklin, she was recommended to the
manager of Smock Lane theatre, Dublin, where her popularity
enabled her to earn as much as forty guineas a night. She returned
to England in 1770 and from then on appeared at various different
venues to great acclaim. During the 1772–3 season she was the
highest paid actress at Covent Garden.

She was married to Major General Lascelles and retired in 1784
with a considerable fortune. She died at Ealing in October 1789.

Lichtenberg was one of the admirers of this 'roguish singer, who
is a great favourite':

I saw at Covent Garden the operetta *Love in a Village*, in which
a certain Miss Catley sang so sweetly that she almost made
me forget the __.[2] She is a black-haired, saucy creature, and
has a charming voice, so powerful that she can make herself
heard, if she will, above the insistent accompagnement and
the applause of an adoring public.[3]

He reports that she had other admirers: 'they say that she plays
"love in the town" on her own account just as well, and it is not
known whether the stage or the bedchamber be the more profitable'.[4]

Miss Catley also caught the attention of a reviewer in *The Town
and Country Magazine*:

… her person is above the middle stature; though perfectly
well made, she is not genteel, there being a carelessness in
her gait, that too nearly approaches the hoyden. Her countenance is remarkably pleasing and expressive, and she has a
wanton wildness in her eye, that cannot fail to captivate. Her
mouth, from whence the most exquisite harmony flows, displays a set of teeth that are unrivalled upon the stage, and
adds charms to a face uncommonly beautiful.

---

[1] *The London Chronicle*, 3 Sept. 1773.
[2] Lichtenberg was severely disabled with a
hunch-back.
[3] Lichtenberg, pp. 53–4.
[4] *ibid.*, p. 52.

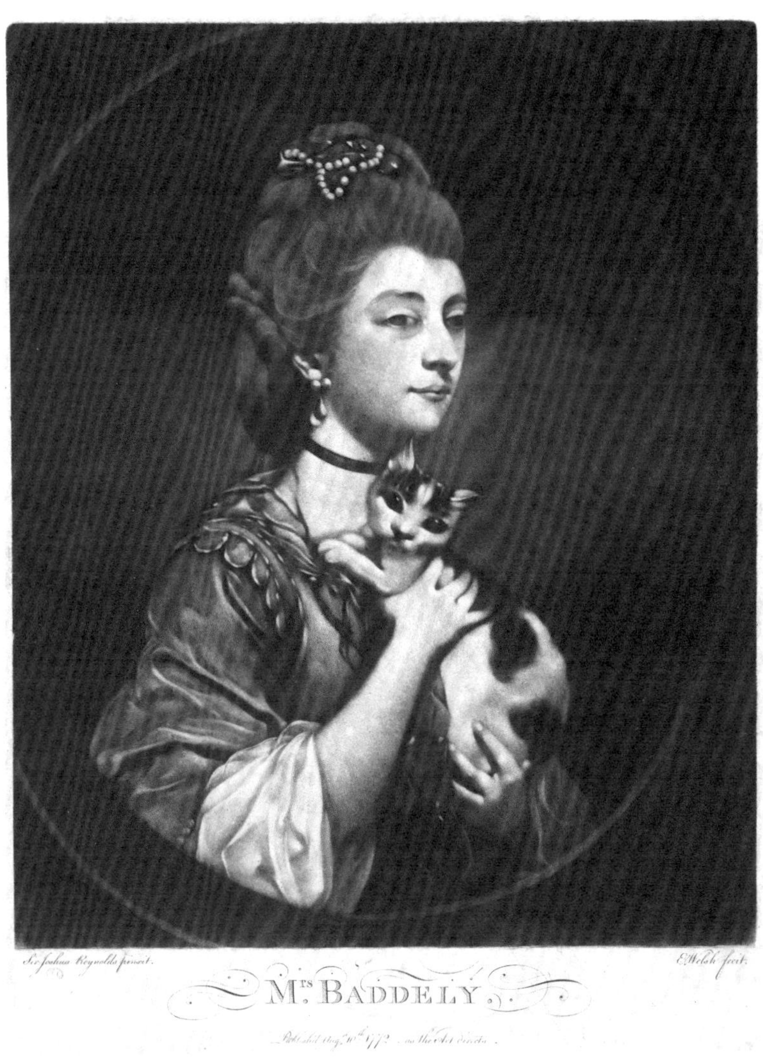

50 Mʳˢ Baddeley

Engraved by Ephraim Welsh
after Sir Joshua Reynolds

Published 10 August 1772

316 x 252 I; 354 x 252 Pl.

References: CS 1; H p. 79; O'D 2

1. Finished proof before all letters.
Impressions: BM.

2. With the engraved inscription: *"Sir Joshua Reynolds pinxit. *** E,, Welsh fecit. / Mʳˢ BADDELY. / Publish'd Augˢᵗ 10:ᵗʰ 1772. as the Act directs."*.
Impressions: CLB P10,979 (impression exhibited); TM.

This print is the only known engraving by Ephraim Welsh, about whom little is known. He exhibited a portrait of a lady in crayon at the Society of Artists in 1771, giving his address as 1 Wimpole Street, Cavendish Square, and at the time that he engraved this print he was a student at the Royal Academy Schools. Reynolds's portrait is poorly served by this engraving and it is very probable that he obtained the commission for Welsh in order to encourage a student. Welsh's plate was not acquired by any printseller and impressions are consequently rare. His style of engraving is coarse, lacking the refinement and delicacy that can be seen in the work of engravers such as John Raphael Smith; the figure of the cat is particularly crudely engraved and could almost be mistaken for a piece of porcelain. In 1773 Thane listed an impression in his catalogue of stock at 2s.

A few weeks after this print came out, Sayer published Robert Laurie's mezzotint of Sophia Baddeley after Zoffany. Although it exhibited some of Laurie's worst defects as an engraver, it became the standard portrait that a theatre-goer might buy. At about the same time, November 1772, Sayer also published Richard Earlom's fine mezzotint of *'Mr. King and Mrs. Baddeley in The Clandestine Marriage'* (see page 41); it is likely that both Sayer's

115

publications were stimulated by the King's delight in Mrs Baddeley's performance in this play (see page 41).

Sophia Snow was born in Westminster in about 1745, the daughter of Valentine Snow, Sergeant-trumpeter to the King and a musician. In 1763, aged eighteen, she ran away with and married an actor, Robert Baddeley, who arranged her first engagement in the following year, the part of Ophelia to Holland's Hamlet. She subsequently became a member of the Drury Lane company.

Mrs Baddeley sang in Arne's oratorio *Judith* at the great Shakespeare Jubilee in Stratford in 1769, and was engaged as a singer on the high salary of twelve guineas a week at Ranelagh and Vauxhall Gardens. Her marriage was extremely unhappy and her husband's unpleasant behaviour towards her caused George Garrick to issue a challenge, resulting in their famous 'bloodless duel'. The Baddeleys separated in 1770 and in the following year Sophia left Drury Lane, to return only occasionally during the rest of her career

Mrs Baddeley was admired for her exceptional beauty, and was both popular and controversial: on one occasion, when she was excluded from the Pantheon because of the management's decision to disallow entry to women of doubtful character, fifty gentlemen armed with swords and headed by Captain George Hangar (noted as one of her lovers), pushed through the constables and 'escorted her in triumph to the rooms', where they demanded an apology from the management.[1]

By 1781 her fortune and health were failing and Mrs Baddeley was forced to flee from her creditors to Dublin. In her later years, according to Wilkinson who saw her acting in York and Edinburgh, she became addicted to laudanum. She fell ill with consumption and died on 1 July 1786.

[1] Two bust portraits of Mrs Baddeley and Captain Hangar were published in *The Town & Country Magazine* in June 1772 to commemorate the event.

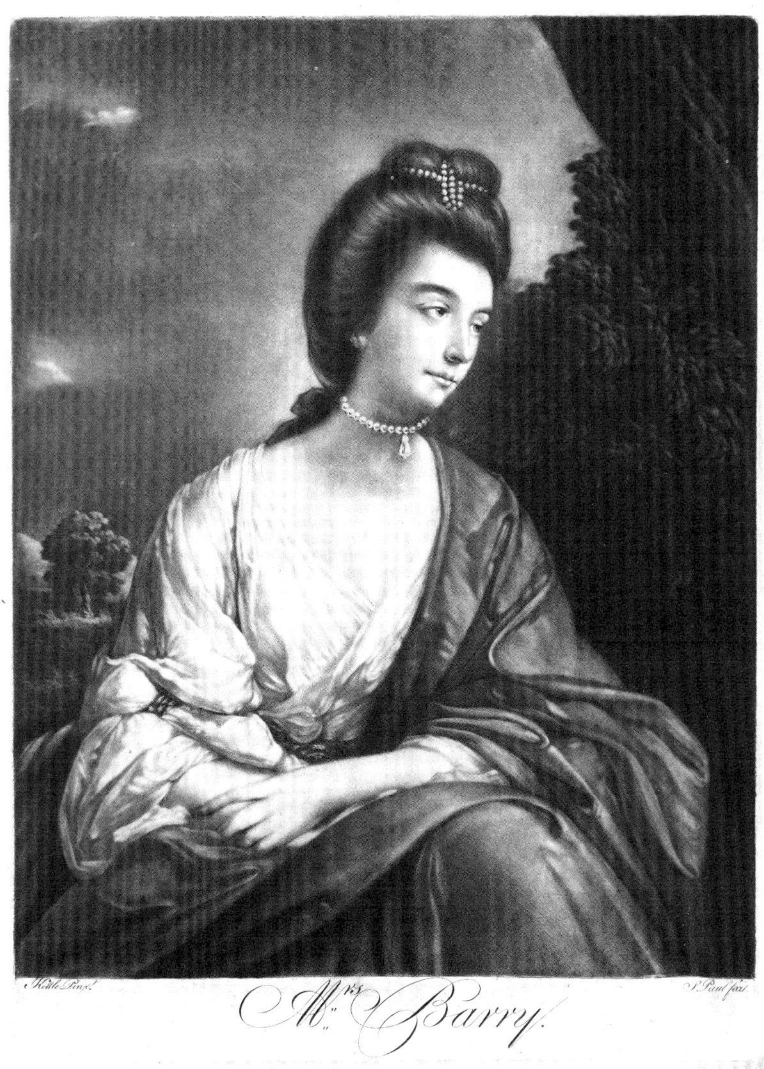

51 Mrs Barry

Engraved by S. Paul [Samuel de Wilde]
after Tilly Kettle

[Published by Samuel de Wilde?]

329 x 251; I; 354 x 251 Pl.

References: CS 1; O'D (Crawford) 3;
Hall (Crawford) 2

1. With the engraved inscription: *"Kettle Pinx!*
**** S Paul fecit | Mrs Barry"*.
Impressions: CLB P4,185 (impression exhibited); BM;
H.

Chaloner Smith states that Samuel de Wilde, best known as a theatrical portrait painter in the 1790s and early 1800s, engraved mezzotints under the pseudonym of S. Paul. This print is a copy, in reverse, of James Watson's mezzotint portrait of '*Lady Molineux*'. There is already confusion over the identity of the sitter in Watson's plate and de Wilde's claim that the sitter in his version is Mrs Barry complicates the matter further. As Chaloner Smith states, Watson's portrait is unlike his later mezzotint of Isabella, Lady Molyneux and therefore may represent another sitter of the same name. The sitter's name was added to Watson's plate in the third and final state, when the plate was probably re-published by Robert Sayer.

Remarkably, despite these two possibly fictitious portraits and a smaller anonymous version of the Kettle/Watson image, no separately published portrait of Mrs Barry exists. Clearly, there was a gap in the market for a mezzotint of Ann Barry who was both newsworthy and popular, a gap which de Wilde was rather brazenly attempting to fill.

A few days before Mrs Barry's (now Mrs Crawford) benefit performance in *Venice Preserv'd*, an advertisement was published by the theatrical portrait painter James Roberts, who is perhaps best

117

PROPOSALS by Mr. James Roberts, for publishing by Subscription, two Mezzotintos, (small whole lengths) viz. one of Mrs. Crawford, (late Mrs. Barry) the other Mrs. Hartley, in the character of Andromache, to be executed by Mr. Val. Green, Engraver in Mezzotinto to his Majesty, &c. and dedicated to Sir Joshua Reynolds.

N. B. As there has never been a print of Mrs. Crawford, it is hoped the dilitanti in general, and the admirers of that great actress in particular, will be speedy in their subscriptions, that they may have the finest and most valuable impressions. A regular series of the most approved dramatic performers will be published. Any Lady or Gentleman is at liberty to subscribe for a single print. Subscriptions received at Mr. James Roberts's, Great Queen-Street, Westminster, (where the original paintings may be seen) and at Mr. Bell's, bookseller.

The Morning Post and Daily Advertiser,
18 March 1779.

known for his small scale drawings to illustrate Bell's *British Theatre.*

If we are to believe Roberts, no portrait of Mrs Barry was available even by 1779 and for some reason his proposal for a mezzotint by Valentine Green failed. Occasionally subscriptions did fail; unlike those for large books that helped underwrite the costs, print subscriptions were often advertised to test the market.

Anne Street was born in 1734 at Bath, the daughter of an eminent apothecary. After the death of her first husband, William Dancer, whom she had married against considerable opposition from her family and friends in 1754, she married Spranger Barry. When he died in 1777, Ann was at the height of her career; it was reported that she earned as much as £1,000 for acting just sixteen nights in Dublin. In July 1778 she married her third husband, Thomas Crawford, an Irish barrister a dozen years her junior, who according to Hannah More was:

> … by his own account not worth a penny, but in debt. He is most desperately in love with his new wife, and in mourning for his old one … Poor man! I believe he thinks her an angel; – pity those fine delusions cannot last.[1]

Lichtenberg considered that:

> Of all the actresses here, Mrs. Barry is, in my opinion, the greatest, or at least the most versatile, being in this respect the only one who could bear comparison with Garrick. She can be trimly laced up like a saucy little waiting maid, and trip about so coyly and with such charming self-complacency that all the young misses and all the tall servants in the house can lose their hearts to her; or, on the other hand, she can sweep in with a cascade of rustling and rippling silk behind her, with an upright carriage and head turned, as though her vanity impelled her to feast her eyes on the set of her train. She is a great beauty, being even by the light of day and without paint, so they tell me, remarkably handsome, and moreover, a born actress … Her beauty has something saint-like about it, and the prevailing impression made by her demeanour and the sound of her excessively charming voice is one of gentle innocence and an obliging amiability. A woman perfect in the sight of God and man! Gentle, yielding, and of a temper as little satirical as heroic … Mr Barry, her husband, an actor who was formerly idolised and is still a favourite, has now become old and stiff. Mr Garrick got rid, therefore, of this excellent lady, probably on account of her husband, who had to be given a large salary and yet was no longer particularly useful, taking in their stead Mr and Mrs Yates from Covent Garden.[2]

He later continues:

> She is a perfect beauty and a great actress; in her ninth year, throwing down her catechism and knitting, she would creep with a Shakespeare into the garret and declaim to the chimneys. If I were rich, I should pack all the German actresses that I know into a ship and take them to London, so that they might learn from Mrs Barry how to use their arms … Her height and bosom could not be better.[3]

She died in 1801.

[1] TDB.
[2] Lichtenberg, pp. 31–32.
[3] *ibid.*, p. 68.

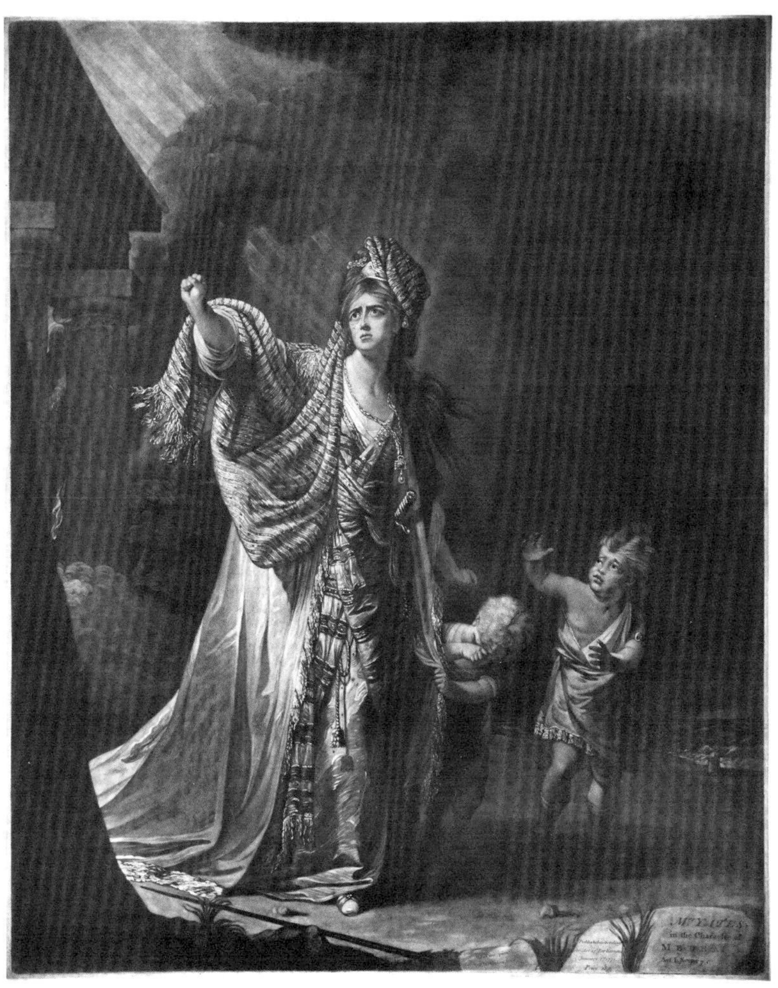

52 Mrs Yates as Medea

Engraved by William Dickinson
after Robert Edge Pine

Published by Robert Edge Pine 1 January 1771

576 x 426 I; 629 x 487 Pl.

References: CS 92; O'D 10; Hall 32

**1. With the engraved inscription at bottom r.
of image:** [to l.] "R.E. Pine pinx.^t / W.
Dickinfon fecit. [in c.] Publish'd according / to
Act of Parliament / *January 1st 1771. / Price 10.^s,
6^d* [to r.] *Mrs YATES,* / in the Charcter of /
MEDEA. / Act I. Scene 7.".
Impressions: BM; H.

2. With the price altered to '*15s 0*'.
Impressions: CLB P37,917 ex. coll. Alfred Morrison
Lugt 151 (impression exhibited).

**3. [False proof with the title and price
erased (R)].**

The painting was exhibited at the Society of Artists in 1770 and
judged by Horace Walpole to be 'a very fine picture'. William
Dickinson showed a drawing of this subject in chalk at the Society
of Artists exhibition in 1771, but the finished print was not exhibited until the following May. Despite the date engraved on the
print, Pine does not seem to have announced the publication until
10 April 1772 (see over).

The advertisement indicates that Pine both published and
organised distribution of this print. The plate remained with
Dickinson and was sold in his sale in 1794 for two guineas.

Richard Glover's *Medea* was first produced on 24 March 1767. It
was then performed only once a year, usually for Mrs Yates's
benefit, which seems to reflect the fact that the play did not
appeal to the public's taste. Hopkins the prompter noted on 29
October 1776, 'This Play was performed the first time for the
Managers – Mrs Yates was fine in her Character; but the Play is too
heavy and will not do'.[1]

The paucity of performances 'enhanced its appeal to connoisseurs'. In 1769 Sylas Neville prolonged his stay in London especially to see the play and found it to be 'inimitably great'. One
reviewer commented:

MEDEA is one of those characters in which the violent passions are continually in agitation; it suits therefore admirably

This Day is published, Price 10s 6d.
A Mezzotinto Print, from an original Whole-Length Portrait, painted by Mr. Pine, of Mrs. Yates, in the Character of Medea.
To be delivered at Mr. Pine's, in St. Martin's Lane. Where also may be had some good Impressions of the Surrender of Calais, and Canute reproving his Flatterers

The Public Advertiser, 10 April 1772.

☞ In Richard Glover's play, Medea, forsaken by Joseph, arrives in Corinth on the day that he is to re-marry. Medea hears Jason telling Theano, Priestess of Juno, of his betrothal. Jason then sees Medea, is seized with guilt and resolves that he will remain faithful to her. He attempts to excuse himself to Medea, but she reacts scornfully. Medea entrusts her children to Theano and with her magic wand invokes Hecate, who promises vengeance: 'What thou'd st love shall perish by thy rage'. Medea cannot bear the idea of destroying Jason and so she summons him and tries to win him back; however he tells her with shame that he has already married. Jason's banishment is re-enforced by the King, and he privately resolves to flee with Medea from Corinth. Suddenly Theano appears and relates that Medea has murdered her own children, in revenge for Jason's betrayal of her. Medea rushes in, faints but then recovers to realise the whole horror of her crime. She is about to stab herself when Juno appears and sweeps her away in a chariot. Also on the verge of suicide, Jason is restrained by Theano, who steels him for the future he must face.

Mrs Yates's stile [sic] of acting, and it is no compliment to say, she, yesterday evening, exerted herself with great success, and gave a dignity to the performance, without which, the Tragedy would have lost its effect ... The chariot in which Medea was borne across the stage, in the fifth act, did Loutherbourg great credit, and gave us an idea of the sublime. The managers have certainly been at much cost in getting up the tragedy of Medea, but, we fear, for little profit ...[2]

Mary Ann Yates was born in 1728, the daughter of William Graham, a captain's steward on a warship. She was apparently hired by Richard Sheridan in Dublin, where she appeared for the first time in 1752. She appeared at Drury Lane for the first time the following December, where she was encouraged by Garrick and Richard Yates, whom she later married.

She was one of the greatest tragic actresses of the century but in comedy even weaker than Mrs Cibber, whose retirement eventually opened up the major roles in tragedy for her. Initially rather timid, she became renowned for her inimitable rage and force. She was unrivalled as Medea, with no other actress attempting this part during her lifetime, as well as being a superb Lady Macbeth.

Charles Dibdin remarked that, 'an emulation of the best French actresses gave her a declamatory air to her delivery',[3] while Lichtenberg claimed that Mrs Yates was, 'so skilled in the management of her arms that from this woman alone could be made an abstract of the art of gesticulation'.[4] Murphy admired her 'statuesque beauty' and Boaden similarly thought that she, 'courted a likeness to the statues of antiquity in the solemn composure of her attitudes'. James Harris[5] praised her more effusively:

for tone and justness of elocution, for uninterrupted attention, for everything that was nervous, various, elegant and true in attitude and action, I never saw her equal but in Garrick, and forgive me for saying I cannot call him her superior.[6]

Garrick had enticed her from Covent Garden in 1774 and paid her a salary of £700, with an extra £50 for providing herself with stylish and fashionable clothes. She grew temperamental and was all too regularly 'indisposed', letting down audiences who often attended specifically to see her. Such behaviour moved Garrick to write that he had no regrets on retiring,

... leaving to Younger Spirits the present race of Theatrical Heroines with all their Airs, indispositions, tricks and importances which have reduc'd the Stage to be a dependent upon the Wills of our inslent[sic], vain, & let me add insignificant female trumpery ...[7]

Yet Davies, on hearing of her imminent retirement, asserted that:

The English theatre will long lament the loss of an actress, whose just elocution, noble manner, warm passion, and majestic deportment, have excited the admiration of foreigners and fixed the affection and applause of Britons.[8]

She died in May 1787 and was buried in Richmond Church.

[1] William Hopkins' Diary quoted in *The London Stage*, V, p. 30.
[2] *The Morning Chronicle*, 30 Oct. 1776.
[3] Joseph Knight, DNB.
[4] A letter of 10 Oct. 1775 in Lichtenberg, p. 14.
[5] James Harris (1709–80), author of Hermes.
[6] DNB.
[7] *Letters*, no. 976, 3 Jan. 1776.
[8] *Dramatic Miscellanies*, III, p. 251.

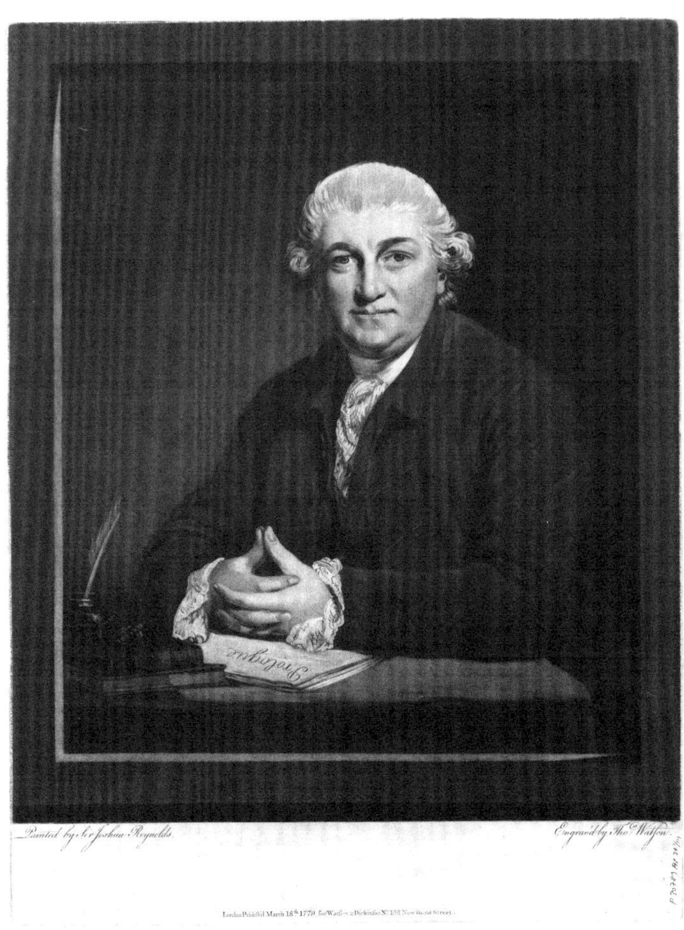

53 David Garrick Esq.[r]

Engraved by Thomas Watson
after Sir Joshua Reynolds

Published by Thomas Watson and
William Dickinson 18 March 1779

337 x 279 I; 380 x 281 Pl.

References: CS 16; R 16; H p. 30; G 35;
O'D 44

**1. [Finished proof before all letters and
before *Prologue* on paper** (said to be in BM)].

**2. Finished proof with the engraved inscrip-
tion:** "*Painted by Sir Joshua Reynolds. ***
Engraved by Tho.[s] Watson.* / London Publifh'd
March 18th 1779, for Watfon & Dickinfon N.[o]
158 New Bond Street.".
Impressions: CLB P30,789 (impression exhibited);
V&A.

3. With the added engraved inscription:
"DAVID GARRICK Efq.[r] / *Engrav'd from the
Original Picture in the pofsefsion of Sir Tho.[s] Mills, /
To whom this Print is with great respect Inscribed, by
his much Obliged Humble Servant –* Tho.[s]
Watson.".
Impressions: CLB.

The mezzotint engraved by Thomas Watson seems to be the authorised version of Reynolds's painting, appearing a little over six weeks after Laurie's print. Watson was a far superior engraver to Laurie and his finished works are excellently drawn; they are superb translations from colour to black and white. The original painting was in the possession of Sir Thomas Mills, to whom the plate was dedicated. This is recorded in an advertisement for Watson's print which also indicates that the painting was exhibited at a monody (written by Sheridan) delivered at Drury Lane; it seems likely that Laurie was thus able to gain access to the original and copy it. Publication of the print was announced in *The Morning Post and Daily Advertiser*, 24 March 1779:

> … in a few days will be published, price five shillings, a mezotinto print of the late DAVID GARRICK, Esq. engraved by Thomas Watson from the original picture painted by Sir Joshua Reynolds, belonging to Sir Thomas Mills. The above picture was exhibited in the monody at Drury-lane Theatre, and is the 1st and most esteemed likeness of him that has been painted. The nobility and gentry desirous of having the first impressions of the above prints, are requested to fend their address to the engravers, Watson and Dickinson, No. 158, New Bond-street (late Mr. Shropshire's) where the pictures may be seen.

In this picture Garrick is seated with his hands resting on a paper inscribed *Prologue*. This alludes to the prologue to Garrick's play, *Taste*.

Thomas Watson, born about 1750, was the son of a printseller. It is not known where he learned to engrave but even his earlier prints, engraved when he was about twenty, show considerable skill. As soon as he came of age, he seems to have been involved in the publication of his own prints, often in partnership with William Dickinson. Their styles are similar and it is possible that Watson was, like Dickinson, a pupil of McArdell. Throughout the 1770s he produced superb mezzotints, excelling in whole-length portraits. If any fault can be found in his work, it is his preference for a cold black ink which makes his soft technique look hard. Watson died young in the summer of 1781.

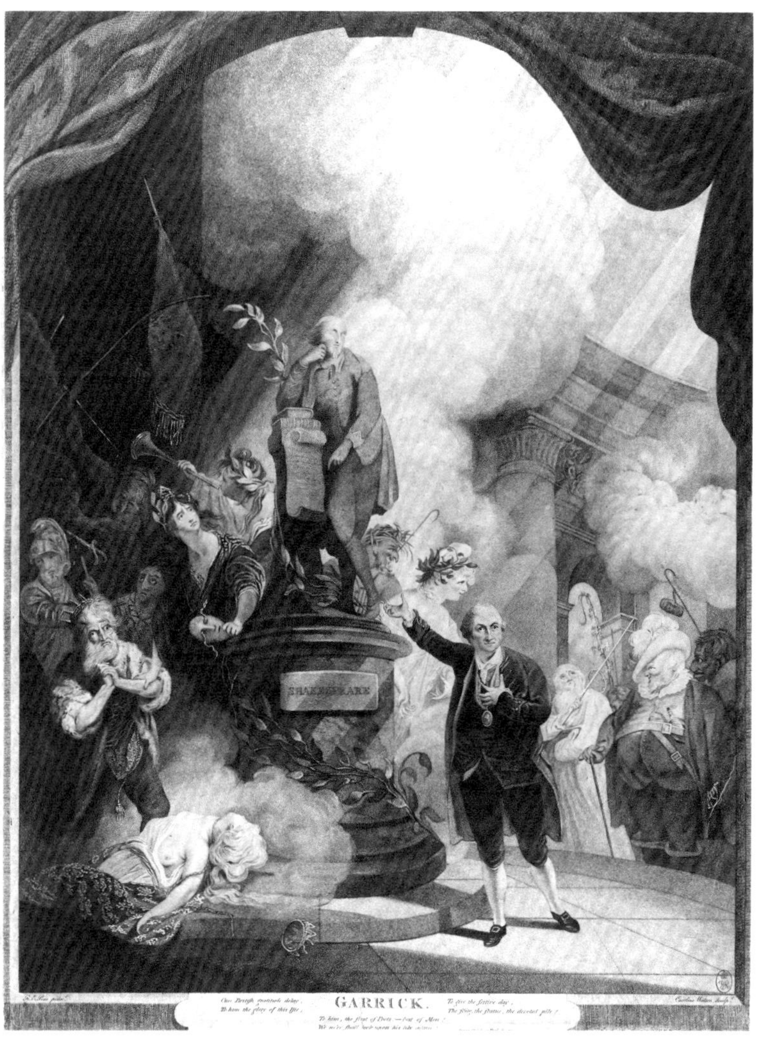

54 [The Apotheosis of Garrick]

Stipple

Engraved by Caroline Watson
after Robert Edge Pine

Published by Robert Edge Pine 1 March 1783

596 x 429 I; 620 x 449 Pl.

References: O'D 33; Hall 55

1. With the engraved inscription: *"R,,E,, Pine pinx.ᵗ, *** Caroline Watson Sculp.ᵗ, | Can British gratitude delay, | To him the glory of this Iſle; *** GARRICK. *** To give the festive day, | The ſong, the ſtatue, the devoted pile! | To him, the first of Poets! – best of Men! | We ne'er ſhall look upon his like again! *** Garrick's Ode to Shakeſpeare. *** London, Publiſhed March 1ˢᵗ 1783 by R E Pine, Albermarle Street.".*
Impressions: CLB P36,004 (impression exhibited).

This print, the only non-mezzotint exhibited, shows the ridiculous levels to which adulation of Garrick rose. Some of its interest lies in the use of Shakespearean characters rather than portraits of players in part. Not since the days of Mercier's Scene from the Careless Husband have dramatic characters been shown, except when accompanying the printed text of a play, without a familiar actor's face. It is as if, now that Garrick is no more, the characters themselves re-appear and the players retire to the periphery. The lavish plates of Boydell's ambitious Shakespeare Gallery were published a few years later, completing the change from prints of actors to prints of plays.

In Caroline Watson's print the imagery is wholly theatrical, with smoke effects and spot-lighting. The comic and tragic muses, Caliban, Falstaff and Prospero are all easily identifiable; Lear weeping over a dead Cordelia and Macbeth staggering at the sight of the dagger floating before him take us back to Shakespeare's original, long-abandoned texts. In the centre Shakespeare appears on his pedestal, but Garrick, dressed as a gentleman and wearing his Shakespeare medallion, upstages him.

Caroline Watson, the daughter and pupil of James Watson, was an accomplished engraver in the stipple manner. Inheriting her father's property and having her own successful career, she died in 1814, a rich woman.

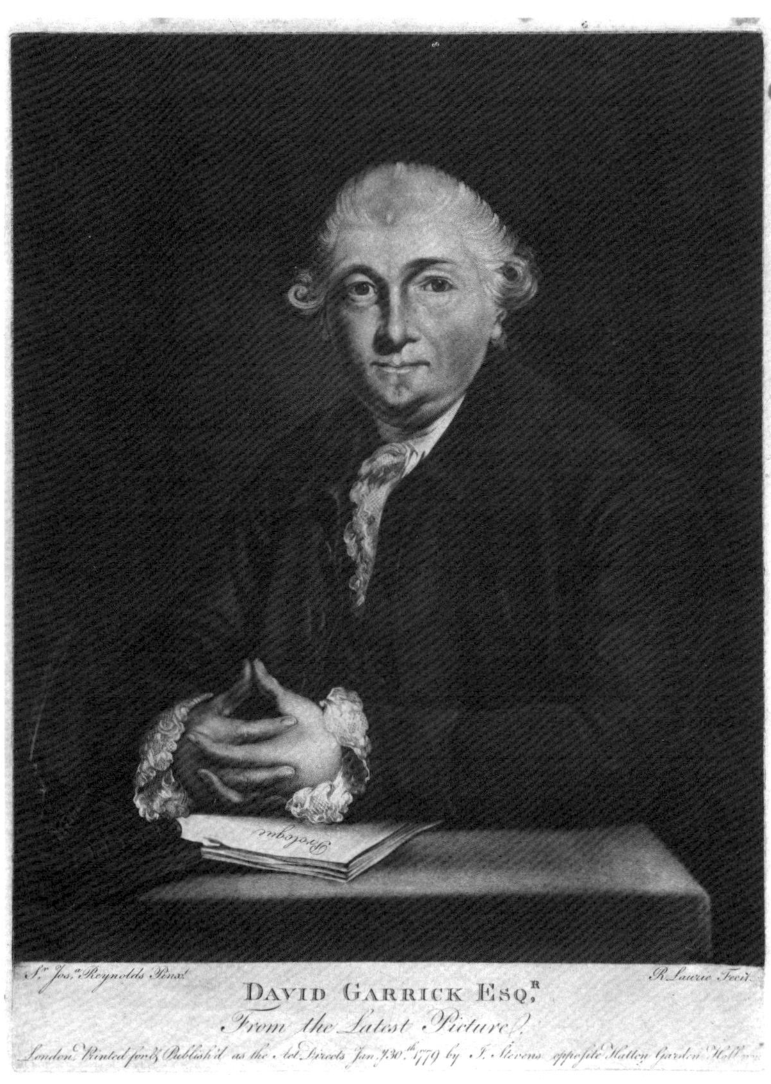

55 David Garrick Esq.r

Engraved by Robert Laurie
after Sir Joshua Reynolds

Published by John Stevens 30 January 1779

319 x 254 I; 355 x 254 Pl.

References: CS 21; H p. 30; O'D 39; Hall 63

1. Before all letters, *Prologue* on paper in image.
Impressions: CLB.

2. With the engraved inscription: "*S.r Jos.a Reynolds Pinx! *** R. Laurie Fecit. /* DAVID GARRICK ESQ.R, / *From the Latest Picture, / London, Printed for & Publish'd as the Act Directs Jan.y 30.th 1779 by J, Stevens oppofite Hatton Garden Holborn.*".
Impressions: CLB P36,005 (impression exhibited); BM.

This piracy was published a few weeks before Watson & Dickinson's authorised version and only ten days after Garrick's death. It was extensively re-worked and re-issued, although impressions on late paper have not been seen. The print is typical of Robert Laurie's brassy technique and poor draughtsmanship and does not do justice to Reynolds's painting, as a glance at Thomas Watson's print will show.

The frame and glass are original and the print is a standard size known as a 'posture', measuring 14 x 10 inches, which would usually have cost 1s plain or 2s coloured. It is likely that frames and glass were available from most printsellers to fit prints of this type; the moulding too is of a common profile used for these cheaper mezzotints. Examples of these were advertised by Laurie & Whittle in their catalogue for 1795 (see over).

Only a handful of mezzotint copper-plates have survived for they were often re-used. This would have involved beating the plate flat and then burnishing and polishing it, a job which was probably given to a copper-plate maker and not carried out in the publisher's establishment. A great number of plates are said to have been melted down for use as shell-cases during the First World War. This plate, purchased from a group of a dozen or more

(91)

COPY-BOOK COVERS.

IN THREE HUNDRED DIFFERENT SUBJECTS,
PRINTED ON HALF-SHEET FOOL'S-CAP PAPER;
CONSISTING OF
VIEWS, SHIPPING, HORSES, HUNTING, BEASTS, BIRDS,
HEADS, DROLL FIGURES, TABLES, &c.
SOLD WHOLESALE ONLY, AT 1s. 8d. A HUNDRED PLAIN, AND 3s. COLOURED.

PAINTINGS ON GLASS,

VERY EXCELLENT ARTICLES FOR COUNTRY TRADE AND EXPORTATION,
BEING
PRINTS PAINTED IN OIL,
The Colours retain their Brilliancy for many Years.
A LARGE ASSORTMENT OF POSTURES AND OCTAVO SIZE, AS MENTIONED IN
THE LATTER PART OF THIS CATALOGUE, IS KEPT
READY FOR MERCHANTS ORDERS.
Posture Size, 14 by 10, in black Frames with gilt Edges, 6s. each; Octavo Size,
6 by 4½, in ditto, 3s. each.

PICTURES AND PRINTS

OF ALL KINDS FRAMED IN THE NEATEST MANNER EITHER IN GOLD, OR BLACK, &c.
Frames for Posture Metzotintos, 14 by 10, with two gilt Edges, 18s. a dozen,
Wholesale.
The same glazed, 36s. a dozen, ditto.
Octave-size Metzotinto frames, 9s. a dozen, Wholesale.
The same glazed, 13s. a dozen, ditto.

DISSECTED MAPS.

FOR THE USE OF SCHOOLS, AND FOR THE MORE EASY METHOD OF TEACH-
ING YOUNG GENTLEMEN AND LADIES GEOGRAPHY.
They are pasted upon Wood, and cut out (or dissected) into the different Kingdoms,
States, Provinces, or Counties, &c. &c. the uniting of which strengthens the
memory very much, as to the Geography of the World.
In square mahogany boxes, 7s. 6d.
Ditto, if dissected a larger size, with the Sea Coast, 10s. 6d.

CONTAINING

ENGLAND	SOUTH AMERICA, SEPARATE
SCOTLAND	FRANCE
IRELAND	SPAIN
THE WORLD	GERMANY
EUROPE	ITALY
ASIA	THE SEVEN UNITED PROVINCES
AFRICA	OF HOLLAND
THE WHOLE CONTINENT OF	THE CATHOLIC NETHERLANDS
AMERICA	THE RUSSIAN EMPIRE, &c.
NORTH AMERICA	SWEDEN, DENMARK and NORWAY

N 2

Laurie & Whittle's catalogue of 1795.

plates which came onto the market a few years ago, was probably
once in the stock of a small printer, and was made by the firm of
Benjamin Whittow and Thomas Large of 48 Shoe Lane. At a later
date this became the address of the important copper-plate manu-
facturing firm established by William Pontifex, who took over the
business and name of his predecessor Jones. In the nineteenth
century the firm, now called William Pontifex, Russell Pontifex &
Co., occupied 46, 47 and 48 Shoe Lane.

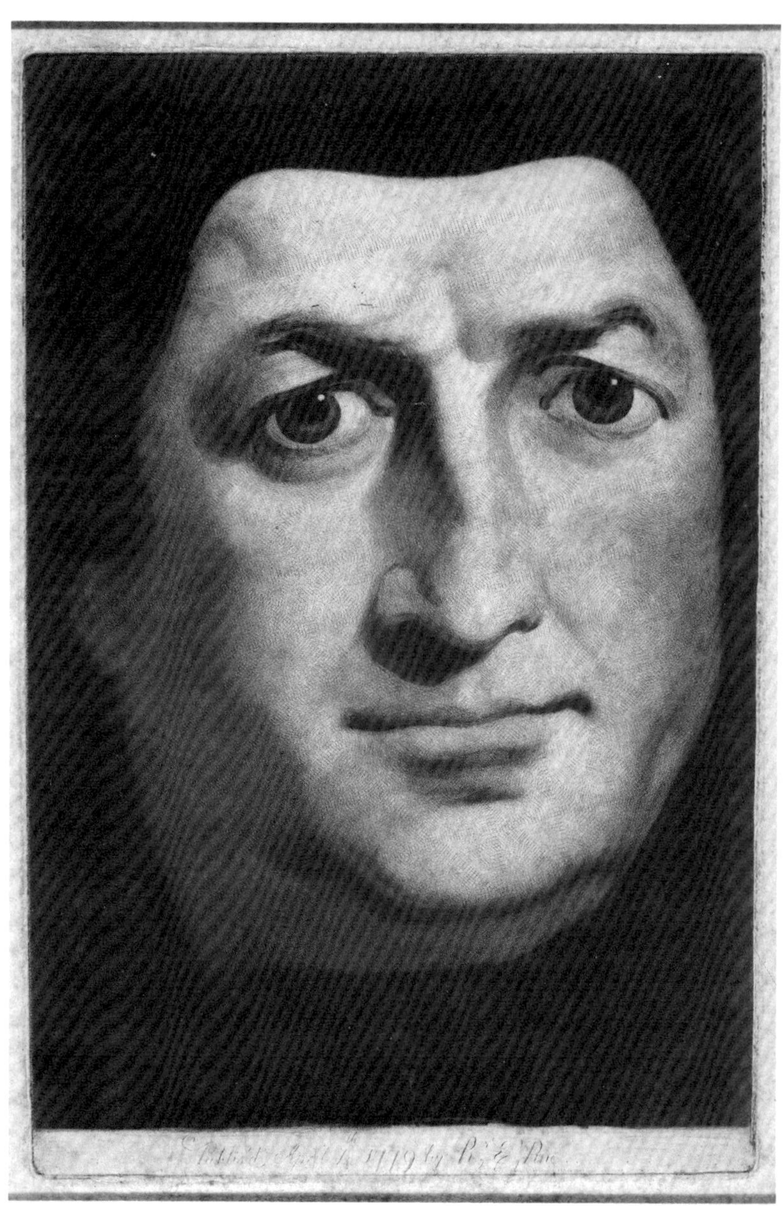

56 [Death Mask of David Garrick]

[Drawn? and engraved by Robert Edge Pine]

Published by Robert Edge Pine 4 April 1779

228 x 154 I; 239 x 155 Pl.

References: CS ENA III 68; O'D 32; Hall 54

1. With the scratched inscription: *"Publis'd, April 4th*[sic] *1779 by R,E, Pine."*.

Impressions: CLB P38,008 (impression exhibited); BM; H.

Very little is known about this print. Death mask prints are extremely rare and this is the only one known to have been engraved in mezzotint. At the time of the publication of the print, the painter Robert Edge Pine was living in Bath. It is possible that the engraving was executed by Pine himself, which would explain the rather crude style; if this was so, it is the only known mezzotint by Pine. The plate is a curious size and the face appears rather squashed.

Although a number of impressions have survived, no early examples have been seen, nor any impressions printed on laid paper which might be expected at this date. Some impressions, particularly one of the copies at Harvard, show considerable wear to the plate which suggests that a great many impressions had already been printed.

The plate may have been a curiosity that was never published but which came on to the market after, or at the time of, Pine's departure for America in 1783. The earliest record of this print is found in Robert Grave's catalogue of prints (1809), where it is priced at 3s 6d. It was eminently suitable for extra-illustrating in books on Garrick, which explains why many libraries with theatrical collections have multiple impressions.

The contrast between Pine's mezzotint and William Sharp's[1] engraved death mask of the impressario John James Heidegger is remarkable: although the former is clearly a death mask, the insertion of the eyes gives it an unnerving vitality. By using mezzotint, Pine successfully describes the contours of the face, but unlike the equally fine but more scientific and graphic result in Sharp's engraving, the face appears soft to the touch indicating flesh and bones.

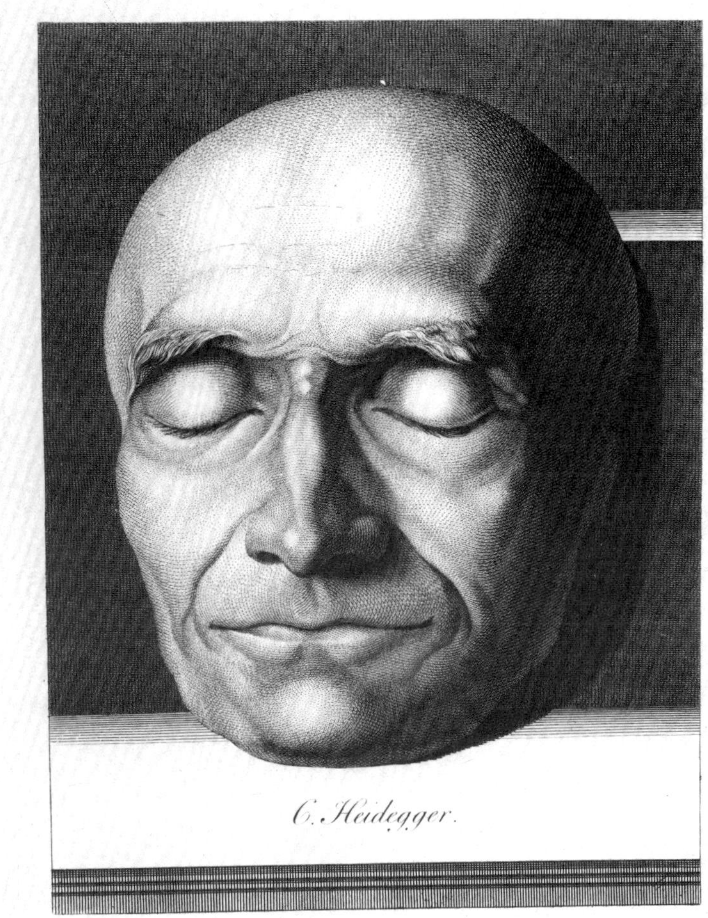

---

[1] William Sharp (1749–1824), engraver.

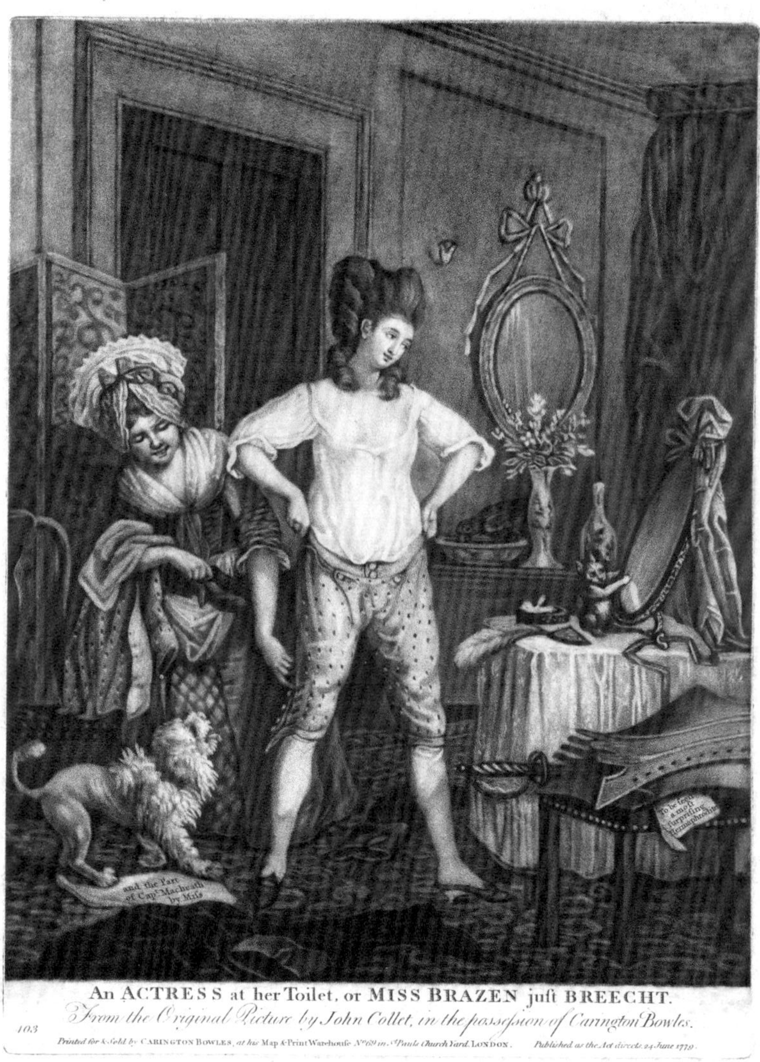

57 An Actress at her Toilet, or Miss Brazen just Breecht

Anonymous mezzotint after John Collet

Published by Carington Bowles 24 June 1779

327 x 249 I; 352 x 250 Pl.

References: B.M. Satires 5622

1. With the engraved inscription: "An ACTRESS at her Toilet, or MISS BRAZEN juſt BREECHT. / *From the Original Picture by John Collet, in the poſſeſsion of Carington Bowles.* / 403 *** / *Printed for & Sold by* CARINGTON BOWLES, *at his* Map & Print Warehouſe Nº 69 in Sᵗ Pauls Church Yard, LONDON.   Published as the act directs, 24 June 1779.".
Impressions: CLB P20,933 (impression exhibited); BM.

John Collet is best known for a large number of designs of low-life subjects that he executed during the 1770s. Some of these designs were used for a series of engravings published by Sayer and his former apprentice John Smith, and by Carington Bowles for his series of half-sheet humorous mezzotints. Bowles also used some of these designs for large 20 x 14 inches line engravings. Perhaps the most commonly cited images after Collet were those engraved by Butler Clowes and published by Sayer and Smith during the late 1760s.

This print is said to caricature the actress Margaret Kennedy.[1] By the time this print was published it had almost become a tradition for the part of Captain Macheath in *The Beggar's Opera* to be played by a woman. Although the print could indeed be a caricature of an actress of the period, it is likely that Collet's main aim was to ridicule fashion and social behaviour; the suggestion is that, after seeing a production of the play, this young woman has decided to wear men's clothes. The artist draws attention to the topsy-turvy world and the lengths to which people will go to be in the forefront of fashion.

[1] *B.M. Satires.*

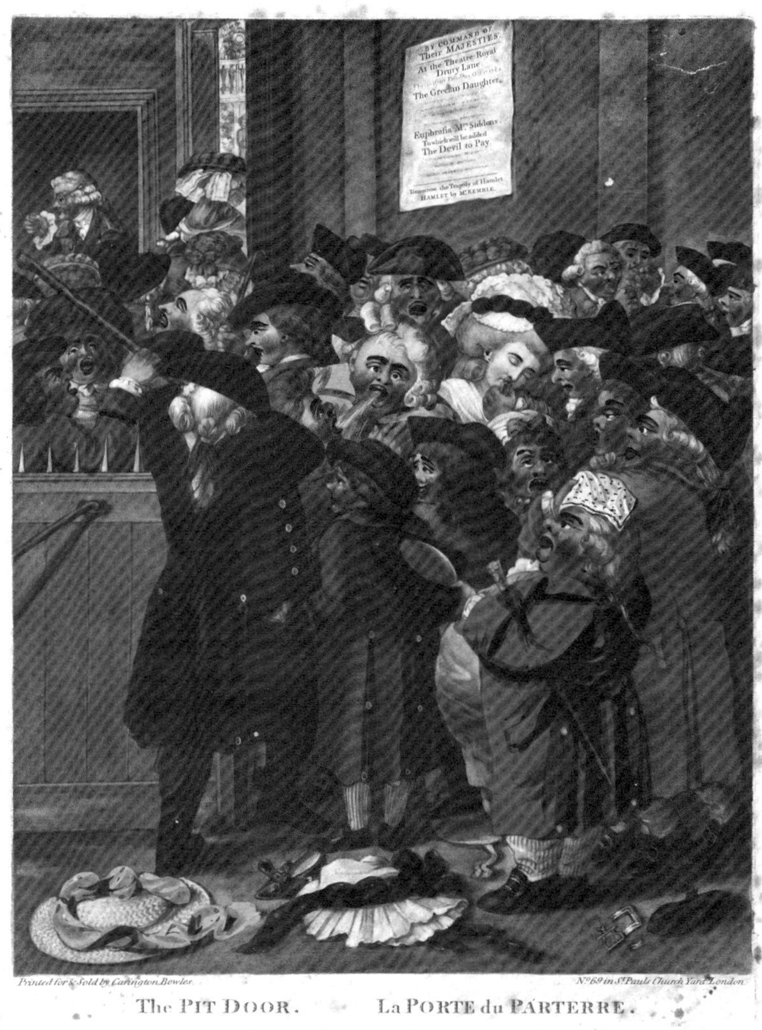

The PIT DOOR. La PORTE du PARTERRE.

58 The Pit Door.
La Porte de Parterre

Anonymous mezzotint after Robert Dighton

Published by Carington Bowles
[9 November 1784]

320 x 249 I; 354 x 250 Pl.

References: BM Satires 6769

1. With the engraved inscription: "*Printed for & Sold by Carington Bowles, ✳✳✳ N.º 69 in S.ᵗ Pauls Church Yard, London. |* The PIT DOOR. ✳✳✳ La PORTE de PARTERRE. *| Publish'd as the Act directs,* [date erased from print, 9 Nov. 1784]".
Impressions: CLB P12,781 (impression exhibited); BM.

Although this satirical print was published some years after Garrick's death, it perfectly illustrates the problems that the audience would have encountered when trying to get into the Pit on a popular night at Drury Lane. As soon as the doors were opened, there was a mad rush to gain entry and the gates would become jammed with people as they shoved and jostled for position. Tempers would fray, fights might be started and injuries could often be quite serious. One man, keen to get his place in the Upper Gallery, pushed through the doors with such gusto that he fell straight over the top and into the Pit. He survived unharmed, but only because he managed to grab a chandelier worth fifty pounds as he fell.

A relatively small percentage of the population attended the theatre in the eighteenth century, certainly far less than one would suppose from the extraordinary interest that was generated by it. The audience comprised only those who could afford the admission price.

When Garrick became manager of Drury Lane in 1747, he immediately enlarged the theatre to hold 1,268 people. The managers of the two patent theatres constantly attempted to make reforms and quite naturally aimed to increase their income.

129

Radical changes, or at least those that the audience considered radical, occasionally had the direst consequences, and on a number of occasions both theatres were almost completely destroyed by disaffected audiences. Even fashion could alter the theatre's revenue: in the mid 1740s the mode for hooped dresses was a concern for the managers since they took up more space. By 1762 Drury Lane had been further enlarged and could hold an audience of approximately 2,360. Covent Garden held just over 1,300 people until it was altered in 1782, when the capacity was increased to 2,170.

The typical audience was both large and heterogeneous, ranging from members of the Royal Family to busy pickpockets. The theatre was made up of Pit, Boxes and Upper and Lower Galleries. The price for a place in the Pit was between 2s and 3s, for a Box 5s and for a place in the Lower Gallery 2s; the 'gods' or Upper Gallery cost 1s. Boxes tended to be for the higher ranks in society and lined both sides of the theatre, extending above and beyond the proscenium. Many of these people came to see and be seen, as Garrick satirised in *Lethe*:

> ... one goes indeed to a Playhouse sometimes, because one does not know how else one can kill one's time – everybody goes, because – all the world's there –.

Garrick was influential in putting aside one tradition that appealed to the more narcissistic playgoers. For years a section of the audience had been allowed to sit on benches at the rear of the stage. Here they not only disturbed the players, often talking both to their friends and to members of the cast, but they also clogged the stage; on one occasion Mrs Cibber as Juliet was unable to enter the Capulets' tomb on account of the crowd.

The Pit and Lower Gallery were occupied by merchants, clerks and tradesmen and on benefit nights the pit and boxes were often put together to increase the places available. The Upper Gallery was regarded by footmen of the gentry as their particular province and to some extent the Pit and Galleries were the most important sections of the audience. Garrick often addressed both prologues and epilogues directly to both the 'gods' and the Pit.

Performances usually started at six o'clock, with the doors being opened between three o'clock and five o'clock. Servants were allowed to reserve places for their masters from about three o'clock. The audience made a terrible noise and always demanded prompt starts. Although the audience of the eighteenth century would appear shocking to us today, it was essentially benevolent. They talked, hissed and heckled, behaviour which was upheld by Lord Mansfield who stated that: 'Every man that is at a Playhouse, has a right to express his approbation or disapprobation instantaneously, according as he likes either the acting, or the Piece – that is a right due to the theatre – an unalterable right.' They threw things at the stage and even at other members of the audience, but despite this when the performance started, 'all noise and bombardment ceases, unless some especial provocation gives rise to further disturbances; and one is bound to admire the quiet attentiveness of such estimable folk'.[1]

Yet the occasional provocation could become very serious indeed. One of the most serious riots occurred at Covent Garden over the managers' decision to abolish half-price tickets. Most main-pieces were five acts long and:

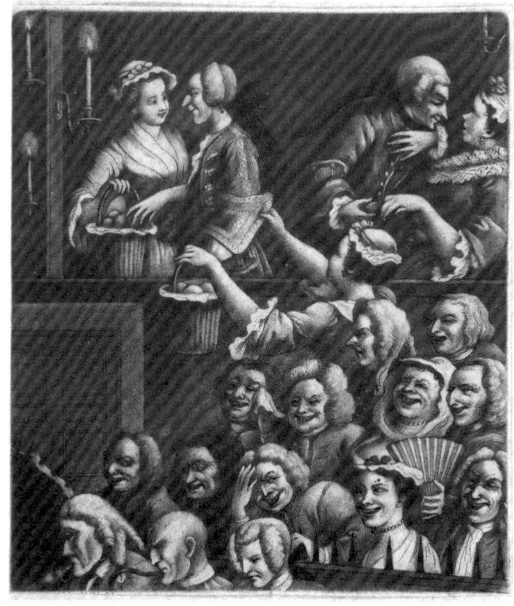

It has been customary, to admit, at the ends of the third act, at half price, all who desired to enter: hence it came to pass, that many persons, not choosing, through a spirit of oeconomy, to come to the first three acts, which are often the least interesting, the theatres were crowded with spectators who paid only half prices for their places; and this the managers by no means found their account in.

The managers declared an end to this practice since they were losing money, but for the eighteenth century audience this was intolerable and seemed to strike at their fundamental liberties: 'This proposal raised as great an alarm in London as the approach of an hostile army ... it extended even to those that did not frequent the theatres'. At the next performance the audience arrived and sat in complete silence until the play began. When the managers refused to back down the turmoil began; fists and cudgels flew, while the actors attempted to continue with the play. The theatre was torn to pieces, benches were destroyed, chandeliers were pulled down and even the supporters of the Royal Arms were torn from the Royal Box; the Unicorn hit the stage, but the Lion, on account of its extra weight, landed in the Pit, destroying the theatre's 'great harpsichord'. The damage was estimated at over two thousand pounds.

[1] J.W. von Archenholz quoted in Kelly, p. 55.

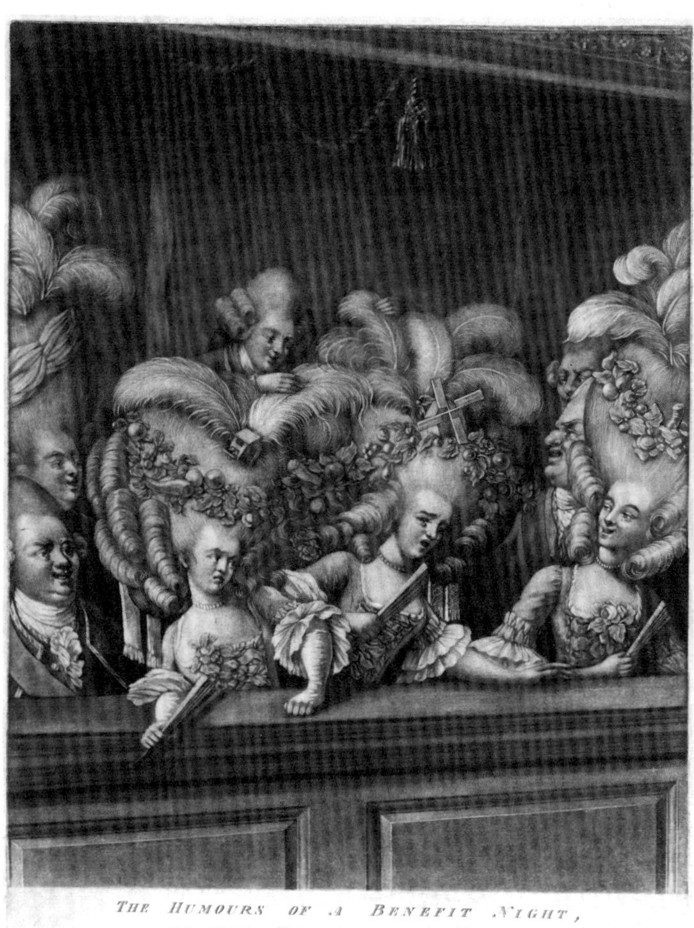

59 The Humours of a Benefit Night, or The Boxes in an Uproar

Anonymous mezzotint

Published by William Humphrey 2 August 1777

321 x 249 I; 350 x 250 Pl.

References: not in B.M. Satires

1. With the engraved inscription: *"THE HUMOURS OF A BENEFIT NIGHT, OR THE BOXES IN AN UPROAR. | Pub,^d 2^d Aug,^t 1777, by W,, Humphrey"*.
Impressions: CLB P9,913.

This print caricatures the over-crowding of boxes at the theatre. The boxes were the domain of the *beau monde*, and would often be targets for the upper galleries:

> The uproar before the play begins is indescribable … Not only orange-peels but sometimes even glasses of water or other liquids are thrown down from the gallery into the pit and boxes, so that frequently spectators are wounded and their clothing is soiled. In short, such outrages are committed in the name of freedom that one forgets one is in a playhouse which claims in its advertisement the title of a Royal theatre. In Germany such disorder would never be tolerated … At Drury Lane I wished to look around the gallery in order to examine its structure, but a heap of orange peels, striking me with considerable force in the face, robbed me of all curiosity. The best plan is to keep your face turned towards the stage and thus quietly submit to the hail of oranges on your back. On one occasion my hat was so saturated (I really do not know with what watery ingredients) that I was compelled to have it cleaned the next day at the hatters.[1]

At benefit nights, all receipts were given to the named person. Such evenings were held for the performers, playwrights, prompters, box-keepers and book-keepers as additional income to their salaries, if they were lucky enough to have one. They were also held to provide financial support for worthy causes and institu-

132

tions. These benefits took place the week before Christmas, with those for members of the company in March and April. There was a conventional order of precedence according to rank, seniority and special accomplishment. Playwrights received a benefit on the third, sixth and ninth nights of the first run of their play.

There were several forms of financial arrangement for benefit performances: a *clear* benefit was free of charges and all income from tickets went directly to the beneficiary; a benefit with *house charges* required the performer to pay a fixed sum of money to the management, plus extra charges for special lighting, music, scenery or costume; a *partial* benefit was when two or more individuals shared the proceeds. Another form was the *half-value-of* tickets, whereby there were no house charges, but the managers received cash sales and half the face value of the tickets at the door.

Not all the tickets were made over to the beneficiary as some were always reserved for sale at the door and there were also free tickets for a number of people. Ticket forgers, known as *scalpers* abounded, so the beneficiaries made doubly sure that their tickets were sold directly by them to their friends. An actor hoped to earn at least one or two months' salary in one night, although occasionally disaster struck: Richard Wroughton found himself in debt to the management to the tune of £5 19s.

The fashion for outrageously high head-dresses was a source of ridicule. Said to have started in France, it was brought to this country by Lady Stanhope. It was all the rage by the early 1760s and the taste survived for nearly twenty years.

The great craftsmen who dressed 'heads' with wool, sheep's tails, cork, false hair and pomatum, soon gained an elevated position in society as they drove in their coaches from one fashionable lady to another, wearing fine suits with ruffles and swords by their sides.

Such creations took hours to prepare and must have been terribly uncomfortable. They sometimes required the wearer to sit up all night, or at best forced them to make use of special blocks of wood to support the structure; doorways and carriages had to be heightened to allow free passage. When plumes, particularly ostrich plumes, became fashionable, caricaturists showed the unhappy birds wandering about with bare rumps or attacking fashionable young women in order to retrieve their feathers.

These 'parcels' of hair remained unopened for days which led to considerable problems: the hair smelt after a while, and insect infestations took hold. One wag reported seeing women fiddling with their hair pins, which he presumed was actually an attempt to spear the more tiresome insects. The opening up of these head-dresses was an hazardous operation. The advertising of special compounds for destroying the vermin and aiding the wearer are proof that the problems were not exaggerated.

Just occasionally there were advantages to the fashion:

A fellow who sat on the sixth row of the Upper Gallery ...
threw a Keg (which he had brought full of liquor into the
House) over the Gallery front. It fell upon a Lady's head, who
sat in that part of the Pit which was railed into the Boxes, but
the Lady's hair being dress'd in high 'ton, the artificial moun-
tain luckily prevented the mischief that otherwise might have
been occasioned ...[2]

The fashion was inevitably satirised on the stage; in Sheridan's St. Patrick's Day[3], for example, a scheming lieutenant remarks:

> ... the London ladies were always too handsome for me; then they are so defended, such a circumballation of hoop, with a breastwork of whalebone that would turn a pistol-bullet, much less Cupid's arrows – then turret on turret on top, with stores of concealed weapons, under pretence of black pins – and above all, a standard of feathers that would do honour to a knight of Bath.

Foote appeared in a Command Performance of his play *Taste* as Lady Pentweazle, wearing an exaggerated head-dress a yard wide, filled with multi-coloured feathers. As he left the stage, he contrived that the head-dress would fall off. The whole scene delighted the Queen and may even have provoked some reform in this absurd fashion.

[1] A letter from Friederick Wilhelm von Shutz, quoted in Kelly, pp. 150–51.
[2] *Lloyd's Evening Post*, 29 Feb. 1776.
[3] 1775.

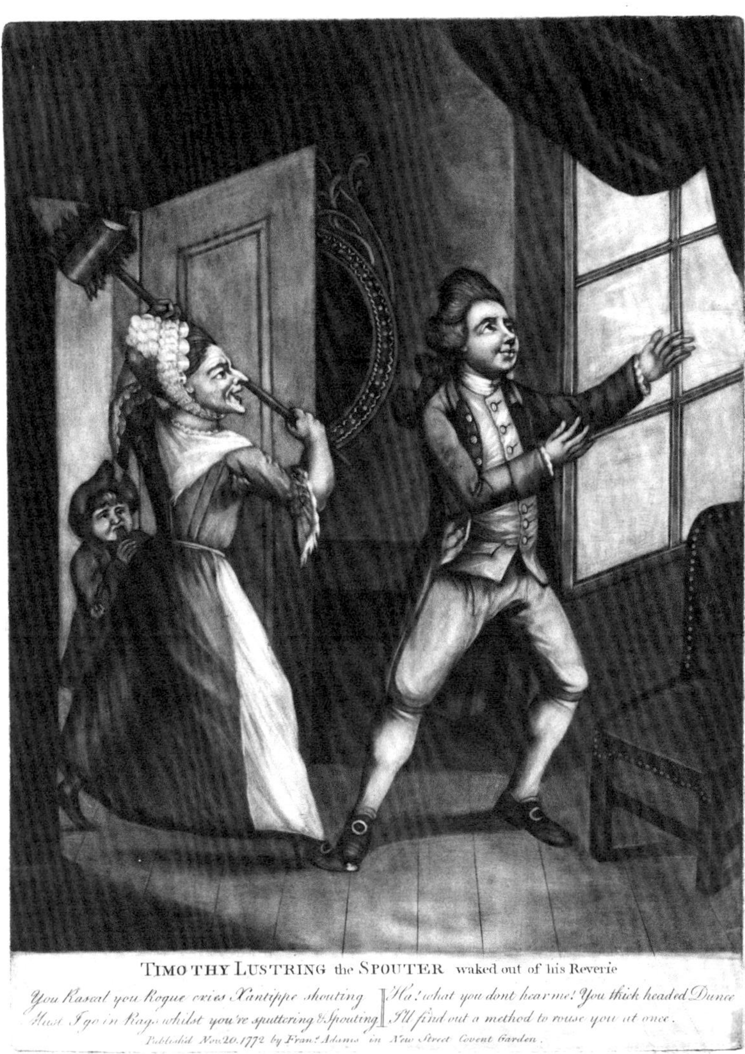

60   Timothy Lustring the Spouter waked out of his Reverie

Engraved by [Francis Edward Adams]

Published by Francis Edward Adams
20 November 1772

320 x 249 I; 354 x 250 Pl.

References: not in B.M. Satires

1. With the engraved inscription.
"TIMOTHY LUSTRING the SPOUTER waked out of his Reverie / [in two columns] *You Rascal you Rogue cries Xantippe shouting / Must I go in Rags whilst you're sputtering & spouting // Ha! what you dont hear me! You thick headed Dunce / I'll find out a method to rouse you at once. /* [and beneath] *Publish'd Nov. 20. 1772 by Fran.s Adams in New Street Covent Garden.*".
Impressions: CLB P36,006 (impression exhibited).

Francis Adams, about whom little is known, may have been the engraver as well as the publisher of this extremely rare print. Chaloner Smith records that he published four prints and suggests that he may have engraved them too; nine mezzotint satires[1] were also published by Adams between November 1772 and August 1774. Like the series of half-sheet humorous mezzotints published by the Bowles family and by Sayer, '*Timothy Lustring*' was targeted at the cheaper end of the market. Generally these prints satirised social behaviour, fashion and morality, with political content being reserved mainly for those examples that documented the conflict over the 'Boston Tea Party' and the early stages of the American War of Independence.

A number of other publishers, William Humphrey, Ryland & Bryer, Sarah Sledge and Robert Pollard published other examples, but those by Adams are some of the most interesting. By the turn of the century, although many of the earlier plates by Bowles and Sayer were still being reissued, the humorous mezzotint declined in popularity in favour of brightly coloured etched satires. Although the 10 x 14 inches mezzotint plate was still used by publishers like John Haines & Son, W.B. Walker and James Fairburn, it tended to be used only for decorative and sentimental genre subjects; by 1810 it had been almost entirely forgotten.

135

DEAR Charles, as I find
You're to Acting inclin'd,
And bewitch'd with the charms of the stage;
Take th' advice of a friend,
And with patience attend,
Ere you play in this Cat-calling Age.

Avoid all stage-traps
To get gallery claps,
And despise the mere noise of hand;
For Plebians aloft,
Are inclin'd very oft,
To applaud what they don't understand.

Let your characters strike,
Don't perform all alike,
But your Manner to vary endeavour;
For those actors who stalk,
In the same formal walk,
To th' applause of true judges rise never.

By each look and each tone
Let expression be shown,
Or your eyes and tongue move in vain;
In sorrow and joy
Evr'y muscle employ,
To be really the man whom you feign.

Neither grumble nor squeak,
But with emphasis speak,
And your voice to all changes adapt;
And beware of a sameness,
It will cause a dull tameness,
and for that you will never be clapt.

If you put on the King,
Your arms do not swing,
With a clumsy and porter-like grace;
Copy Garrick; and try,
With a turn of your eye,
To throw meaning all over your face.

In a scene of despair,
Do not horridly stare,
Nor in chains look as meekly as a lamb;
If you passions transpose,
And make these clash with those,
The fiercest critics, with justice, will damn.

With a plume and great wig,
You in vain will look big,
If there's nothing alive in your features;
For the actors who owe
All their merit to show,
Are indeed most contemptible creatures.

In a scene full of love,
When you bill like a dove,
Burlesque not the passion with pining;
Express what you feel,
And your raptures reveal
In a masculine way without whining.

If these few rules are miss'd,
You'll surely be hiss'd,
Take kindly then what I have hinted;
Or else for the play,
In the bills of the day,
You'll ne'er be in capitals printed.

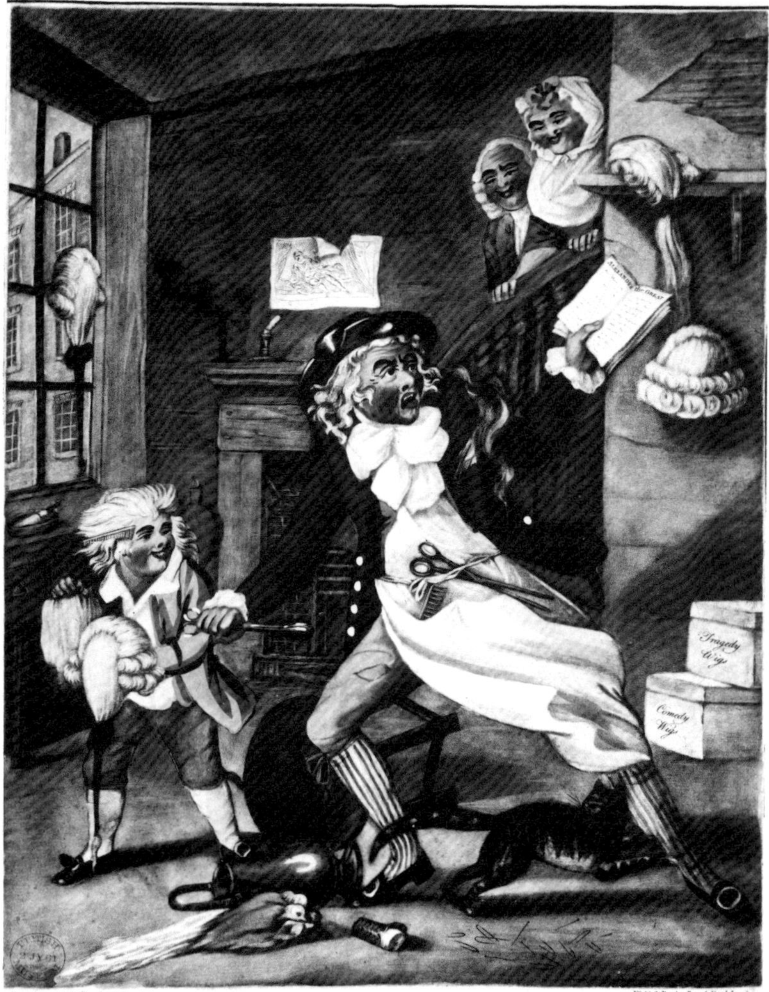

TRAGEDY BURLESQUED, or the BARBER turned ACTOR.

This print is probably intended to depict a mercer who, remembering the balcony scene from the previous evening's performance at Drury Lane, imagines himself as the fond lover. Like the barber in Bowles's print (see above), his addiction to all things theatrical causes his business to fall to rack and ruin. It is interesting to note that an impression of Grignion's '*Garrick in the Character of Richard III*' is pasted to the wall above the fireplace (see page 68). This was an age when people from all walks of life were captivated by the theatre. As Arthur Murphy declared, the theatre '… engrossed the minds of men to such a degree, that it may now be said, that there existed in England a fourth estate, King, Lords, and Commons, and Drury Lane play house'.

The acting company during the middle of the eighteenth century was a fairly stable body and the numbers of actors small (at Drury Lane 1755–6 there were one hundred and eight in the company, including dancers and singers, whilst the company at Covent Garden was made up of about seventy-five individuals). The two London patent theatres were the most prestigious, followed by Dublin and then a number of provincial venues. Since opportunities for preferment were limited, players who had gained a foothold within a company were extremely jealous of their prerogatives, whether this was for parts, salaries, costumes or any other privilege. In many cases, when one theatre was dominated by a coterie of 'capital' players, a young and talented actor would be obliged to either alternate between both patent houses, or go to Dublin where, more often than not, they would be well received.

Each company had its first-rate players, the 'stars' of the day, but also relied on a core of solid and dependable lesser players. Only a few actors were thought to excel in both tragedy and comedy, although some attempted to try both, often with disastrous effects. An actor who showed particular merit in a role would often become associated with it. They would be seen on the stage again and again and after a short time the audience would become almost intimately acquainted with them, knowing their foibles and failings. The audience was extremely powerful and could often ruin an actor's career; if for some reason, often just on a whim, the audience felt affronted by an actor or felt his performance to be inadequate, he would be hissed from the stage not able to return until he made a public apology. In contrast, a bad play or a poor production could often be carried by the merit of a single performer; this particularly applied to Garrick, whose appearance in a play could ensure its success, although on occasion he was accused of deliberately gathering together a poor cast to offset his own skills.

The balance of a particular company could also determine the repertory, either by prolonging the life of a particular piece, or by inspiring playwrights to cater for an individual talent. The loss of a player to a rival company would have immediate effect. Illness of the actors, real or feigned, could have the most terrible financial consequences for the managers and also affected the repertory. On many occasions when an actor was ill, the audience would not be satisfied with the substitution of the leading player for a less able member of the company, and instead might insist on a complete change of main piece, ensuring that another 'star' would take the stage.

In the late 1760s the leading actors at Covent Garden, Powell and Woodward, received two pounds fifteen shillings a day, not including returns from benefit performances. Players' salaries differed enormously from around a shilling a day to the huge sum of forty guineas a performance which Ann Catley earned at the height of her career – in 1777 Mrs Barry was reputed to have earned £1,100 for sixteen nights at Dublin. Most actors on the other hand struggled for a living. A few years earlier in 1774 one writer had drawn attention to the miserable income of a country comedian, who he reported:

> ... played at Chesterfield in Derbyshire, the character of Richard III. At the end of the play he undressed[changed costume], and danced a minuet, read the Lecture on Heads, acted the character of Petruchio, and concluded with a hornpipe, which was insisted by the upper gallery ...[2]

For this he was paid a mere four pence halfpenny.

[1] *B.M. Satires*, no. 4783. This and a number of other examples are in the collection of Christopher Lennox-Boyd.
[2] *The London Chronicle*, 1–3 Sept. 1774.

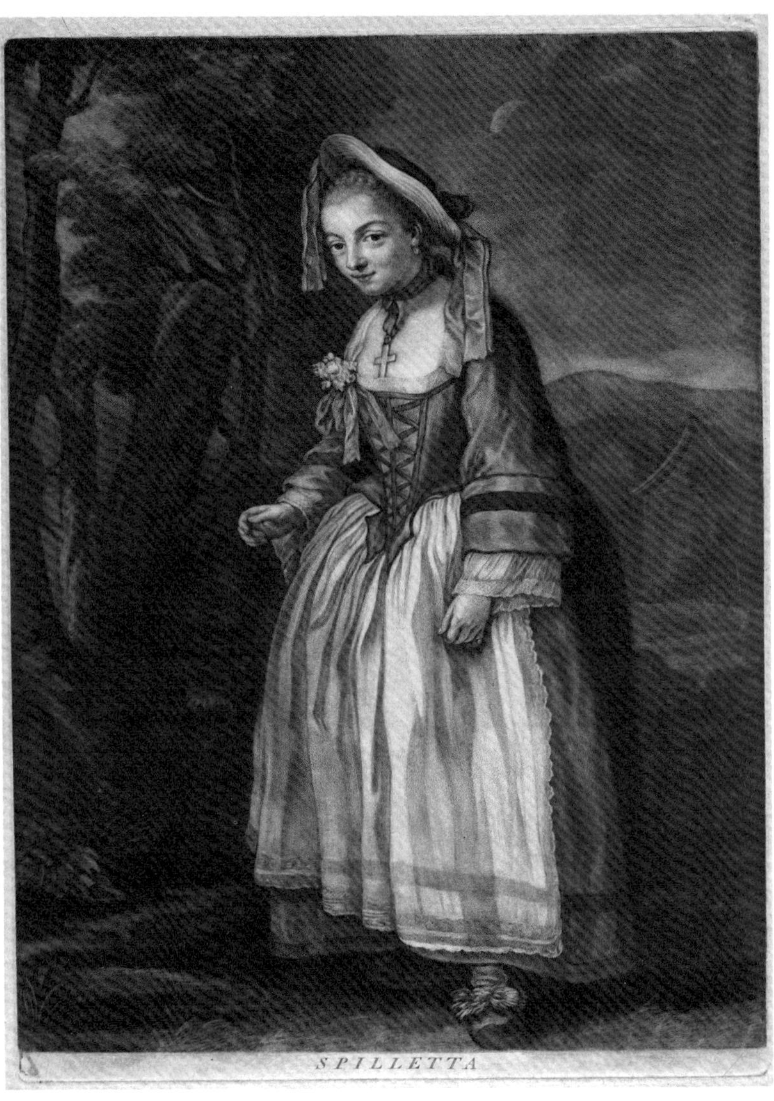

61 Spiletta

Engraved by Richard Purcell
after Jean-Baptiste van Loo

Published by Robert Sayer [after 1768]

341 x 250 I; 351 x 250 Pl.

References: CS 27; Hall 3

1. [With the inscription: "Vanloo pinxt.
Corbut fecit. Spiletta. London, Printed for Robt
Sayer at No. 53 Fleet Street."(CS)].

2. With the title only: "SPILETTA".
Impressions: CLB P5,854 (impression exhibited); H.

This print is copied, in reverse, from Jean Daullé's[1] line engraving
after van Loo of Marie Justine Favart. Although Daullé's print was
published in 1754 (see over), Sayer's was probably not published
until after 1768. It is interesting to note that Sayer accompanied
Thomas Jefferys,[2] the map publisher, to Paris in October 1768,
returning to England in December. On his return, Jefferys advertised that he had prints 'lately imported from France'; it is unlikely
that Sayer would have missed such a good opportunity to purchase
continental stock, and had he not already obtained an impression,
it is possible that Daullé's print was amongst these. The print was
listed in Sayer & Bennett's 1775 catalogue as *Spiletta, a celebrated
Italian comedian*: its omission from Sayer's catalogue of 1766 helps
to confirm that it was published after that date. Sayer's mezzotint
was the basis for a small print, a small head and shoulders version,
published on 1 February 1782 by W. Turner, a frame maker in
Snow Hill. It is difficult to know whether Sayer published this
mezzotint as a portrait of Madame Favart, a celebrated French
actress, or whether he was merely using an interesting image
which would appeal to the market; if it was the former, why did he
add the title *Spiletta*? The title may suggest that Sayer issued the
print as a portrait of Mlle Giordani, who took the part of Spiletta in

138

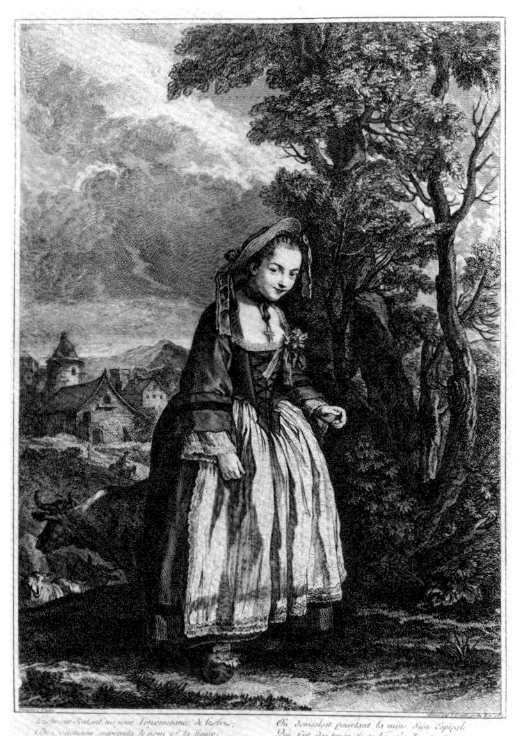

Cochi's burletta *Gli Amanti Gelosi* in 1756, but since this was at least ten years before the print was published, it seems unlikely. The conclusion must be that he issued an attractive print and gave it a title that associated it with a successful stage interpretation in order to enhance its appeal.

Madame Favart was one of the giants of the Paris stage. Her husband Charles Simon Favart was engaged in 1743 by Jean Monnet at the Opéra Comique in Paris, where he acted as author, reader of plays and stage manager. The Opéra Comique was suppressed as its success threatened the well established Comédie Italienne. In 1750, after an enforced absence, Madame Favart returned to the stage at the Comédie Italienne and with her husband set about a number of reforms. This print illustrates one of the important changes that she instigated in theatre costume: she eschewed extravagant court costume and chose to wear the simple linen dress of a Savoyard peasant with bare arms and wooden clogs when she played Bastienne in *Bastien et Bastienne* (1754).

Garrick is likely to have met the Favarts on his continental trip 1763–5; it is known that he was corresponding with Charles Simon Favart by at least 1767. Madame Favart died in 1772 and in that year, in the guise of an old woman, she appears along with thirty or so of her colleagues in *The Dramatic Characters of the English, French and Italian Stages*. This series of prints was issued, with characters added from time to time, from 1769 onwards. Madame Favart, like most of the other players from the Comédie Francais and the Comédie Italienne, was added in 1772. It had probably reached its full extension in 1774 when it was advertised.

[1] Jean Daullé (1703–63), French engraver.
[2] Thomas Jefferys (c. 1718–71), map and printseller, geographer to the King 1780.

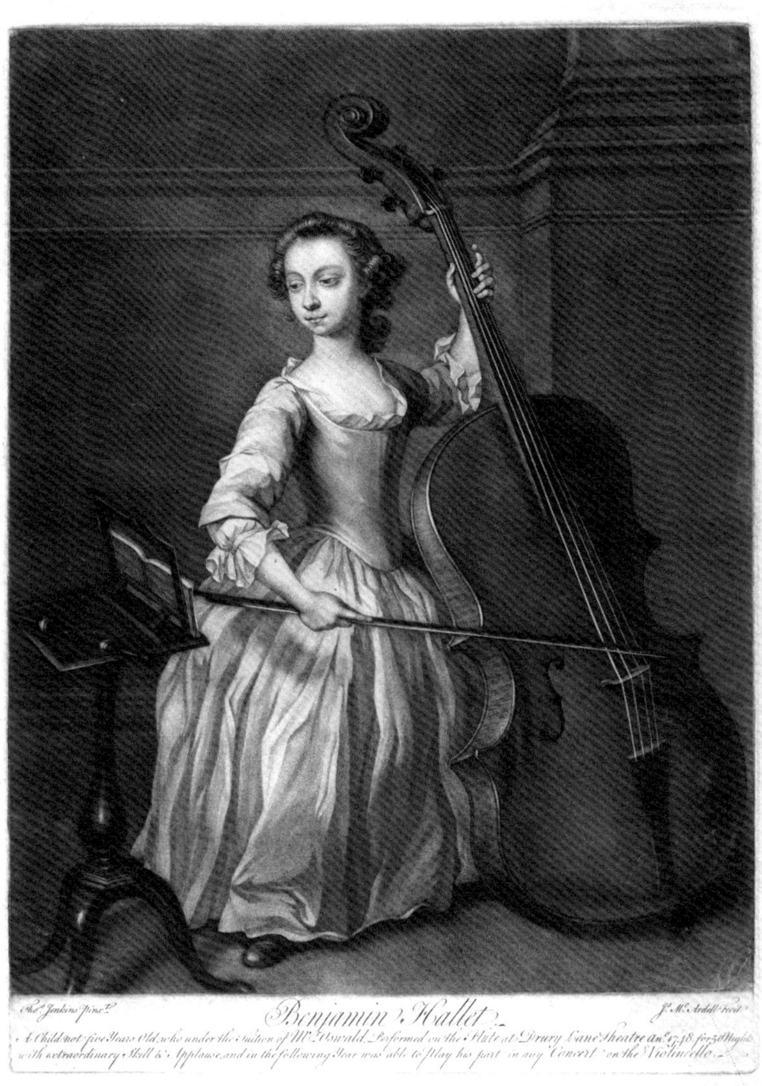

62 Benjamin Hallet

Engraved by James McArdell
after Thomas Jenkins

[Private plate c. 1751–2]

396 x 301 I; 428 x 302 Pl.

References: CS 96; R 96; G 7; O'D 1; Hall 1

1. With the engraved inscription: *"Tho.! Jenkins Pinx! *** J.! M.! Ardell Fecit | Benjamin Hallet, | A Child not five Years Old, who under the Tuition of M.! Oswald, Performed on the the Flute at Drury Lane Theatre An.? 1748: for 50 Nights | with extraordinary Skill & Applause, and in the following Year was able to Play his part in any Concert on the Violincello.".*
Impressions: CLB P13,780 (impression exhibited); BM; H.

This print, with impressions recorded in only one state, was probably a private plate, for if it had ever fallen into the hands of a print publisher it is likely that he would have added his own publication details. In 1774 Shropshire listed an impression, 'very fine & scarce' at the high price of 10s 6d. Prints of this size and type would normally have cost 5s and the higher price charged by Shropshire not only indicates its rarity and quality, but adds weight to the suggestion that this print was published as a private plate.

Soon after painting this portrait Thomas Jenkins (1722–98) moved to Rome where, like many artists, he took to dealing; his success was considerable and he became one of the greatest dealers in paintings and antiquities, before becoming a banker.

The infant prodigy Benjamin Hallett is shown on stage in 1749, playing the cello. He is dressed in skirts, at an age when most boys would have started to wear breeches. This was probably done to make him look even younger than he was, for by 1751 when he received a benefit, he is described as nine years of age – a remarkable increase in age over three years! Performances by infant prodigies such as Hallet, 'musical' entertainers such as Skeggs playing on his 'broomsticado', tight-rope walkers and performing animals, as well as serious musical pieces, made up the playbill. Although these 'spectacles', which in the modern sense might be termed 'theatrical reviews', lacked a main-piece or anything else of substance, in the eighteenth century they made up a significant part of a visit to the theatre. The best known of these were produced by 'Mrs Midnight', the frivolous poet Christopher Smart. Their popularity can be gauged from the fact that there are prints of musical entertainers (see page 142), performing dogs and tight-rope walkers (see below).

Hallet disappeared from the stage in 1753 and his career is hard to follow, but we do know that he appears on London bills in December 1751, when he played a solo on the cello and delivered an epilogue, something that he often performed, at the Haymarket Theatre. He continued to play both there and at the Castle Tavern for the rest of his short and distinguished career.

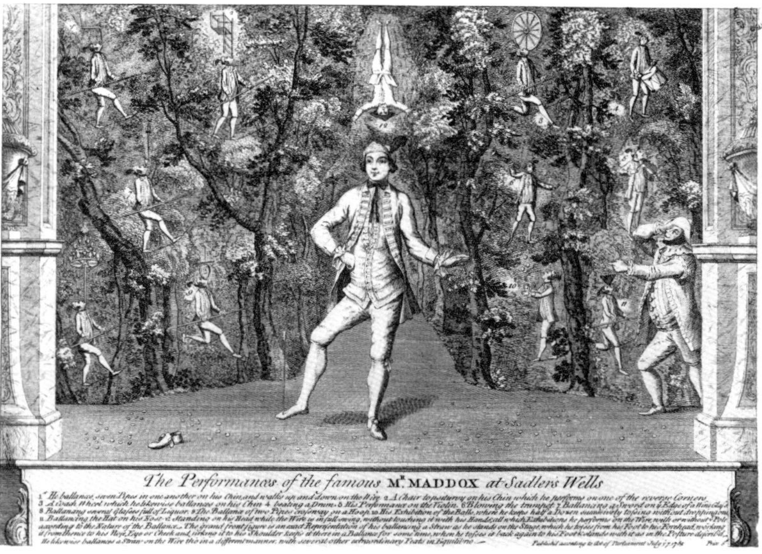

Anthony Maddox, published 1752 by R. Marshall.

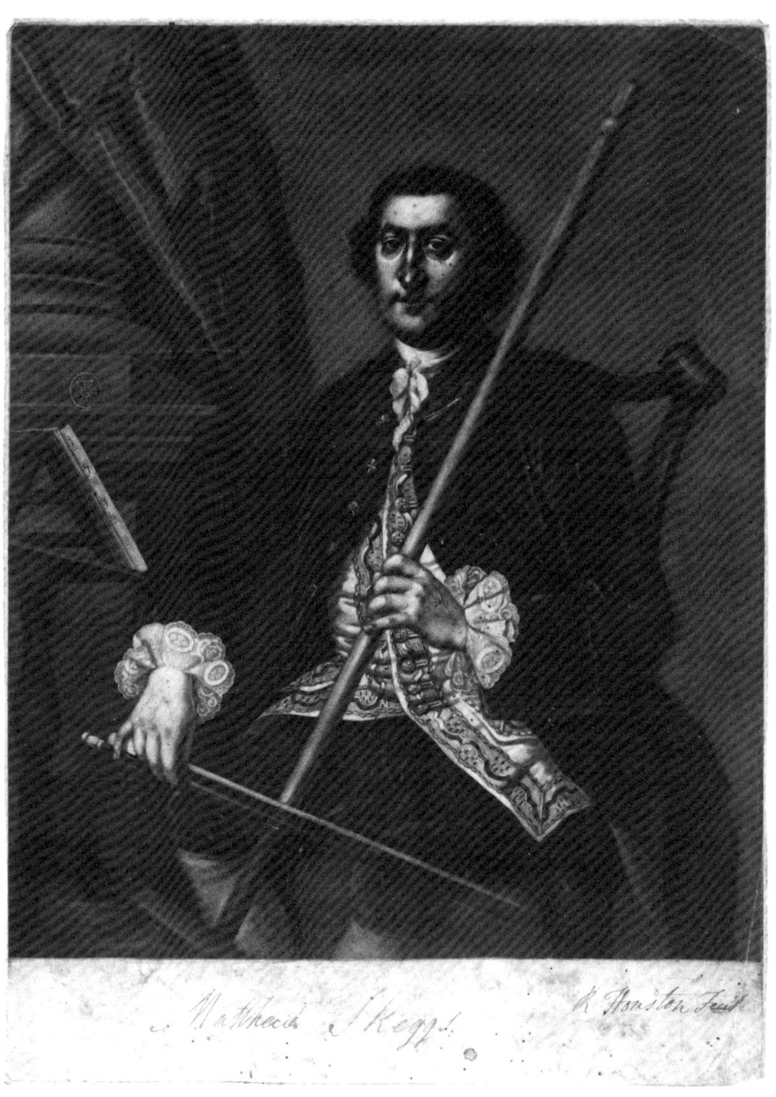

63 Skeggs, in the Character of Seignor Bumbasto

Engraved by Richard Houston
after Thomas King

[Published by] Michael Jackson, and
Matthew Skeggs c.1752–60[1]

314 x 252 I; 356 x 253 Pl.

References: CS 111; O'D 1; Hall 1

**1. Un-finished proof before all letters. The
background, waistcoat hands and lace cuffs
finished, but the face, coat, breeches, stockings, broom and bow are before additional
lights and finishing.**
Impressions: CLB P37,988 (impression exhibited);
BM

2. With the engraved inscription: *"Thos. King
pinx! *** Richd Houston fecit. / SKEGGS, / In the
Character of Seignor Bumbasto. / Sold by the*

This un-finished proof is a good example of Richard Houston's
method of engraving: every feature has been put in roughly and
the background, waistcoat, hands and lace cuffs have been finished, but the face, coat and many other features still need
working on. In the finished state, highlights have been added,
there are fewer contrasts on the face and Skeggs's vacuous expression is emphasised (see over). Progress proofs for English prints in
general are scarce although mezzotint progress proofs appear to
survive, possibly because the method required more to be made. It
was easier to lay in the general details and finish the features
piece-meal, as Houston does, taking proofs at regular intervals; any
alterations to the plate could be marked on the progress proof,
known as 'touching', either by the engraver himself (see page 22),
or by the painter.

This print is scarce and it is likely that its appeal was limited
since the plate was never taken up by a large printseller. An
impression was listed in Walter Shropshire's catalogue for 1774,
'very fine, proof' at 4s. A second mezzotint plate of Skeggs exists, a
broadsheet with a short half-length portrait in a circle and verses
below, thought to be engraved by Houston (as *G Pigganinni fecit*)
and published by John Ryall.

Impression: CLB; BM.

3. With the address of Jackson altered: *Bride
Court* replaced by *Chancery Lane.*

Impressions: BM.

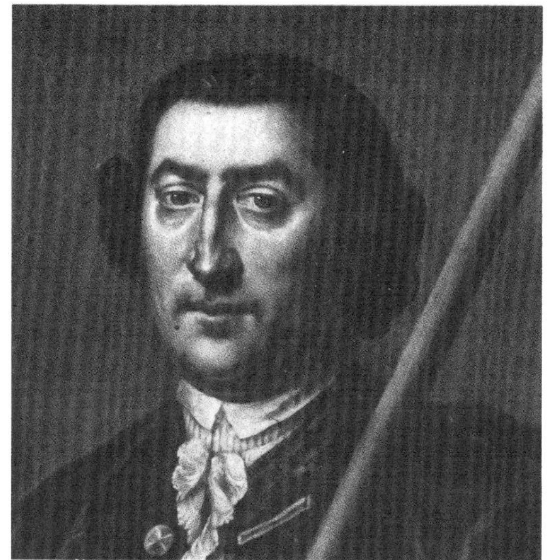

Detail of the finished state.

Each Buck and jolly Fellow,
as heard of Skegginello,
The famous Skegginello that grunts so pretty
Upon his Broomsticado.
Such music he has made, O
'Twill spoil the fiddling trade, O
And that's a Pity.
But have you heard of or seen, O.
His Phyz, so pretty
In Picture Shops so grinn, O,
With comic Nose and Chin, O.
Who'd think a Man cou'd shine so . . .

It is possible that this even rarer plate pre-dates the Jackson and Skeggs co-publication.

Michael Jackson is thought to have come from Ireland, like McArdell, Houston, Purcell and Spooner. He may have returned to Dublin, for his printselling business at Rembrandt's Head, Fleet Street and later at Chancery Lane was short-lived; his premises in Fleet Street had been taken over by George Pulley by about 1760. His Irish connections are evident in his publication of the Dublin scene painter John Lewis's portrait of Peg Woffington and in his mezzotint of Spranger Barry as Macbeth after a drawing by the Irish designer James Gwinn, both published in 1753.

Skeggs, at one time a publican,[2] is pictured in one of his most successful burlesque parts in the entertainments known as medley concerts, which were very popular between 1752–60. These were produced mainly at the Haymarket by Christopher Smart, using a variety of pseudonyms, particularly 'Mrs Midnight' or the 'Old Woman' (see page 140).

Walpole's opinion was scathing; he wrote in a letter in May 1752 of such a performance, 'it appeared the lowest buffonery in the world ...'. Skeggs was presumably involved in the part when, 'two or three men intend to persuade you that they play on a broomstick, which is drolly brought in, carefully shrouded in a case, so as to be mistaken for a bassoon, or a bass viol, but they succeed in nothing but the action'. Johnson's friend Mrs Thrale thought more of the performance, considering that it 'pretended to nothing better, and was wondrous droll, and what the wags call funny'.[3]

Matthew Skeggs eventually retired to Shefford in Bedfordshire, where he was still living in 1772.

[1] A search in the Poor Rate Books for Pall Mall indicates that Skeggs had taken over the premises of John Tompkinson by 5 April 1759 and that by October 1760 assessment the name of Stephen Massey was substituted for that of Skeggs; he is not listed thereafter.

[2] Hotten, J.C. and Larwood, J. *A History of Signboards*, 1985, p. 85.

[3] Mrs Thrale, Hester, later Piozzi, quoted in the DNB.

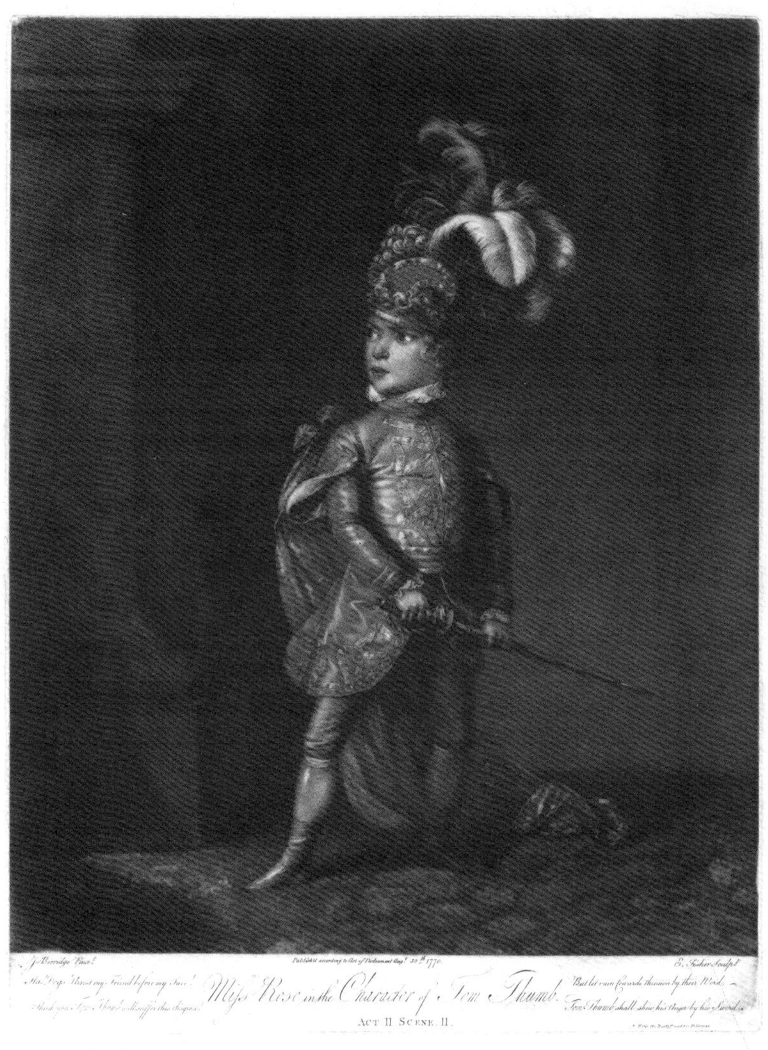

64 Miss Rose in the Character of Tom Thumb

Engraved by Edward Fisher after John Berridge

Published 30 August 1770

362 x 290 I; 400 x 290 Pl.

References: CS 53; O'D 1; Hall 1

1. Finished proof before all letters.
Impressions: TM.

2. [Finished proof with the scratched inscription: "Publish'd according to Act of Parliament August 30th 1770" (CS)].

3. With the engraved inscription: *"Publish'd according to Act of Parliament Aug.! 30.th 1770. | J Berridge Pinx.,! *** E, Fisher Sculp.,! | [to l.] Ha! Dogs! Arrest my Friend before my Face! | Think you Tom Thumb will suffer this disgrace! *** Miſs Rose in the Character of Tom Thumb. | ACT II. SCENE II. *** [to r.] But let vain Cowards threaten by their*

The painting by John Berridge, a pupil and imitator of Reynolds, was exhibited at the Society of Artists in 1770. Few of his works have the force and character of this charming picture. Fisher's mezzotint was published a few months later but was not exhibited.

Edward Fisher was born in Dublin in 1722; although originally a hatter he later turned to engraving. His earliest print is dated 1758, and since there is no confirmation that any of his engravings were executed in Ireland it is possible that he learned the art in London from his fellow countryman James McArdell. Reynolds accused him of being 'injudiciously exact', finishing his prints too highly in areas of the plate which the painter considered unimportant; Chaloner Smith considers this criticism to be unfair and allows Fisher, 'a high place for both breadth of treatment and delicacy of finish'. Where a decorative background mattered, as in Stubbs's *'A French Fox Dog'*, Fisher was inimitable. After his death in 1785 his plates were dispersed amongst several printsellers and it is said that a number of these were 'dishonestly tampered with' to create false proofs.

Henry Fielding's *Tom Thumb the Great* was first performed at the Haymarket in 1730. Its title was later altered to *The Tragedy of Tragedies, or the Life and Death of Tom Thumb the Great* and it received an additional act in 1731. The plot of the play is extraordinary, with the leading characters being Lilliputians who are victorious over giants. Amongst the characters are Noodle, Doodle and Foodle, foolish courtiers, King Arthur who is a tavern bully, his 'lickerish' Queen called Dollalolla, their sentimental daughter, Huncamunca and Lord Grizzle, Tom Thumb's main rival for the hand of the Princess. Tom fights the giants and resolves to kill a bailiff (the moment depicted in the print), who has attempted to arrest Noodle at the suit of his tailor. Tom determines to, 'clear the town of bailiffs and render the streets safe for poor gentlemen, even at noonday'. The climax in the last scene, modelled on Hamlet, is a mass stabbing at the Court, after the marriage of Tom Thumb and Huncamunca is prevented by the death of Tom, who is swallowed by a cow. Apparently its reception by the audience was so enthusiastic that, 'it was very difficult for the actors to escape without a second [stage] slaughter'.

The after-piece, described as an 'exuberant farce in the mock-heroic manner', was judged to be Fielding's most successful work, ridiculing the 'bombastic style of tragic performances that predominated at the time'. Reputedly, one of the only two times upon which Dean Swift, 'one of the most thoroughgoing of pessimists', was ever seen to laugh was at a performance of this play. His *Travels ... by Lemuel Gulliver ...* had been published four years before the first performance.

'Miss Rose' has been identified as Rose de Francetti, who first appeared as 'the Author, a five year old Girl', delivering an epilogue to a performance of Bickerstaffe's *Dr Last in his Chariot* at the Haymarket on 21 June 1769. On 7 August of that year, Miss Rose appeared for the first time as Tom Thumb. According to Gentleman she excelled in this part, being of 'diminutive size, archness of look, and peculiar shrewdness of expression'.[1]

[1] Gentleman, II, p. 58.

Bibliography

In preparing this catalogue we have, of course, relied on the remarkable works, *The London Stage* and *A Biographical Dictionary of Actors, Actresses...*, both published by Southern Illinois Press, the final volumes of the latter arriving on library shelves late last year. Many of our references in manuscript diaries to both plays and players were originally found there.

For the prints we have relied on the standard catalogues raisonées. We have also read many of the contemporary catalogues, both those of publishers and of dealers. For the painters, we have used Professor Waterhouse's *Dictionary of Eighteenth Century British Painters* and for both we have consulted Algernon Graves's *Royal Academy* and *Society of Artists...*

Other sources are acknowledged in the text. The most commonly used books are included with the abbreviations listed below. With books published in the eighteenth and nineteenth centuries we presume that they were published in London. As many later books are published by academic presses we have, where appropriate, identified the publisher rather than the place.

Allen Allen (Brian): Francis Hayman, Yale University Press, 1987.

B.M. Satires Stephens (Frederick George) & George (Dorothy) eds: Catalogue of Prints & Drawings in the British Museum, ... Political and Personal Satires, 1870–1954.

Bradshaw Bow Bradshaw (Peter): Bow Porcelain Figures, 1748–1774, London, 1992.

Bradshaw Derby Bradshaw (Peter): Derby Porcelain Figures, 1750–1848, London, 1990.

CS Chaloner Smith (John): British Mezzotinto Portraits, 1883.

Cumberland Cumberland (Richard): Memoirs of Richard Cumberland, 1807.

Davies Davies (Thomas): Memoirs of the Life of David Garrick, 1780.

DNB The Dictionary of National Biography, 1885–1900.

Dramatic Miscellanies Davies (Thomas): Dramatic Miscellanies ..., 1783–4.

Festival of Wit, 1806.

G Goodwin (Gordon): T. Watson, J. Watson & E. Judkins, London, 1904, or J. McArdell, London, 1903.

Garrick Garrick (David): An Essay on Acting, 1744.

Genest [Genest (John)]: Some Account of the English Stage, Bath, 1832.

Gentleman Gentleman (Francis): The Dramatic Censor, 1770.

Hall Hall (Lilliana H): Catalogue of Dramatic Portraits ... Harvard University Press, 1930–1934.

Hill [Hill (Sir John)]: The Actor, 2nd ed., 1755.

Hotten 'Larwood (Jacob)' [i.e. Schevichaven (Herman Diederik J. van) and Hotten (John Camden): The History of Signboards, 1866.

Hp Hamilton (Edward): The Engraved Works of Sir Joshua Reynolds, 1884.

Kelly Kelly (J.A.): German Visitors to English Theatres in the 18th Century, Princeton University Press, 1936.

Letters Little (David M.) & Kahrl, (George M.): Letters of David Garrick, Oxford University Press, 1963.

Lichtenberg Lichtenberg (Georg Christoph): Lichtenberg's Visits to England, Oxford, Clarendon Press, 1938.

Lugt Lugt (Fritz): Les Marques des Collections, Paris, 1921 (reprinted The Hague 1956).

Murphy Murphy (Arthur): Life of David Garrick, 1801.

O'D O'Donoghue (Freeman): Catalogue of Engraved British Portraits ... British Musuem, London, 1908–1925.

Pasquin 'Anthony Pasquin pseud.' [i.e. John Williams]: The Pin Basket. To the Children of Thespis, 1796.

Penny Penny (Nicholas) ed: Reynolds, exhibition catalogue, Royal Academy of Arts, London 1986.

R Russell (Charles E.): British Mezzotint Portraits and their States, London, 1926.

Rational Rosciad, L. (F.B.): The Rational Rosciad, 1767.

Stone & Kahrl Stone (George Winchester jnr) & Kahrl (George M.): David Garrick, a critical biography, Southern Illinois University Press, 1979.

TDB Highfill (Philip, jnr), Burnim (Kalman) & Langhans (Edward A.) eds: A Biographical Dictionary of Actors, Actresses ... London, Southern Illinois University Press, 1973–1993.

Theatrical Biography Theatrical Biography, 1772.

Theatrical Review [Potter (John)]: The Theatrical Review, 1772.

Victor Victor (Benjamin): The History of the Theatres of London and Dublin, 1771.

W Whitman (Alfred): Valentine Green, London, 1902.

Waterhouse Waterhouse (Ellis): Dictionary of Eighteenth Century British Painters, Woodbridge, 1981.

Wilkinson Wilkinson (Tate): Memoirs of his own Life, York, 1790.

Index

We have indexed names of actors, dramatists, artists, engravers, printsellers and print publishers. The plays and a few other subjects have also been added. The principal entries cited are printed in bold.